MAKE THE RIGHT CALL

With Foreword by Paul Tagliabue, NFL Commissioner

and

Commentary by Jerry Seeman, NFL Director of Officiating

TRIUMPH
BOOKS
CHICAGO

Special thanks for editorial assistance to Jason Leighton.
Design by Mike Mulligan Design.

This book is available at special discounts for your group or organization.
For further information, contact:
Triumph Books
601 South LaSalle Street
Suite 500
Chicago, IL 60605
(312) 939-3330
(312) 663-3557 (fax)

Printed in the U.S.A.

It is not surprising that fans of America's most popular sport have a strong interest in understanding the NFL's Official Playing Rules.

Familiarity with the rules creates a better understanding of the action on the field and, therefore, more enjoyment of the game. This updated version of the rule book—specially designed in a "reader friendly" presentation—will answer all your questions about the intricate framework of the game.

Along with our annual review of the rules, the NFL is committed to the highest level of officiating through the top-flight training program conducted by NFL Director of Officiating Jerry Seeman.

I hope readers of this new edition of *Make the Right Call* will gain a new appreciation for the rules of football and for the expertise and judgment of our NFL officials in administering them.

Paul Tagliabue

Commissioner
National Football League

The best way to understand the rules of any sport is to *see them in action*. This new edition of *Make the Right Call* gives the reader a mental picture of the on-field action by including <u>hundreds of realistic (though not historical) game situations.</u>

The material for these game situations comes from the NFL's interpretations — known officially as "Approved Rulings" or "A.R.s" — of the Official Playing Rules. The A.R.s are periodically issued by the NFL specifically to supplement and illustrate the basic language of the rules.

The A.R.s form the basis here for the running series of "Plays," followed by "Rulings" that appear after many sections of the Official Playing Rules material in this book, as shown in this example:

MAKE THE RIGHT CALL   PLAY **1**   Fourth-and-10 on Patriots' 35. On a field goal attempt, Cowboys' offensive tackle Flozell Adams and offensive guard Nate Newton lock their legs as they line up. The field goal is good.

Ruling: Field goal good, no foul.

Penalty situations are indicated as shown in this example:

PENALTY: FOR VIOLATION OF SNAP FORMATION: LOSS OF FIVE YARDS FROM PREVIOUS SPOT.

Note: <u>All playing situations in this book are purely hypothetical and for purposes of example only. Likewise, all names of NFL players and teams are purely for illustration purposes and are not based on actual historical games</u>.

References such as "15-4-1" refer to Rule 15, Section 4, Article 1. Headings at the top of left-hand pages refer to the Rule under discussion; right-hand headings refer to the particular Section discussed on that page.

This new edition of *Make the Right Call* contains all current rules governing the playing of professional football that are in effect for the 1999 NFL season. Because interconference games are played throughout the NFL season, all rules contained in this book apply uniformly to both the American and National Football Conferences.

ORDER OF THE RULES

CHAPTER 1
THE FIELD

Once the seven NFL game officials are out on the field, coordination of efforts between the officials is the only way to make sure every play is being covered properly.

The key to good coverage is being in correct field position: If you can't see the play, you can't make the call.

Jerry Seeman
NFL DIRECTOR OF OFFICIATING

Section 1   Dimensions

PLAYING
LINES

FIELD OF PLAY

The game shall be played upon a rectangular field, 360 feet in length and 160 feet in width. The lines at each end of the field are termed End Lines. Those on each side are termed Sidelines. Goal Lines shall be established in the field 10 yards from and parallel to each end line. The area bounded by goal lines and sidelines is known as the Field of Play. The areas bounded by goal lines, end lines, and sidelines are known as the End Zones.

The areas bounded by goal lines and lines parallel to, and 70 feet 9 inches inbounds, from each sideline, are known as the Side Zones. The lines parallel to sidelines are termed Inbound Lines. The end lines and the sidelines are also termed Boundary Lines.

The playing field will be rimmed by a solid white border a minimum of 6 feet wide along the end lines and sidelines. An additional broken limit line 6 feet further outside this border is to encompass the playing field in the non-bench areas, and such broken line will be continued at an angle from each 32-yard line and pass behind the bench areas (all benches a minimum 30 feet back from the sidelines). In addition, within each bench area, a yellow line 6 feet behind the solid white border will delineate a special area for coaches, behind which all players, except one player charting the game, must remain. If a clubs solid white border is a minimum of 12 feet wide, there is no requirement that the broken restraining line also be added in the non-bench areas. However, the appropriate yellow line described above must be clearly marked within the bench areas.

Section 2   Markings

LINE
MARKINGS

At intervals of 5 yards, yard lines (3-41-2) parallel to the goal lines shall be marked in the field of play. *These lines are to stop 8 inches short of the 6-foot solid border.* The 4-inch wide yard lines are to be extended 4 inches beyond the white 6-foot border along the sidelines. Each of these lines shall be intersected at right angles by short lines 70 feet, 9 inches long (23 yards, 1 foot, 9 inches) in from each side to indicate inbounds lines.

INBOUND
LINES

In line with the Inbound Lines there shall be marks at 1-yard intervals between each distance of 5 yards for the full length of the field. These lines are to begin 8 inches from the 6-foot solid border and are to measure 2 feet in length.

Bottoms of numbers indicating yard lines in multiples of 10 must be placed beginning 12 yards in from each sideline. These are to be 2 yards in length.

Two yards from the middle of each goal line and parallel to it, there shall be marked in the Field of Play, lines 1 yard in length.

All boundary lines, goal lines, and marked lines are to be continuous lines. These, and any other specified markings, must be in white, and there shall be no exceptions without authorization of the Commissioner. Field numerals must also be white.

Care must be exercised in any end-zone marking or decoration or club identification at the 50-yard line that said marking or decorations do not in any way cause confusion as to delineation of goal lines, sidelines, and end lines. Such markings or decorations must be approved by the Commissioner.

The four intersections of goal lines and sidelines must be marked, at inside corners, by pylons mounted on flexible shafts. In addition, two such pylons shall be placed on each end line (four in all).

SUPPLEMENTAL NOTES

GOAL LINE

All measurements are to be made from the inside edges of the line marking the boundary lines. Each goal line marking is to be in its end zone so that the edge of the line toward the field of play (actual goal line) is 30 feet from the inside edge of the end line. Each goal line is to be eight inches wide.

All lines are to be marked with a material that is not injurious to eyes or skin. It is desirable that the yard-line markers be flexible in order to prevent injury. No benches or rigid fixtures should be nearer than ten yards from sidelines.

In league parks where ground rules are necessary, because of fixed conditions that cannot be changed, they will be made by the Commissioner. Otherwise they will be made by mutual agreement of the two coaches. If they cannot agree, the Referee is the final authority after consulting his crew.

Section 3   Goal

CROSSBAR

In the plane of each end line there shall be a centrally placed horizontal Crossbar 18 feet 6 inches in length the top face of which is 10 feet above the ground. The goal is the **vertical plane** extending indefinitely above the crossbar and between the lines indicated by the outer edges of the goal posts.

GOAL POSTS

All goal posts will be the single-standard type, offset from the end line and bright gold in color. The uprights will extend 30 feet above the crossbar and will be no less than 3 inches and no more than 4 inches in diameter. A ribbon 4 inches by 42 inches is to be attached to the top of each post.

NOTE: GOAL POSTS MUST BE PADDED IN A MANNER PRESCRIBED BY THE LEAGUE.

Section 4   Players' Benches

PLAYERS'
BENCHES

At the option of the home team, both the players' benches may be located on the same side of the field. In such a case, the end of each bench shall start at the 45-yard line and continue towards the adjacent goal line.

NOTE: WHEN BOTH BENCHES ARE SO LOCATED, CHAIN CREW AND LINESMEN ARE TO OPERATE DURING ENTIRE GAME ON OPPOSITE SIDE TO BENCHES. SEE 15-4-1.

Section 5   Chain Crew and Ball Boys

CHAIN CREW
AND BALL
BOYS

Members of the chain crew and the ball boys must be uniformly identifiable as specified by the Commissioner. White shirts are to be worn by members of the chain crew.

Section 6   Sideline Markers

SIDELINE
MARKERS

The home club must provide and use the standard set of sideline markers that have been approved by the Commissioner.

Plan of the Playing Field

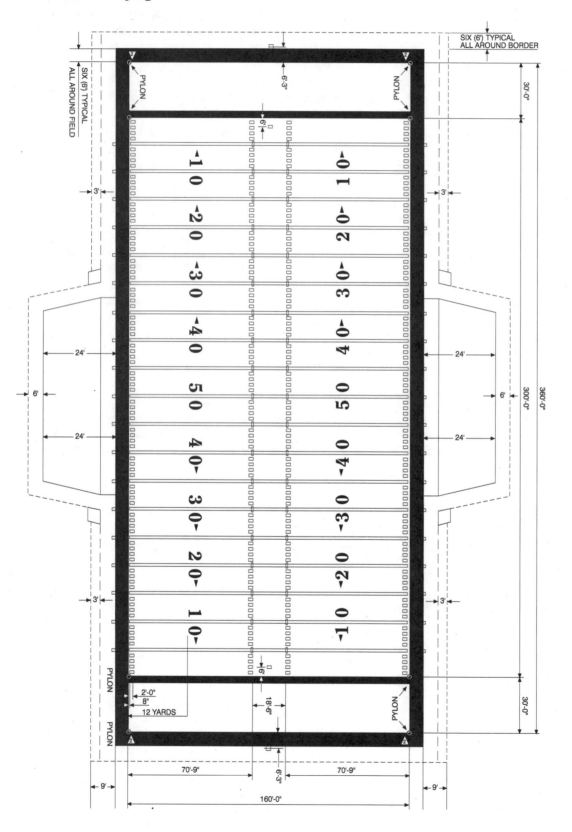

Field Markings

1. The playing field will be rimmed by a solid white border six feet wide along the end lines and sidelines. There will be an additional broken yellow line nine feet farther outside this border along each sideline in the non-bench areas, and such broken line will be continued at an angle from each 30-yard line and pass behind the bench area (all benches a minimum of 30 feet back from the sidelines) at a distance of six feet. In each end zone, this broken yellow line is six feet from the solid white border. These yellow broken lines are to be two feet long with a space of one foot between them.

   In addition, within each bench area, a solid yellow line six feet behind the solid border will delineate a special area for coaches, behind which all players, except one player who is charting the game, must remain. Furthermore, a broken white line four feet long with a space of two feet intervals will be marked three feet inside the nine foot restriction line on the sideline, extending to meet the existing yellow broken line six feet behind both end zones and at each television box outside the bench area.

2. All lines are to be 4 inches wide, with the exception of the goal line and yellow line, which are to be 8 inches wide. Tolerance of line widths is plus one-fourth inch.

3. All line work is to be laid out to dimensions shown on the plan with a tolerance of one-fourth inch. All lines are straight.

4. All boundary lines, goal lines, and marked yard lines are to be continuous lines.

5. The four intersections of goal lines and sidelines must be marked at inside corners of the end zone and the goal line by pylons mounted on flexible shafts. Pylons must be placed at inside edges of white lines and should not touch the surface of the actual playing field itself.

6. All lines are to be marked with a material that is not injurious to eyes or skin.

7. No benches or rigid fixtures should be nearer than 10 yards from the sidelines. If space permits, they may be further back.

8. Player benches can be situated anywhere between respective 35-yard lines. Where possible, a continuation of the dotted yellow line is to extend from the 30-yard lines to a point six feet behind the player benches thereby enclosing this area.

9. A white arrow is to be placed on the ground adjacent to the top portion of each number (with the exception of the 50) with the point formed by the two longer sides pointing toward the goal line. The two longer sides measure 36 inches each, while the crossfield side measures 18 inches. The 18-inch crossfield side is to start 15 inches below the top, and 6 inches from the goalward edge of each outer number (except the 50).

10. The location of the inbounds lines is 70'9" for professional football, 53'4" for college football. On fields used primarily by the NFL, the professional inbound lines should be 4 inches wide by 2 feet long. Alternate college lines, if they are to be included, should be 4 inches wide by 1 foot long.

11. Care must be exercised in any end zone marking, decoration, or club identification at the 50-yard line, that said marks or decorations do not in any way cause confusion as to delineation of goal lines, sidelines, and end lines. Such markings or decorations must be approved by the Commissioner.

Inbound Yard Markers

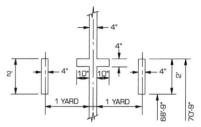

Dimensions for Numerals on the Playing Field

Dimensions for the Directional Arrows

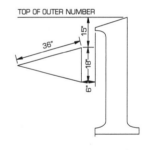

NFL Bench Area Showing Restricted Zones

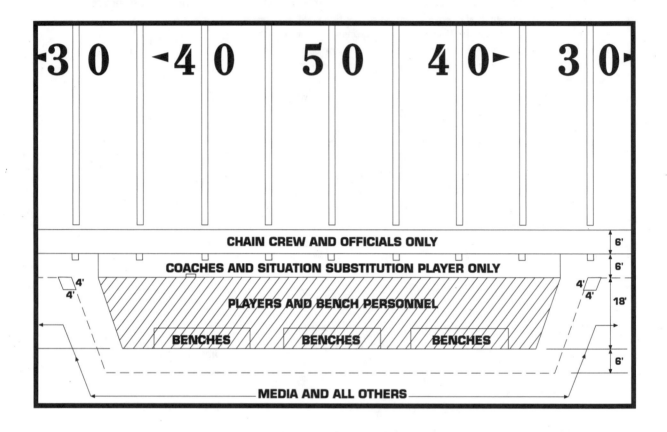

CHAPTER 2

THE BALL

Some fans may know that the game balls, prior to game time, are checked for proper inflation by the referee and the officiating crew in the locker room.

Fans might not know that the officials also rub down each game ball with a damp cloth so that the tackiness will come to the surface of the ball.

Jerry Seeman
NFL DIRECTOR OF OFFICIATING

**BALL
DIMENSIONS**

The Ball must be a "Wilson," hand selected, bearing the signature of the Commissioner of the league, Paul Tagliabue.

The ball shall be made up of an inflated (12½ to 13½ pounds) rubber bladder enclosed in a pebble grained, leather case (natural tan color) without corrugations of any kind. It shall have the form of a prolate spheroid and the size and weight shall be: long axis, 11 to 11¼ inches; long circumference, 28 to 28½ inches; short circumference, 21 to 21¼ inches; weight, 14 to 15 ounces.

The Referee shall be the sole judge as to whether all balls offered for play comply with these specifications.

BALL SUPPLY

The home club shall have 24 balls available for testing with a pressure gauge by the Referee one hour prior to the starting time of the game to meet with league requirements.

A pump is to be furnished by the home club, and balls shall remain with and be returned to the ball attendant prior to the start of the game by the Referee.

In the event a home team ball does not conform to specifications, or its supply is exhausted, the Referee shall secure a proper ball from visitors and, failing that, use the best available ball. Any such circumstances must be reported to the Commissioner.

In case of rain or a wet, muddy, or slippery field, a playable ball shall be used at the request of the offensive team's center. The Game Clock shall not stop for such action (unless undue delay occurs).

NOTE: IT IS THE RESPONSIBILITY OF THE HOME TEAM TO FURNISH PLAYABLE BALLS AT ALL TIMES BY ATTENDANTS FROM EITHER SIDE OF THE PLAYING FIELD.

CHAPTER 3
DEFINITIONS

Definitions are important. Fans sometimes get confused over the difference between a fumble and a muff, for example. A fumble means a player had possession and then lost it. A muff means the player never actually had possession of the ball.

Jerry Seeman
NFL DIRECTOR OF OFFICIATING

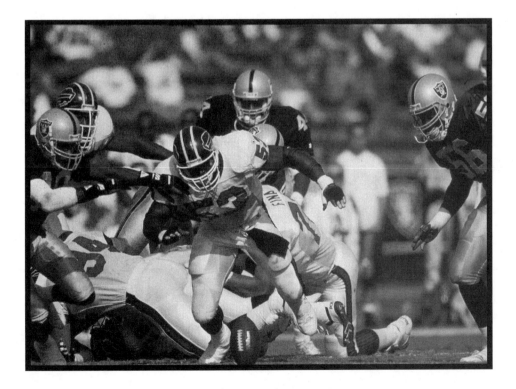

Section 1   Approved Ruling (A.R.)

APPROVED
RULING

An Approved Ruling (A.R.) is an official decision on a given statement of facts and serves to illustrate the intent, application, or amplification of a rule. Supplemental notes are often used for the same purpose (3-32).

TECHNICAL
TERMS

Technical Terms are such terms that have a fixed and exact meaning throughout the code. Because of their alphabetical arrangement in Rule Three, certain ones are used prior to being defined. In such cases they are accented only the first time they are used.

Section 2   Ball in Play, Dead Ball

BALL IN PLAY

Article 1   The Ball is in Play (or Live Ball) when it is:

(a) legally free kicked (6-1-1 and 2), or

(b) legally snapped (7-3-1).

It continues in play until the down ends (3-7-1 and 7-4-1).

DEAD BALL

Article 2   A Dead Ball is one that is not in play. The time period during which the ball is dead is Between Downs. This includes the interval during all time outs (including intermission) and from the time the ball becomes dead until it is not in play.

LOOSE BALL

Article 3   A Loose Ball is a live ball that is not in player **possession**, i.e., any **kick, pass,** or **fumble**. A loose ball that has not yet struck the ground is In Flight. A loose ball (either during or after flight) is considered in **possession** of team **(offense)** whose **player kicked, passed**, or **fumbled**. It ends when a player secures possession or when **down ends** if that is before such possession.

FUMBLE

Article 4   A Fumble is any act, other than a pass or legal kick, which results in loss of player possession. The term Fumble always implies possession.

NOTE: IF A PLAYER PRETENDS TO FUMBLE AND CAUSES THE BALL TO GO FORWARD, IT IS A FORWARD PASS AND MAY BE ILLEGAL (8-1-1-PEN. A, C).

MAKE THE RIGHT CALL

PLAY **1**   While the Steelers' Jerome Bettis is in possession, the Cardinals' Eric Swann grabs the ball away from him.

PLAY **2**   While the Steelers' Jerome Bettis is in possession, the Cardinals' Eric Swann bats or kicks the ball away from him.

Ruling 1: Fumble.

Ruling 2: A foul during a fumble. Kicking a ball in player possession is a foul (12-1-7).

MUFF

Article 5   A Muff is the **touching** of the ball by a player in an unsuccessful attempt to obtain **possession** of a loose ball.

NOTE: ANY BALL INTENTIONALLY **MUFFED** FORWARD IS A **BAT** AND MAY BE A **FOUL**. (3-2-5-G, 12-1-6, 9-1-10-EXC, 3-14-3-NOTE).

TOUCHING THE BALL	Touching the Ball refers to any contact. Ordinarily there is no distinction between a player touching the ball with his hands or any part of his body being touched by it except as specifically provided for (9-10-Exc. and 3-14-3-Note).

NOTE: THE RESULT OF THE TOUCHING IS SOMETIMES INFLUENCED BY THE INTENT OR THE LOCATION.

TOUCHING FREE KICK	(a) See 6-2-1 and 4, for touching a free kick.
INTENT OR LOCATION OF TOUCHING	(b) See 6-3-1-Exc., for touching a free kick before it goes **out of bounds** between the goal lines.
INELIGIBLE PLAYER TOUCHING A PASS	(c) See 8-1-5, for **ineligible offensive player** touching a forward pass **on, behind,** or **beyond** the line.
PUSHED INTO A KICK	(d) See 9-1-6,7,8, for touching a scrimmage kick on or behind the line, and also 9-1-10, for being pushed into a kick by an opponent.
TOUCHING KICK DURING ATTEMPTED FIELD GOAL	(e) See 11-5-1-b, for touching a kick during an attempted **field goal.**
SIMULTANEOUS TOUCHING	(f) Simultaneous touching by two opponents of a fumble, pass, or kick is treated under their respective sections.
BAT OR PUNCH	(g) A Bat or Punch is the intentional striking of the ball with hand, fist, elbow, or forearm. See 12-1-6.

NOTE: IF THERE IS ANY QUESTION BY THE COVERING OFFICIAL(S) AS TO WHETHER A DEFENDER IS STRIPPING OR BATTING A BALL IN PLAYER POSSESSION, OFFICIALS WILL RULE WHETHER THE ACTION IS A LEGAL ACT (STRIPPING THE BALL).

PLAYER POSSESSION	**Article 6** A player inbounds other than an eligible receiver is in possession when he has held the ball firmly in his grasp long enough to have established control. In order for an eligible receiver of a forward pass to be in possession, he must control the ball throughout the act of clearly touching both feet, or any other part of his body other than his hand(s), to the ground inbounds. If the Player is hit causing the ball to come loose simultaneously while clearly touching inbounds both feet or any other part of the body except the hand(s), there is no possession. If, when the ball comes loose, there is any question whether the above acts are simultaneous, the ruling shall be no possession. This definition would apply whether on the field of play or in the end zone. The terms Catch, Intercept, Recover, Advance, and Fumble denote player possession (as distinguished from touching or muffing).
CATCH	(a) A *Catch* is made when a player inbounds secures possession of a pass, kick, or fumble in flight. See 3-20, 8-1-6-S.N.5.
INTERCEPTION	(b) An *Interception* is made when a pass or fumble is caught by an opponent of the passer or fumbler.
RECOVER	(c) The term *Recover* indicates securing possession of a loose ball after it has touched the ground by either the offense or defense.

NOTE 1: IF THERE IS ANY QUESTION BY THE COVERING OFFICIAL(S) AS TO WHETHER A PASS IS COMPLETE, INTERCEPTED, OR INCOMPLETE, IT WILL ALWAYS BE RULED INCOMPLETE.

NOTE 2: RECOVER AS USED IN AN APPROVED RULING (3-1) DOES NOT IMPLY ADVANCE UNLESS SO STATED.

NOTE 3: IF A PLAYER WOULD HAVE CAUGHT, INTERCEPTED, OR RECOVERED A BALL INBOUNDS BUT WAS FORCED OUT OF BOUNDS, PLAYER POSSESSION WOULD BE GRANTED.

TEAM
POSSESSION

Article 7   A team is in possession when a player of that team is in possession of a live ball and also while the ball is loose following such player possession (3-2-3, 3-2-6).

> NOTE: FOR BREVITY, TERMS SUCH AS KICK, PASS, FUMBLE, ETC., ARE USED TO DENOTE THE BALL DURING THE TIME IT IS AFFECTED BY THE ACT. HENCE, REFERENCE IS MADE TO A PLAYER TOUCHING, CATCHING, OR RECOVERING A "KICK."

Section 3   Blocking

BLOCKING

(1) During a legal block, contact can be made with the head, shoulders, hands and/or outer surface of the forearm, or any other part of the body.

(2) Hands (open or closed) can be thrust forward initially to contact an opponent on or outside the opponent's frame, but the blocker must work to bring his hands on or inside the frame.

> NOTE: PASS BLOCKING: HAND(S) THRUST FORWARD THAT SLIP OUTSIDE THE BODY OF THE DEFENDER WILL BE LEGAL IF BLOCKER WORKED TO BRING THEM BACK INSIDE. HAND(S) OR ARM(S) THAT ENCIRCLE A DEFENDER I.E., HOOK AN OPPONENT ARE TO BE CONSIDERED ILLEGAL AND OFFICIALS ARE TO CALL A FOUL FOR HOLDING. BLOCKER CANNOT USE HIS HANDS OR ARMS TO PUSH FROM BEHIND, HANG ONTO, OR ENCIRCLE AN OPPONENT IN A MANNER THAT RESTRICTS HIS MOVEMENT AS THE PLAY DEVELOPS.

(3) Hands cannot be thrust forward *above* the frame to contact an opponent on the neck, face, or head.

> NOTE: THE FRAME IS DEFINED AS THE PART OF THE OPPONENTS BODY BELOW THE NECK THAT IS PRESENTED TO THE BLOCKER.

(4) As the play develops, a blocker is permitted to work for and maintain position on an opponent as long as he does not push from behind or clip (outside legal clip zone). A blocker lined up more than two yards outside the tackle is subject, also, to the crackback rule *and cannot move into the clip zone and push or clip from behind. (See 12-2-10).*

(5) By use of up and down action of the arm(s), the blocker is permitted to ward off the opponent's attempt to grasp his jersey or arms.

> NOTE: SEE 12-1-2.

Section 4   Chucking

CHUCKING

Chucking is a means of warding off an opponent who is in front of a defender by contacting him with a quick extension of arm or arms followed by the return of arm(s) to a flexed position, thereby breaking the original contact. See 12-1-4-Exc. 1.

Section 5   Clipping

CLIPPING

Clipping is throwing the body across the back of the leg of an opponent or charging or falling into the back of an opponent below the waist after approaching him from behind, provided the opponent is not a *runner* or it is not *close line play.*

> NOTE: SEE SUPPLEMENTAL NOTES UNDER 12-2-9, FOR ADDITIONAL INTERPRETATIONS OR RESTRICTIONS CONCERNING CLIPPING.

MAKE THE RIGHT CALL PLAY **1** Carolina's William Floyd advances 10 yards and is hit from behind by the Ravens' Tony Siragusa, who throws his body across the back of Floyd's leg.

Ruling 1: *Legal and not a clip, because Floyd was a runner. If Floyd was not a runner, it would have been a clip.*

Section 6   Disqualified Player

DISQUALIFIED PLAYER

A Disqualified Player is one who is banished from further participation in the game and must return to his dressing room within a reasonable period of time for any of the following:

(a) flagrant striking, kneeing, or kicking an opponent (12-2-1);

(b) flagrant roughing of a kicker, passer, or any other opponent (12-2-6 and 12-2-11);

(c) a palpably unfair act (12-3-3);

(d) flagrant unsportsmanlike conduct by players or non-players (Rule 13); or

(e) repeat violation of a suspended player (Rule 5-3-Pen. c).

NOTE: DISQUALIFIED PLAYER IS NOT TO REAPPEAR IN HIS TEAM UNIFORM NOR RETURN TO ANY AREA OTHER THAN TO WHICH SPECTATORS HAVE ACCESS.

Section 7   Down

DOWN

Article 1   A Down (or Play) is a period of action that starts when the ball is put in play (3-2-1) and ends when ball is next dead (7-4-1).

SCRIMMAGE DOWN

A down that starts with a snap is known as a Scrimmage Down (3-29).

FREE KICK DOWN

A down that starts with a free kick is known as a Free Kick Down (6-1-1 and 2).

SERIES OF DOWNS

Article 2   A Series of Downs is the four consecutive charged scrimmage downs allotted to the offensive team during which it must advance the ball to a yard line called the necessary line in order to retain possession (7-1-1).

NECESSARY LINE

The Necessary Line is always 10 yards in advance of the spot of the snap (which starts the series) except when a goal line is less than 10 yards from this spot. In that case the necessary line is the goal line.

CHARGED DOWN

When the offensive team has been in possession constantly during a scrimmage down, the down is counted as one of a series except as provided for a foul (14-8), and is known as a Charged Down.

FIRST DOWN

The initial down in each series is known as the First Down, and if it is a charged down, subsequent charged downs are numbered consecutively until a new series is declared for either team (7-1-1 and 2).

Section 8   Drop Kick

DROP KICK

A Drop Kick is a kick by a kicker who drops the ball and kicks it as or immediately after it touches the ground.

Section 9   Fair Catch

FAIR CATCH

A Fair Catch is an unhindered catch by any player of the receivers of a free kick or of a scrimmage kick except one that has not crossed the line of scrimmage (3-17-3), provided he has legally signalled his intention of attempting such a catch (10-1-1).

MARK OF THE CATCH

Article 1   The Mark of the Catch is the spot from either:

(a) where the ball is actually caught by a receiver after a fair catch signal, valid or invalid (10-1-2); or

(b) the spot of ball after a penalty for fair catch interference (10-1-4).

Section 10   Field Goal

FIELD GOAL

A Field Goal is made by kicking the ball from the field of play through the plane of the opponents' goal by a drop kick or a placekick either:

(a) From behind the line on a play from scrimmage; or

(b) During a fair catch kick. See 11-5-3 and 3-9.

Section 11   Foul and Spots of Enforcement

FOUL

Article 1   A Foul is any infraction of a playing rule. Spot of Enforcement (or Basic Spot) is the *spot* at which a *penalty* is *enforced*. Four such spots are commonly used. They are:

SPOTS OF ENFORCEMENT

(a) Spot of Foul—The spot where a foul was committed or is so considered by rule (14-1-1).

(b) Previous Spot—The identical spot where the ball was last put in play.

(c) Spot of Snap, backward pass, or fumble—The spot where the foul occurred or the spot where the penalty is to be enforced.

(d) Succeeding Spot—The spot where the ball would next be put in play if no distance penalty were to be enforced.

ENFORCEMENT AFTER TOUCHDOWN

Exception: If a foul occurs after a touchdown and before the ready for play signal for a try, the succeeding spot is the spot of the next kickoff.

NOTES: A PENALTY IS NEVER ENFORCED FROM THE SPOT OF A LEGAL KICK FROM SCRIMMAGE (9-1-17). AN ENFORCEMENT INCLUDES A DECLINATION (14-6). SEE 14-1-5, FOR DEFINITION OF BASIC SPOT AND 3 AND 1 RULE.

Article 2   Types of Fouls

CONTINUING ACTION FOUL

(a) A Continuing Action Foul (or a subsequent foul) is spiking the ball, or a *personal* foul (12-2) that occurs during the continuing (subsequent) action immediately after a down ends (14-5). See 14-1-7 to 10.

NOTE: A CONTINUING ACTION FOUL MAY OCCUR WITH THE GAME CLOCK EITHER RUNNING OR STOPPED, AND IS ALWAYS ENFORCED FROM THE SUCCEEDING SPOT.

MULTIPLE FOUL

(b) A Multiple Foul is two or more fouls by the same team during the same down, unless they are part of a double foul (14-4).

DOUBLE FOUL

(c) A Double Foul is a foul by each team during the same down and includes any multiple foul by either team, including continuous action fouls (14-3).

FOUL
BETWEEN
DOWNS

(d) A Foul Between Downs is one that occurs after a down has definitely ended and before the next snap or free kick (3-2-2).

MAKE RIGHT CALL

PLAY ❶ Eagles' ball second-and-5 on their 25. The Eagles' Duce Staley runs out of bounds on his 45, after which his teammate Jamie Asher clips on the 30.

PLAY ❷ The Packers' Santana Dotson holds an offensive player on the line of scrimmage. The Packers' Vonnie Holiday was offside.

PLAY ❸ The offensive team is offside. The defensive team interferes with an eligible receiver downfield. The pass falls incomplete.

PLAY ❹ The Raiders clip after their running back, Napoleon Kaufman, scored.

Ruling 1: Philadelphia's ball first-and-25 on its 30. A continuing action foul. See 14-1-7. It happened after the down ended and was a personal foul. See A.R. 14.55

Ruling 2: A multiple foul because it was two fouls by the same team during the same down. See 14-4.

Ruling 3: A double foul because each team committed a foul during the same down. See 14-3.

Ruling 4: A foul between downs because the down ended when the score was made. Penalize on subsequent kickoff. See 14-1-7 and 14-5.

Section 12   Free Kick

FREE KICK

Article 1   A Free Kick is one that puts the ball in play to start a free kick down (3-2-1 and 6-1-1):

It includes:

(a) kickoff;

(b) safety kick; 6-1-2-a

(c) fair catch kick (6-1-3-3), (3-9).

FREE KICK
LINES

Article 2   The Free Kick Line for the offensive team is a yard line through the most forward point from which the ball is to be kicked (6-1-4).

The Free Kick Line for the defensive team is a yard line 10 yards in advance of the offensive team's free kick line (6-1-4).

Section 13   Huddle

HUDDLE

A Huddle is the action of two or more players of the offensive team who, instead of assuming their normal position for the snap, form a group for getting the signal for the next play or for any other reason (7-2-5).

Section 14 In Touch and Impetus

IN TOUCH

Article 1 A Ball is In Touch when:

(a) after it has come from the field of play, it touches a goal line (plane) while in player possession; or

(b) while it is loose, it touches anything on or behind a goal line.

NOTE: IF A PLAYER WHILE STANDING ON OR BEHIND HIS GOAL LINE TOUCHES A BALL THAT HAS COME FROM THE FIELD OF PLAY AND THE OFFICIAL IS IN DOUBT AS TO WHETHER THE BALL ACTUALLY TOUCHED THE GOAL LINE (PLANE), HE SHALL RULE THAT THE BALL WAS IN TOUCH.

BALL DEAD IN TOUCH

Article 2 A Ball Dead in Touch is one dead on or behind a goal line and it is either a *touchdown*, a *safety*, a *touchback*, a *field goal*, or the termination of a *try* (11), or a loss of down at previous spot (8-1-5).

NOTE: SOMETIMES A SAFETY, TOUCHDOWN, OR TRY (UNSUCCESSFUL) IS AWARDED BECAUSE OF A FOUL. IN SUCH CASES THEY ARE PENALTIES. ALSO NOTE EXCEPTIONS 8-4-2-EXC. 3, AND 8-4-2-S.N.

IMPETUS

Article 3 Impetus is the action of a player that gives momentum to the ball and sends it in touch.

The Impetus is attributed to the offense except when the ball is sent in touch through a new momentum when the defense *muffs* or *bats*:

(a) a kick or fumble;

(b) a backward pass after it has struck ground; or

(c) when the defense illegally kicks any ball (12-1-7).

NOTE: IF A PLAYER IS PUSHED OR BLOCKED INTO ANY KICK OR FUMBLE OR INTO A BACKWARD PASS AFTER IT HAS STRUCK GROUND, AND IF SUCH PUSHING OR BLOCKING IS THE PRIMARY FACTOR THAT SENDS SUCH A LOOSE BALL IN TOUCH, THE IMPETUS IS BY THE PUSHER OR BLOCKER, AND THE PUSHED (BLOCKED) PLAYER WILL NOT BE CONSIDERED TO HAVE TOUCHED THE BALL. SEE 9-1-10.

Section 15 Kicker

KICKER

A Kicker is the player of the offensive team who legally punts, placekicks, or dropkicks the ball. The offensive team is known as the Kickers during a kick.

A Receiver is any defensive player during a kick. The defensive team is known as the Receivers during a kick.

Section 16 Kickoff

KICKOFF

A Kickoff is a free kick used to put the ball in play:

(a) At start of the first and third periods;

(b) After each Try; and

(c) After a successful field goal (6-1-1-c).

NOTE: ONSIDE KICK (SEE 6-3-1, NOTE).

ONSIDE KICK

If a kicker obviously attempts to kick a ball short and it goes less than 20 yards, it is defined as an onside kick (this also applies to a safety kick).

Section 17   Line of Scrimmage

SCRIMMAGE LINE

Article 1   The Line of Scrimmage for each team is a yard line (plane) passing through the end of the ball nearest a team's own goal line. The term *scrimmage line*, or *line*, implies a play from scrimmage.

PLAYER ON LINE

Article 2   A Player of Team A is on his line when:

(a) his shoulders face Team B's goal line, and

(b) if he is the snapper, no part of his body is beyond Team B's line at the snap,

(c) if he is a non-snapper, he is not more than one foot behind his line. (For a non-snapper to be on the line of scrimmage, the guideline officials will use is that his helmet must break a vertical plane that would pass through the beltline of the snapper.)

NOTE: INTERLOCKING LEGS ARE PERMISSIBLE.

 PLAY **1**   The Buccaneers' Dave Moore assumes a three-point stance with his shoulders facing the Vikings' goal line. One hand is on the ground and it is on or not more than one foot behind his line. Neither of his feet or the other hand is within one foot of his line.

Ruling 1: Moore is legally on his line.

BALL CROSSES LINE

Article 3   The ball has crossed the scrimmage line *(crosses line)* when, during a play from scrimmage, it has been passed or legally kicked by a Team A player, through the plane of their line and has then touched the ground or anyone *behind* Team B's line.

NOTE: AT THE SNAP THE SCRIMMAGE LINES ARE DEFINITELY FIXED. AFTER THE SNAP THE LINES ARE NO LONGER DEFINITE AND THE OFFICIAL MAY CONSTRUE THE LINE OF SCRIMMAGE AS AN INDEFINITE AREA IN THE IMMEDIATE VICINITY OF THE TWO LINES.

Section 18   Neutral Zone, Start of Neutral Zone, and Encroaching

NEUTRAL ZONE

The Neutral Zone is the space the length of the ball between the offense's and the defense's scrimmage lines (planes). It **starts** when the ball is ready for play. (See neutral zone infraction, 7-2-2).

ENCROACHING

A player is Encroaching (7-2-2) on the neutral zone when any part of his body is in it and contact occurs prior to the snap. The official must blow his whistle immediately.

Exception: The **snapper** is not considered in the neutral zone if no part of his body is beyond Team B's line at the snap (7-2-2).

NOTE: THE FIELD JUDGE IS RESPONSIBLE FOR THE 40/25-SECOND COUNT WITH THE START OF THE NEUTRAL ZONE (4-3-9 AND 4-3-10).

Section 19   Offside

OFFSIDE

A player is Offside when any part of his body or his person is beyond his scrimmage or free kick line when the ball is put in play.

Exceptions: The *snapper* may be beyond his line provided he is not beyond the defensive line (3-18-Exception).

The *holder* of a *placekick* for a free kick may be beyond it (6-1-5-b).

The *kicker* may be beyond the line, but his kicking foot may not be (6-1-5-b).

Section 20   Out of Bounds and Inbounds Spot

PLAYER OR OFFICIAL OUT OF BOUNDS

Article 1   A player or an official is Out of Bounds when he touches:

(a) A boundary line; or

(b) Anything other than a player on or outside a boundary line.

BALL OUT OF BOUNDS

Article 2   The Ball is Out of Bounds when:

(a) the runner is out of bounds;

(b) while in player possession it touches a boundary line or anything other than a player on or outside such line; or

(c) a loose ball touches a boundary line or anything on or outside such line.

INBOUNDS SPOT

Article 3   The Inbounds Spot is a spot 70 feet 9 inches in from the sideline on the yard line passing through the spot where the ball or a runner is out of bounds between the goal lines.

Under certain conditions, the ball is dead in a side zone or has been placed there as the result of a penalty. See 7-3-7 and 7-5-1 to 6.

NOTE: ORDINARILY THE OUT-OF-BOUNDS SPOT IS THE SPOT WHERE THE BALL CROSSED A SIDELINE. HOWEVER, IF A BALL, WHILE STILL WITHIN A BOUNDARY LINE, IS DECLARED OUT OF BOUNDS BECAUSE OF TOUCHING ANYTHING THAT IS OUT OF BOUNDS, THE OUT-OF-BOUNDS SPOT IS ON THE YARD LINE THROUGH THE SPOT OF THE BALL AT THE INSTANT OF SUCH TOUCHING.

 PLAY **1**   The Bears' Ty Hallock, with his feet inbounds, touches an official who is touching a sideline.

PLAY **2**   The Bears' Ty Hallock, with his feet inbounds, touches any player who is touching a sideline.

PLAY **3**   The Bears' Ty Hallock fumbles and the loose ball touches the Cowboys' Dexter Coakley who is standing on sideline, and then ball rebounds into the field of play where Coakley falls on it.

PLAY **4**   Bears' Ty Hallock touches the shaft of the Cowboys' goal line marker with any part of his body.

Ruling 1: Out of bounds.

Ruling 2: Inbounds.

Ruling 3: *Dead ball and out of bounds as soon as the loose ball touches the player on sideline. Bears' ball at inbounds spot.*

Ruling 4: *Dead in touch. Position of ball determines. If, at instant of touching, any part of the ball is on or behind defensive goal line, it is a touchdown (11-2). If, at the instant of touching, any part of the ball is one foot from the goal line, it is Bears' ball on the Cowboys' one-foot line.*

Section 21   Pass and Passer

PASS AND
PASSER

Article 1   A Pass is the movement of the ball caused by handing, throwing, shoving (shovel pass), or pushing (push pass) by a runner (3-27-1). Such a movement is a pass, even though the ball does not leave his hand or hands, provided a teammate takes it (hand to hand pass).

NOTE: THE TERM IS ALSO USED TO DESIGNATE THE ACTION OF A PLAYER WHO CAUSES A PASS AS IN, "HE WILL PASS THE BALL."

FORWARD
PASS

Article 2   A Forward Pass (8-1-1) is a pass that:

(a) moves forward (to a point nearer the opponent's goal line) after leaving the passer's hands and before touching another player; or

(b) is handed (regardless of the direction of movement of the ball) to a player who is in advance of a teammate from whose hands he takes or receives it.

Exception: When the ball is handed forward to an eligible pass receiver (8-1-2) who is behind his line, it is not a forward pass. If the receiver muffs, it is treated as a fumble. (See 8-1-6-S.N. (1) for ball handed forward to ineligible behind the line.)

NOTE: A FUMBLE OR MUFF GOING FORWARD IS DISREGARDED AS TO ITS DIRECTION, UNLESS THE ACT IS RULED INTENTIONAL. IN SUCH CASES, THE FUMBLE IS A FORWARD PASS (8-1-1) AND THE MUFF IS A BAT (12-1-6).

PLAY **1**   A pass legally handed forward to an eligible pass receiver is followed by a forward pass in flight from behind the line.

PLAY **2**   A pass is legally handed forward to an eligible pass receiver, who muffs the ball and it is recovered by the defensive team.

Ruling 1: *A legal pass because the first handoff is not considered a forward pass (see Exception above).*

Ruling 2: *Not an incomplete pass. It is treated as a fumble and the defensive team keeps the ball.*

PASSER,
PASSING
TEAM

Article 3   A player who makes a legal forward pass is known as the Passer until the pass ends. The teammates of any player who passes forward (legally or illegally) are known collectively as the Passing Team or Passers.

BACKWARD PASS

Article 4 A Backward Pass (8-4-1) is any pass that is not a forward pass.

SUPPLEMENTAL NOTES

FORWARD, BEYOND, IN ADVANCE

(1) Forward, Beyond, or In Advance Of are terms that designate a point nearer the goal line of the defense unless the defense is specifically named. Converse terms are Backward or Behind.

(2) A pass parallel to a yard line or an offensive player moving parallel to it at the *snap* is considered backward.

(3) If a pass is batted, muffed, punched, or kicked in any direction, it does not change its original designation. However, such an act may change the impetus (3-14-3) if sent in touch or may be a foul (12-1-6, 7).

PLAY 1 The ball, moving backwards in the hands of the Packers' Brett Favre, is possessed by teammate Robert Brooks who is in advance of Favre.

PLAY 2 The ball, moving forward in the hands of the Packers' Brett Favre, is possessed by teammate Robert Brooks who is behind Favre.

Ruling 1: A forward pass unless Brooks is behind his line and is eligible to receive a forward pass.

Ruling 2: A backward pass.

Section 22 Piling On

PILING ON

Piling On is causing the body to fall upon any prostrate player (other than the runner), or upon a runner after the ball is dead (12-2-7).

Section 23 Placekick

PLACEKICK

A Placekick is a kick made by a kicker while the ball is in a fixed position on the ground except as provided for a permissible manufactured tee at kickoff (6-1-5). The ball may be held in position by a teammate. See 11-5-4.

Section 24 Pocket Area

POCKET AREA

The Pocket Area applies from a point two yards outside of either offensive tackle and includes the tight end *if* he stays on or drops off the line of scrimmage to pass protect. Pocket extends longitudinally behind the line back to the offensive team's own end line.

Section 25 Post-Possession

POST-POSSESSION FOUL

A foul by the receiving team that occurs after a ball is legally kicked from scrimmage prior to possession changing. The ball must cross the line of scrimmage and the receiving team must retain the kicked ball. See 9-1-17-Exception 2.

Section 26 Punt

PUNT

A Punt is a kick made by a kicker who drops the ball and kicks it while it is in flight (9-1-1).

Section 27 Runner and Running Play

RUNNER

Article 1 The Runner is the offensive player who is in possession of a live ball (3-2-1), i.e., holding the ball or carrying it in any direction.

RUNNING PLAY

Article 2 A Running Play is a play during which there is a runner and which is not followed by a kick or forward pass from behind the scrimmage line. There may be more than one such play during the same down (14-1-12).

SUPPLEMENTAL NOTES

(1) The exception to a running play is significant only when a foul occurs while there is a runner prior to a kick or pass from behind the line (8-3-2, 9-1-17, and 14-1-12).

(2) The statement, a player may advance, means that he may become a runner, make a legal kick (9-1-1), make a backward pass (8-4-1), or during a play from scrimmage, an offensive player may forward pass (8-1-1) from behind his scrimmage line, provided it is the first such pass during the down and the ball had not been beyond the line of scrimmage previously.

MAKE THE RIGHT CALL

PLAY 1 The Raiders' James Jett catches a kickoff, advances, and fumbles. The Bills' Kamil Loud recovers and advances.

Ruling 1: While Jett and Loud were in possession, there were two running plays during the same down.

Section 28 Safety

SAFETY

A Safety is the situation in which the ball is dead on or behind a team's own goal line provided:

(a) the impetus (3-14-3) came from a player of that team;

(b) it is not a touchdown (11-2); or

(c) it is not a pass violation by Team A behind its own goal line (8-1-1-Pen. A).

Section 29 Scrimmage, Play From Scrimmage

SCRIMMAGE DOWN

A Scrimmage Down is one that starts with a snap (3-31). From Scrimmage refers to any action from the start of the snap until the down ends or if Team A loses possession and Team B secures possession. Any subsequent action during the down, after a change of team possession, is **Not From Scrimmage.**

SCRIMMAGE LINE

NOTES: THE TERM *SCRIMMAGE LINE* OR *LINE* IMPLIES A PLAY BY A *FROM SCRIMMAGE. LINE* IS USED EXTENSIVELY FOR BREVITY AND IS NOT TO BE CONFUSED WITH SIDE, END, OR YARD LINE. *LINE* IS ALSO USED FOR FREE KICK LINE. FOR GIVEN REASONS, ACTION DURING A FREE KICK DOWN (6-1), IS SOMETIMES REFERRED TO AS A PLAY *NOT FROM SCRIMMAGE.*

Section 30 Shift

SHIFT

A Shift is the action of two or more offensive players who (prior to a snap), after having assumed a set position, simultaneously change the position of their feet by pivoting to or assuming a new set position with either one foot or both feet (7-2-5).

Section 31　Snap and the Snapper

SNAP AND
THE SNAPPER

A Snap is a backward pass that puts the ball in play to start a scrimmage down. The Snapper is the offensive player who attempts a snap. See 7-3-3, for conditions pertaining to a legal snap.

Section 32　Supplemental Notes (S.N.)

SUPPLEMENTAL
NOTES

Supplemental Notes (S.N.) are descriptive paragraphs used to amplify a given rule, which would otherwise be too cumbersome or involved in its scope or wording.

An Approved Ruling (A.R.) is often used for the same purpose (3-1). Additional Approved Rulings are found in *The Official Casebook of the National Football League.*

A Note or Notes are usually more specific and apply to a particular situation. They are also used to indicate pertinent references to other rules.

Section 33　Suspended Player

SUSPENDED
PLAYER

A Suspended Player is one who must be withdrawn, for at least one down, for correction of illegal equipment (5-3).

Section 34　Tackling

TACKLING

Tackling is the use of hands or arms by a defensive player in his attempt to hold a runner or throw him to the ground (12-1-4).

Section 35　Team A and B, Offense and Defense

OFFENSE AND
DEFENSE

Article 1　Whenever a team is in possession (3-2-7), it is the Offense and, at such time, its opponent is the Defense.

TEAM A
AND
TEAM B

Article 2　The team that puts the ball in play is Team A, and its opponent is Team B. For brevity, a player of Team A is referred to as A1 and his teammates as A2, A3, etc. Opponents are B1, B2, etc.

NOTE: A TEAM BECOMES TEAM A WHEN IT HAS BEEN DESIGNATED TO PUT BALL IN PLAY, AND IT REMAINS TEAM A UNTIL A DOWN ENDS, EVEN THOUGH THERE MIGHT BE ONE OR MORE CHANGES OF POSSESSION DURING THE DOWN. THIS IS IN CONTRAST WITH THE TERMS *OFFENSE* AND *DEFENSE*. TEAM A IS ALWAYS THE OFFENSE WHEN A DOWN STARTS, BUT BECOMES THE DEFENSE IF AND WHEN B SECURES POSSESSION DURING THE DOWN, AND VICE VERSA FOR EACH CHANGE OF POSSESSION.

Section 36　Time Out or Time In

TIME OUT

Article 1　A Time Out is an interval during which the Game Clock is stopped (4-3-1) and includes the intermissions (4-1-1 to 6).

NOTE: THE TERM *TIME OUT* (GENERAL) IS NOT TO BE CONFUSED WITH A CHARGED TEAM TIME OUT, WHICH IS SPECIFIC (4-3-3).

TIME IN

Article 2　Time In is the converse (4-3-2) and is also used to indicate when the clock operator is to start his clock.

Section 37　Touchback

TOUCHBACK

A Touchback is the situation in which a ball is dead on or behind a team's own goal line, provided the impetus came from an opponent and provided it is not a touchdown (11-6).

NOTE: SEE 8-1-1 TO 5 FOR EXCEPTIONS TO TOUCHBACK, WHEN IMPETUS BY AN OPPONENT IS AN INCOMPLETE PASS.

Section 38 Touchdown

TOUCHDOWN

A Touchdown is the situation in which any part of the ball, legally in possession of a player inbounds, is on, above, or behind the opponent's goal line (plane), provided it is not a touchback (11-2).

Section 39 Tripping

TRIPPING

Tripping is the use of the leg or foot in obstructing any opponent (including a runner) below the knee (12-1-3).

Section 40 Try

TRY

A Try is an opportunity given a team that has just scored a touchdown to score an additional one or two points during one scrimmage down (11-3).

Section 41 Yard Line, Own Goal

OWN GOAL

Article 1   A team's Own Goal during any given period is the one it is guarding. The adjacent goal line is known as its (own) goal line.

YARD LINE

Article 2   A Yard Line is any line and its vertical plane parallel to the end line. The Yard Lines (marked or unmarked) in the field of play are named by number in yards from a team's goal line to the center of the field.

NOTE: THE YARD LINE 19 YARDS FROM TEAM A'S GOAL LINE IS CALLED A'S 19-YARD LINE. THE YARD LINE 51 YARDS FROM A'S GOAL LINE IS CALLED B'S 49-YARD LINE. (FOR BREVITY, THESE ARE REFERRED TO AS A'S 19 AND B'S 49.)

MAKE THE RIGHT CALL

CHAPTER 4
GAME TIMING

In NFL games, there are two categories of time: the period inside the two-minute warning at the end of each half, and all the other time. When you're inside the two-minute warning period, special rules apply.

An example is fumbling the ball. Unlike the rules before the two-minute warning, only the fumbling player can recover the ball and advance once the warning period has started. That special rule keeps teams from trying to gain an advantage by fumbling the ball forward for a teammate to recover.

Jerry Seeman
NFL DIRECTOR OF OFFICIATING

Section 1　Length of the Game

LENGTH OF GAME AND INTERMISSIONS

Article 1　The length of the game is 60 minutes, divided into four periods of 15 minutes each, with intervals of 2 minutes between the first and second periods (first half) and between the third and fourth periods (second half). During these intermissions all playing rules continue in force and no representative of either team shall enter the field unless he is an incoming substitute. See 13-1-5.

PENALTY: FOR ILLEGALLY ENTERING FIELD: LOSS OF 15 YARDS FROM SUCCEEDING SPOT (13-1-6, PEN.).

TIMING THE INTERMISSIONS

Article 2　The Field Judge is to time the 2-minute intermissions and shall sound his whistle (or signal visibly) at 1 minute and 50 seconds. The Referee shall sound his whistle immediately thereafter for:

(a) play to start; and

(b) Clock operator to start the timing of 25 seconds. See 4-3-10-S.N. 1.

OFFICIAL TIME

Article 3　The stadium electric clock shall be the official time. The clock operator shall start and stop the clock upon the signal of any official in accordance with the rules. The Line Judge (15-5-2) shall be responsible for supervision of the timing and in case the stadium clock becomes inoperative, or for any reason it is not being operated correctly, he shall take over the official timing on the field.

HALFTIME

Article 4　Between the second and third periods, there shall be an intermission of 12 minutes. During intermission, play is suspended, and the teams may leave the field. This is to be timed by the Line Judge. See 15-5-4.

NOTE: SEE 13-1-1 TO 4, FOR FOULS BY NON-PLAYERS BETWEEN HALVES.

KICKOFF ON SCHEDULE

Article 5　Both teams must be on the field in ample time to kick off at the scheduled time for start of each half. Ample time prior to the start of the game is construed to be at least 15 minutes prior to the initial kickoff in order to ensure sufficient time for proper warm-up. Head coaches must be notified personally before the start of each half by designated members of the officiating crew.

PENALTIES: FOR DELAYING START OF HALF:

> **(A) LOSS OF 15 YARDS FROM THE SPOT OF THE KICKOFF AS DETERMINED BY RULE 4, SECTION 2.**
>
> **(B) LOSS OF COIN TOSS OPTION FOR BOTH HALVES AND 15 YARDS IF A TEAM IS NOT ON THE FIELD IN AMPLE TIME PRIOR TO THE SCHEDULED KICKOFF AS INDICATED.**

SUDDEN DEATH

Article 6　Provisions for the sudden death method of determining the winner in case of certain tie scores at the end of game will be found under Rule 16.

Section 2   Starting Each Period

TOSS OF COIN

Article 1   Not more than three minutes before the kickoff, the Referee, in the presence of both teams' captains (limit of six per team, all of whom must be uniformed members of the active list) shall toss a coin at the center of the field. The toss shall be called by the captain of the visiting team or by the captain designated by the Referee if there is no home team. The winner of the toss must choose one of two privileges and the loser is given the other. The two privileges are:

(a) which team is to receive; or

(b) the goal his team will defend.

PENALTY: FOR FAILURE TO COMPLY: LOSS OF COIN TOSS OPTION, BOTH HALVES, AND LOSS OF 15 YARDS FROM SPOT OF KICKOFF FOR FIRST HALF ONLY.

SECOND HALF CHOICE

For the second half, the captain who lost the pregame toss is to have the first choice of the two privileges listed in (a) or (b) unless one of the teams lost its first and second half option under 4-1-5. Immediately prior to the start of the second half, the captains of both teams must inform the Referee of their respective choices.

SUPPLEMENTAL NOTE

(1) When the teams first appear on field for the start of second half, the Referee is to assume a position on one side at the numbers and indicate which team will receive.

CHANGE OF GOALS

Article 2   At the end of the first and third periods, the teams must change goals. Team possession, number of succeeding down, and relative position of the ball on the field of play and of the necessary line remain unchanged.

Section 3   Timing

TIME OUT, STOP CLOCK

Article 1   The clock operator shall stop the game clock (time out) when upon his own positive knowledge or signal or upon a signal by any official:

(a) the ball is out of bounds;

(b) a receiver catches after a fair catch signal (10-1-2);

(c) ball is dead in touch;

(d) at end of down during which a foul occurs;

STATUS OF GAME CLOCK AFTER PENALTY ENFORCEMENT

NOTE: IF THE CLOCK WAS STOPPED FOR A FOUL BY EITHER TEAM (WHETHER PENALTY IS ACCEPTED OR DECLINED), IT WILL BE STARTED WHEN THE BALL IS DECLARED READY FOR PLAY; EXCEPT WHEN THE FOUL OCCURRED DURING THE LAST TWO MINUTES OF THE FIRST HALF, OR THE LAST FIVE MINUTES OF THE SECOND HALF, IN WHICH CASE THE CLOCK STARTS ON THE SNAP.

(e) whenever a forward pass is incomplete;

(f)   at the time of a foul, for which the ball remains dead or is dead immediately;

(g) upon referee's signal of two minutes remaining for a half;

(h) when a period expires;

(i)   when any official signals a time out for any other reason;

(j)   when a kicked ball is recovered illegally and/or surrounded; or

(k) upon the completion of a down involving a change of possession.

PLAY 1 Second-and-10 on the Browns' 30. Their running back Terry Kirby goes to his 40 where he is tackled. During Kirby's run, teammate Leslie Shepherd clipped the Redskins' Dana Stubblefield at the Browns' 35.

PLAY 2 Second-and-10 on the Browns' 30. Their running back Terry Kirby goes to his 40 and steps out of bounds there. During Kirby's run, teammate Leslie Shepherd clipped the Redskins' Dana Stubblefield at the Browns' 35.

Ruling 1: *The Browns' ball second-and-20 on their 20. Game Clock starts on ready to play signal after penalty is enforced.*

Ruling 2: *Browns' ball second-and-20 on their 20. Game Clock starts with referee's ready signal as ball was dead when Kirby ran out of bounds, except in last two minutes of first half or last five minutes of second half.*

CHANGE OF POSSESSION

NOTES: CHANGE OF POSSESSION INCLUDES:

(1) RECOVERY OF LOOSE BALL BY TEAM NOT PUTTING BALL IN PLAY;

(2) FORWARD PASS INTERCEPTION;

(3) FREE KICK OR KICK FROM SCRIMMAGE RECOVERED AND/OR ADVANCED BY THE RECEIVING TEAM OR THAT GOES OUT OF BOUNDS; AND

(4) LEGAL TOUCHING, MUFF, OR FUMBLE BY RECEIVING TEAM OF ANY KICKED BALL THAT IS RECOVERED BY THE KICKING TEAM.

TIME IN, START CLAOCK

Article 2 The clock operator shall start his clock (time in) when the ball is kicked off to start the game. Thereafter, following any time out (3-36), the clock shall be started when the ball is next snapped or free-kicked.

Exceptions:

1) After a field goal, safety, or touchdown, the clock is started at kickoff following a Try except as provided for the last two minutes of a half (6-3-1-Note).

2) After the two-minute warning of a half, the clock is not started until a kickoff or safety kick is legally touched in the field of play (6-3-1, and 11-5-3).

TIME IN AFTER OUT OF BOUNDS

3) Except in the last two minutes of the first half and the last five minutes of the game, on a play from scrimmage whenever a runner goes out of bounds, the Game Clock is started when an official spots the ball at the inbounds mark and the Referee gives the ready signal.

TIME IN ON REFEREE'S WHISTLE

4) After the two minute warning of each half, if there is an illegal substitution penalty (5-1-5 and 5-2-1) or an excess time out (See 4-3-10 for exception), the game clock is started with the referee's whistle, if the clock was running.

5) After a referee's time out (4-3-7), the game clock is started with the referee's whistle if the clock was running.

PLAY 1 During the last two minutes of the game the offensive team safety kicks from its 20.

Ruling 1: Time in starts when the safety kick is legally touched by any player in the field of play (6-3-1-Note).

No extension of the automatic time outs in Article 1 shall be allowed unless any player requests a team time out, or a Referee orders a team time out or suspends play himself.

CONSECUTIVE
TIME OUTS

NOTE 1: IN CASE OF CONSECUTIVE TIME OUTS BETWEEN DOWNS, TIME IS IN ACCORDING TO THE CLASSIFICATION OF THE LAST TIME OUT (4-3-1-NOTE 1).

NOTE 2: CONSECUTIVE TEAM TIME OUTS BETWEEN DOWNS BY EITHER TEAM ARE ALLOWED SO LONG AS IT IS NOT BY THE SAME TEAM. SUCH A TIME OUT MAY FOLLOW AN AUTOMATIC TIME OUT (4-3-1) OR REFEREE'S TIME OUT (4-3-7) AND MAXIMUM LENGTH OF THE SECOND TIME OUT WILL BE 40 SECONDS. NO ADDITIONAL CONSECUTIVE TEAM TIME OUTS CAN BE TAKEN DURING THE SAME DEAD BALL PERIOD.

PLAY 1 Following a Referee's time out after a change of possession after a punt:
a) The Browns take their third team time out.
b) The Browns take their fourth team time out prior to last two minutes.

Ruling 1a: *Time in with snap.*

Ruling 1b: *The Browns are penalized 5 yards and time is in with snap.*

CHARGED
TIME OUTS

Article 3   The Referee shall declare a charged team time out when he suspends play while the ball is dead:

(a) After or upon a request for a time out by any player;

(b) Should a player appear injured on the field, official will call time out for an injured player. Time out shall not be charged to team unless:

TIME OUT FOR
INJURY NOT
CHARGED

(1) players on field or from bench attempt to assist injured player from the field unless directed to by team physician or trainer in consultation with official;

(2) injury occurs after two-minute warning of either half;

Exception: Time out is not charged if a foul committed by opponent caused the injury.

(3) injured player remains in the game.

NOTE: MEMBERS OF BOTH TEAMS MAY GO TO THE SIDELINE FOR CONFERENCE WITH COACHES DURING AN INJURY TIME OUT, BUT MUST BE READY TO PLAY WHEN REFEREE SIGNALS BALL IN PLAY AS SOON AS TREATMENT IS COMPLETED OR INJURED PLAYER HAS LEFT THE FIELD.

Exceptions: Following a time out as in (a) or (b), the Referee may order a charged time out for injury or for repair of legal equipment, but only in an obvious emergency (4-3-4 and 5), and especially so during the last two minutes of a half (4-3-10).

PLAY **1** A runner is tackled and appears injured since he doesn't move.

Ruling 1: Official should call time out for injured player. Official should not try to determine if player is injured. Time out is not charged if conditions of 4-3-3-b, are not violated.

THREE TIME
OUTS
ALLOWED

Article 4 Three charged team time outs are allowed a team during each half without a distance penalty (4-3-5). When any team time out occurs, the Field Judge shall start his watch and sound his whistle (or signal visibly) at the expiration of 1 minute and 50 seconds. The Referee shall not sound his whistle for play to start before such a signal from the Field Judge.

Exception 1: Whenever a team time out is called after the two-minute warning in a half, the time out shall last 40 seconds unless more time is required because of an injury or television utilizes a commercial opportunity.

Exception 2: The Referee may allow:

INJURY AND
EQUIPMENT
TIME OUT

(a) necessary time to attend to an injured player; or

(b) repair legal equipment.

NOTE: IN THE JUDGEMENT OF THE REFEREE, IF SUCH A PLAYER IS NOT READY FOR PLAY IN A REASONABLE AMOUNT OF TIME, HE MUST BE WITHDRAWN.

SUPPLEMENTAL NOTES

(1) In the case of extended team time outs ordered by the Referee for exceptions (a) and/or (b), the Field Judge shall not sound his whistle until the expiration of extra time is allowed.

(2) The Referee shall sound his whistle for play to start immediately upon Field Judge's signal for the expiration of any team time out.

(3) On all requested time outs, the Referee shall not signify that the ball will be put in play prior to 1 minute and 50 seconds of elapsed time, or 40 seconds during the last two minutes of a half.

EXCESS TIME
OUTS PRIOR TO
LAST TWO
MINUTES

Article 5 Team time outs prior to the last two minutes of a half, in excess of three, for either team, is a foul unless the time out is for an injured player who is removed from the game (except injury time out caused by a foul, 4-3-3-Exception).

NOTE: IF A TEAM DESIRES TO TAKE AN EXCESS TIME OUT PRIOR TO THE TWO-MINUTE WARNING, THEY MAY DO SO AND LEAVE THE INJURED PLAYER IN THE GAME, WITH APPROPRIATE PENALTY.

REFEREE
WHISTLE AFTER
EXCESS

After the first three time outs during a half, all team time outs regardless of the reason are to be counted in determining the fourth or subsequent time outs. After the two-minute warning of each half, if there is an excess time out by either team, time is in with the Referee's whistle for play to start, if the clock had been running. (See 4-3-10 for exception).

EXCESS TIME
OUTS DURING
LAST TWO
MINUTES

Article 6 Team time outs after two-minute warning of half.

(a) During the last two minutes of either half, additional time outs by either team after the third legal one are not allowed unless it is for an injured player who must be immediately designated and removed. A fourth time out under these conditions is not penalized. Subsequent requests (fifth or more) under these same conditions are allowed, but are penalized five yards. On all excess time outs against the defense, the play clock is reset to 40 seconds.

EXCESS TIME OUTS DURING LAST TWO MINUTES, 10-SECOND HOLD

(b) During the last two minutes of either half while time is in, if the score is tied or the team in possession is behind in the score and the offensive team has exhausted its legal time outs, an additional time out may be requested and granted under (a) above. However, the ball shall not be put in play until the time on the game clock has been reduced by 10 seconds. (The Referee, in a position between the center and the quarterback, will advise [by using the microphone] the game clock operator to take 10 seconds off the clock. During this time interval, the Umpire will be directly over the ball. After 10 seconds have been taken off the clock, both officials will back away with the Umpire raising his arm above his head. After a momentary delay, the Umpire will quickly lower his arm and give the wind-the-clock signal. This signal indicates to the game clock operator to restart the game clock and also to the offensive team that it may legally snap the ball.)

NOTE: THERE CAN NEVER BE A 10-SECOND RUN OFF AGAINST THE DEFENSIVE TEAM.

PENALTY: FOR EACH EXCESS TIME OUT: LOSS OF FIVE YARDS FROM SUCCEEDING SPOT FOR DELAY. NECESSARY LINE AND NUMBER OF DOWN REMAIN THE SAME.

SUPPLEMENTAL NOTES

(1) Either half can end during the 10-second period between time in and permissible play resumption, as well as during enforcement or declination of penalty for offensive team fouls.

(2) This applies to Sudden Death Rule (Rule 16) in force for Wild Card Playoffs, Divisional Playoffs, Conference Championship Games, the Super Bowl, and the Pro Bowl.

FEIGNING INJURIES

(3) The Rules Committee deprecates feigning injuries, with subsequent withdrawal, to obtain a time out without penalty and even so when done to conserve time. Coaches are urged to cooperate in discouraging this practice. The Referee should refuse such a request when it is an obvious evasion of the rules.

(4) The Referee must notify both captain and head coach when their team has been charged with three time outs, and no penalty is to be enforced for an excess time out unless such notice has been given. The Referee shall not delegate this notification to any other person.

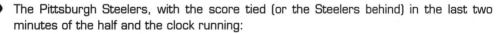

PLAY **1** The Pittsburgh Steelers, with the score tied (or the Steelers behind) in the last two minutes of the half and the clock running:
(a) Request their fourth time out due to an injured player.
(b) Request their fifth time out due to an injured player.

Ruling 1a: Granted. No five yard penalty. Player has to be removed. Referee's ready signal starts the clock, but the ball is not put into play for at least 10 seconds.

Ruling 1b: Granted. Five yard penalty. Player has to be removed. Referee's whistle starts the clock and the ball shall not be put into play for at least 10 seconds.

Article 7 Play may be suspended by Referee (Referee's Time Out) at any time without penalty to either team when playing time is being destroyed because of delay not intentionally caused by either team, provided it does not violate some specific rule.

SUPPLEMENTAL NOTES

The following situations are automatic Referee's time outs:

(1) Where there is a change of possession. The clock will start on the snap.

(2) Any possibility of a measurement for first down or in consulting a captain about one.

(3) Any time the player who originally takes the snap is tackled behind the line of scrimmage.

NOTE: THE PLAY CLOCK STARTS AT 40 SECONDS AFTER THE TACKLE.

Exception: During the last two minutes of a half, the Game Clock shall be restarted as soon as the ball has been spotted for the succeeding down, at which time the Referee is to give the ready signal. In all cases, a minimum of five seconds must have elapsed before the ball is made ready for play.

NOTE: PRIOR TO THE LAST TWO MINUTES OF A HALF, THE REFEREE WILL ALLOW RECEIVERS TO *APPROACH THE LINE OF SCRIMMAGE* BEFORE GIVING THE "WIND THE GAME CLOCK" SIGNAL.

(4) Undue pileups on the runner or ball, or determining possession after a fumble during time in.

(5) Undue delay by officials in spotting ball for the next snap.

(6) Illegal recovery of any kicked ball from scrimmage.

(7) The snap made before the Referee can assume his position (not a repeated act). See 4-3-9-h.

(8) Injury to an official or member of the chain crew.

(9) Captain's choice of a free kick or snap after a fair catch. See 11-5-3.

(10) Official's conference for a rules interpretation or an enforcement (15-1-6). Clock starts as original status dictates.

(11) Repairing or replacing game equipment (not player equipment).

(12) Line Judge's signal of two minute warning for a half; the Game Clock starts on the snap.

(13) Obvious inability of the offense to hear team signals because of crowd noise. When such situations prevail, the following procedures must be followed:

(a) If the quarterback (or other signal-caller) of the offensive team indicates to the Referee that his teammates cannot hear his signals, and the Referee deems it reasonable to conclude the players on the offense (other than wide receivers) cannot hear, the Referee will extend his right arm fully over his head to indicate disruptive crowd noise. The Referee then will signal a Referee's time out and ask the defensive captain to use his best effort to quiet the crowd. The Referee then will announce over his wireless microphone that he has asked the defensive team to assist in quieting the crowd so that the game can continue. He then will return to his position behind the offensive team.

(b) If, after the public announcement described in (a) above, crowd noise conditions in that same ball possession are deemed by the Referee, with or without appeal by the offensive signal-caller, to be disruptive to the offense, he again will use the upraised-arm signal and will announce over his wireless microphone that any further crowd noise which is disruptive will result in forfeiture by the defense of one of its remaining time outs in the half or, in the absence of time outs, a five-yard penalty against the defense for delay of the game.

(c) If, after the public announcement described in (b) above, crowd noise conditions in that same ball possession are deemed by the Referee, with or without appeal by the offensive signal-caller, to be disruptive to the offense, he again will use the upraised-arm signal and will, if such signal does not quiet the crowd, assess the appropriate penalty provided for in (b) above.

(d) Thereafter if disruptive crowd noise recurs in the same ball possession, the Referee, with or without appeal from the offensive signal-caller, will use the upraised-arm signal while remaining in his normal position behind the offensive formation and without calling a Referee's time out. Following a momentary pause to confirm that disruptive noise conditions are continuing, he will assess the appropriate penalty provided for in (b) above.

(e) If, upon any appeal from the offensive signal-caller, the Referee deems that noise conditions are not sufficiently disruptive to apply the crowd-noise procedures, he will deny the appeal and proceed with normal game timing. The Referee's signal that he is denying the appeal will be to point toward the defensive team's goal line.

(f) During the time out described in (a) above, the offensive team may huddle. When the offensive team again attempts to run a play, the game clock will start on the snap. The 40/25-second clock will not be used.

(g) If, in any ball possession subsequent to the first possession of the game that involves disruptive crowd noise, the Referee, either with or without an appeal by the offensive signal-caller, deems it to be reasonable to conclude that the players on offense (other than wide receivers) cannot hear, the Referee will signal a Referee's time out and announce over his wireless microphone that the defensive team is now subject to appropriate crowd noise penalties. Any crowd-noise interruption thereafter in that same ball possession will result in the Referee using his upraised-arm signal, followed, if necessary, by a penalty against the defense.

(h) Once the procedures of (a) and (b) above have been followed in a given game, disruptive crowd-noise incidents in any subsequent ball possession will be handled by the procedures of (g). In effect, for each ball possession during which disruptive crowd noise occurs (with the exception of the first in the game), the Referee will make one public announcement after which he may assess a penalty, and he will thereafter always precede any such penalty by the upraised-arm signal but not by a public announcement. As specified in (a) and (b) above, he will make two public announcements before assessing a penalty on the first ball possession of the game during which disruptive crowd noise occurs.

(i) In any instance where the Referee is signaling with upraised arm, the offensive signal-caller may, if he chooses, continue to play. Such signal indicates that disruptive crowd-noise conditions prevail; it does not automatically stop play nor does it automatically result in a penalty. Conversely, if the Referee's arm is not upraised, the penalty situation does not prevail and the offense must attempt to continue play.

(14) On a play from scrimmage, if a fumble goes out of bounds forward by any player, the clock stops on the official's time out signal, then restarts on the wind of the clock signal. (See 7-5-6-Note)

(15) On a play not from scrimmage, if a fumble goes out of bounds forward by any player, the clock stops on the official's time out signal and will restart at the snap.

TIME IN AFTER
REFEREE'S
WHISTLE

Article 8   After a Referee's time out, time in starts with his whistle (clock signal).

Exception: After a time out for a change of possession, notification of two minutes remaining for a half, stopping the clock for inability to hear signals, and after enforcement (when appropriate) time is in with the snap. See 11-5-3 and 15-1-10.

PLAY ❶   The Redskins' Brad Johnson drops back to pass and is tackled behind his line.

PLAY ❷   The Cowboys' Deion Sanders gives a fair-catch signal and catches ball.

PLAY ❸   At the instant a runner is contacted by a defensive player, ball is inbounds. He then:
a)   Slides across side line.
b)   Loses possession after he touches ground and ball crosses sideline.

Ruling 1: Referee's time out. Stop the clock until the ball can be respotted at succeeding spot. (40 second clock starts when time out signal is given).

Ruling 2: Referee's time out. Stop clock. When ready for play, start clock with snap or fair-catch kick.

Ruling 3a: Not a time out.

Ruling 3b: Not a time out unless it is evident that undue time will be consumed in spotting ball (Referee's time out).

DELAY OF
GAME

Article 9   The ball must be put in play promptly and any action or inaction by either team that tends to prevent this is a delay of game. It is delay of game if the ball is not put into play within 40/25 seconds:

(a)   by snap after the neutral zone starts (3-18);

(b)   after a Referee's time out.

Other examples of action or inaction that are to be construed as delay of game or attempts to conserve playing time are:

(c)   Repeatedly charging into the neutral zone prior to the snap when not otherwise ruled encroaching (7-2-2).

(d)   With time in, start of neutral zone is unduly delayed by failure of players of either team to assemble promptly.

HURRY UP
OFFENSE AND
SNAP

NOTE: DURING LAST TWO MINUTES OF HALF, ONCE THE BALL HAS BEEN RESPOTTED FOR THE SUCCEEDING DOWN AND THE HEAD LINESMAN HAS PLACED HIS BEAN BAG ON THE GROUND AT THE NEW LINE OF SCRIMMAGE, THE UMPIRE, UPON SIGNAL FROM THE REFEREE, IS TO STEP AWAY FROM THE BALL. AT THIS POINT A SNAP MAY BE MADE. IF BALL IS SNAPPED BEFORE ALL MEMBERS OF DEFENSIVE TEAM HAVE TAKEN THEIR PROPER POSITION ON LINE OF SCRIMMAGE, PLAY IS TO BE STOPPED IMMEDIATELY AND THAT TEAM PENALIZED FIVE YARDS FOR OFFSIDE.

(e)   When a player remains on a dead ball or on a runner who has been downed.

(f)   Failure to play immediately when ordered, including not kicking off within the designated 25 seconds on the play clock.

(g)   Player exercising rights of captain except in emergency.

(h)   Repeatedly snapping ball after the neutral zone is established before the Referee can assume his position (7-3-3-c-2).

(i) A runner repeatedly attempts to advance after he is so held that his forward progress is stopped.

(j) When one of the kickers recovers a kick (unless one recovered behind line other than a Try-kick), and carries it in any direction. See 9-1-4 Note; 9-1-6.

(k) Undue advance by a receiver who catches after a fair catch signal (valid or invalid) unless after touching kickers in fight. See 10-1-2-Exception.

(l) Opponent taking ball from runner after it is dead, causes a loose ball or scramble that consumes playing time to re-spot the ball (7-4-1-d).

(m) Undue delay in assembling after a time out.

(n) Substitute entering during play unless interference (12-3-3).

(o) Defensive player(s) aligned in a stationary position within one yard of the line of scrimmage cannot make quick and abrupt actions that are not part of normal defensive player movement in an obvious attempt to cause an offensive player(s) to foul (false start). (Blow whistle immediately)

PENALTY: FOR DELAY OF GAME: LOSS OF FIVE YARDS:

(A) FROM SUCCEEDING SPOT IF BETWEEN DOWNS AND BALL REMAINS DEAD; OR

(B) FROM PREVIOUS SPOT IF BALL WAS IN PLAY. NUMBER OF DOWN AND NECESSARY LINE REMAIN THE SAME.

NOTE: AFTER AN ENFORCEMENT FOR DELAY OF GAME BY THE DEFENSE, PRIOR TO OR AT THE SNAP, NUMBER OF DOWN AND NECESSARY LINE REMAIN THE SAME. SEE 14-8-5.

ACTION TO CONSERVE TIME

Article 10 There shall be no unusual action or inaction during the last two minutes of a half to conserve time.

PENALTY: FOR ATTEMPTS TO CONSERVE TIME: LOSS OF FIVE YARDS FOR DELAY. WHEN EFFORTS ARE MADE BY THE OFFENSIVE TEAM TO CONSERVE TIME, OFFICIALS WILL RUN 10 SECONDS OFF THE GAME CLOCK BEFORE PERMITTING THE BALL TO BE PUT IN PLAY ON THE READY SIGNAL. IF THE ACTION IS BY THE DEFENSE, THE PLAY CLOCK WILL BE RESET TO 40 SECONDS AND THE GAME CLOCK WILL START ON THE READY SIGNAL.

NOTE: THERE NEVER CAN BE A 10-SECOND RUN OFF AGAINST THE DEFENSIVE TEAM.

SUPPLEMENTAL NOTES

PLAY CLOCK 40/25-SECOND COUNT

(1) The Play Clock operator shall time the 40/25-second intervals between plays upon signal from game official(s). The 40-second interval is to start when one play ends. If certain administrative stoppages or other delays occur such as change of possession, team time out, Referee's time out, injury, measurement, or any unusual delay that interferes with the normal flow of play, a 25-second interval is to be used (even if the 40-second clock was already counting down). The 40/25-second clock is to start when:

a) neutral zone starts with Referee's whistle (3-18);

b) Referee's whistle indicates that play may start following any time out.

If the ball is not put in play within this time, he sounds his whistle for the foul and the ball remains dead. When the foul is prior to a snap, defensive team may decline distance penalty, in which case down is replayed. See 14-6 Exception (4).

(2) More than two successive penalties, during the same down, after a warning is unsportsmanlike conduct (12-3-1-h, i).

**BACKWARD
PASS OUT OF
BOUNDS**

(3) When the ball is dead during time in, the Referee must determine immediately if a measurement is indicated, unless there has been a change of possession. If indicated, he declares a Referee's time out. Otherwise, he immediately signals start of neutral zone before approximating distance to be gained. The distance and the number of down are to be announced as he assumes his normal stance.

(4) Certain acts of delay may involve stopping the clock immediately. Repeated violations of substitution rule to conserve time are unsportsmanlike conduct (12-2-13-g, h and 4-3-9).

(5) During a play from scrimmage a backward pass going out of bounds during the last two minutes of a half stops the clock. Time is in with the Referee's whistle (clock signal) when the ball is ready for play.

NOTE: TIME FOR A HALF CAN EXPIRE BEFORE A BALL CAN BE PUT IN PLAY FOLLOWING REFEREE'S WHISTLE FOR PLAY TO START.

PLAY **1** With eight seconds remaining in the first half, Buffalo quarterback Doug Flutie throws a backward pass out-of-bounds to stop the game clock.

PLAY **2** With seven seconds remaining in the first half, offensive guard Ruben Brown commits a false start in order to stop the game clock.

Ruling 1: Half over, 10-second runoff for conserving time

Ruling 2: Half over, 10-second runoff for conserving time

**EXTENSION
OF PERIOD**

**DEFENSIVE
FOUL AT END
OF PERIOD**

**OFFENSIVE
FOUL AT END
OF PERIOD**

Article 11 If at the end of any period, time expires while the ball is in play, time is not called until down ends. During such a down:

(a) If there is an accepted foul (not one of a double foul) by defense, the offended team may choose to extend period by one down (enforcement as usual). If the first or third period is not so extended, any penalty (unless declined) is enforced before the start of the succeeding period.

(b) If there is a foul by offense, there shall be no extension of the period. If the foul occurs on the last play of the half, no score made by offense is counted.

Exception: If offensive foul is (1) illegal touching of a kick, (2) fair catch interference, (3) palpably unfair act, or (4) foul followed by a change of team possession, the period may be extended by an untimed down, if defense so chooses.

PLAY 1 Fourth-and-10 on the Bills' 40. On the last play of the first quarter the Seahawks miss an attempted field goal. The Bills were offside. There is a strong wind at their back.

PLAY 2 Third-and-10 on the Dolphins' 45. The Dolphins are offside. Dolphins' quarterback Dan Marino throws a legal pass which is complete to O. J. McDuffie who runs for a score. Time for second half expired during play.

PLAY 3 Fourth-and-10 on the Oilers' 20. A punt is touched illegally by Titans' kicking team player Rodney Thomas on his 45 who falls on the ball as time runs out in second half.

PLAY 4 The Dolphins' Brock Marion intercepts at midfield on the last play of either half. On runback, teammate John Avery clips at the Broncos' 40. The Broncos' Rod Smith piles on after Marion is tackled on the Broncos' 30.

PLAY 5 The Cowboys punt as time for the half expires. The Redskins' Darrell Green gives a valid fair catch signal and catches the ball on the Cowboys' 35.

Ruling 1: Seahawks have option of extending period by an untimed down. It can put ball in play from the Bills' 35 and kick the same way. If the period is not extended, it would be fourth and five on the Bills' 35 at start of second period.

Ruling 2: No score and game over as it was an offensive foul on last play of half.

Ruling 3: One scrimmage down allowed, if desired, by receivers from the Titans' 45. Untimed down as it was an illegal touch.

Ruling 4: Extend the period with an untimed down from the Broncos' 40. Dolphins' ball. See 14-3-3.

Ruling 5: The receiving team may extend the period by a fair catch kick (6-1-2-b). If the ball is kicked out of bounds, the half is over.

DOUBLE FOUL AT END OF PERIOD

(c) If a double foul (14-3) occurs on the last play of the first or third periods, the period is not extended. If a double foul occurs during the last play of either half, extend the period.

Exception: The half is not extended if:

(1) Both fouls are continuous action fouls;

(2) 5 vs. 15, with major foul on the offense (14-3-1-Exc. 1);

(3) Double foul with change of possession, clean hands rule (14-3-2).

TOUCHDOWN ON LAST PLAY

(d) If a touchdown is made, the try shall be allowed (except during a sudden-death period).

FAIR CATCH ON LAST PLAY

(e) If a fair catch is signaled and made, team may choose to extend the period by one free kick down (6-1-2-b). If the first or third period is not so extended, the choice of a snap or free kick (10-1-6) to start the succeeding down is not vitiated.

EXTENSION OF FIRST OR THIRD PERIODS

(f) If no fair catch signal is given and the kickers interfere with the receiver's opportunity to catch a scrimmage kick, the receiving team may extend the period by one down from scrimmage.

(g) If the first or third period is extended for any reason, or if a touchdown occurs during the last play of such a period, any additional play, including a Try, shall be completed before change of goal. If a period is extended for any reason, it shall continue until a down free from any foul specified in (a) to (f) is completed.

SAFETY ON
LAST PLAY

(h) If a safety occurs during the last play of a half, the score counts. No safety kick is made unless it resulted from a foul, and even so unless receivers request that kick be made.

DEFENSIVE
FOULS
DURING LAST
40/25
SECONDS OF
HALF

Article 12 In the last 40/25 seconds of either half, with the Game Clock running, and the defensive team behind with no time outs remaining, a defensive foul prior to the snap cannot prevent the termination of a half except for the normal options available to the offensive team.

CHAPTER 5

PLAYERS, SUBSTITUTES, AND EQUIPMENT

Here's another part of the officials' job: we examine all the players' equipment during the pre-game warm up a half-hour before the kickoff. This year, special procedures have been established to ensure the legality of player equipment/uniform.

Jerry Seeman
NFL DIRECTOR OF OFFICIATING

Section 1   Number of Players

NUMBER OF PLAYERS

Article 1   The game is to be played by two teams of 11 players each. If a snap or free kick is made while a team has:

(a) fewer than 11 players on field, ball is in play and there is no penalty;

(b) more than 11 players on field, ball is in play and there is a five-yard penalty (5-2-1); or

(c) a player who fails to inform the Referee of a change of his eligibility when required by rule, no official is to notify team of this fact before play starts and there is a penalty (7-2-3).

TEAM CAPTAINS

Article 2   Each team must designate its captain(s), and that player(s) is the sole representative of his team in all communications with Officials. See Rule 18.

FIRST CHOICE

Article 3   A captain's first choice from any alternative privileges which may be offered his team, before or during the game, is final and not subject to change.

PLAYERS NUMBERED BY POSITION

Article 4   All players must wear numerals on their jerseys in accordance with Rule 5, Section 3, Article 3(c), and such numerals must be by playing position as follows: quarterbacks, punters, and placekickers, 1-19 (and 10-19 for wide receivers if 80-89 are all otherwise assigned); running backs and defensive backs, 20-49; centers, 50-59 (60-79 if 50-59 unavailable); offensive guards and tackles, 60-79; wide receivers and tight ends, 80-89; defensive linemen, 60-79 (90-99 if 60-79 unavailable); and linebackers, 50-59 (90-99 if 50-59 unavailable).

If a player changes his position during his playing career in the NFL and such change moves him out of a category specified above, he must be issued an appropriate new jersey numeral.

Any request to wear a numeral for a special position not specified above (e.g., H-back) must be made to the Commissioner.

During the preseason period when playing rosters are larger, the League will allow duplication and other temporary deviations from the numbering scheme specified above, but the rule must be adhered to for all players during the regular season and postseason. Clubs must make numerals available to adhere to the rule, even if it requires putting back into circulation a numeral that has been retired or withheld for other reasons. See 7-2-3 for reporting change of position.

PLAYERS WITHDRAWN AND SUBSTITUTED

Article 5   A player must be withdrawn and substituted for when he is disqualified (12-2,3) or suspended (5-3). A suspended player may re-enter when legal. A disqualified player must leave the playing field enclosure and go to the team locker room within a reasonable time.

PENALTIES:

(A) **FOR ILLEGAL RETURN: LOSS OF FIVE YARDS FROM SUCCEEDING SPOT AFTER DISCOVERY.**

(B) **FOR RETURN OF A DISQUALIFIED PLAYER: LOSS OF 15 YARDS AND EXCLUSION FROM PLAYING FIELD ENCLOSURE.**

SUPPLEMENTAL NOTES

COACHES
RESPONSIBLE
FOR LEGAL
SUB

(1) Coaches are to assume full responsibility for the legality of substitutions, but this does not preclude a penalty if discovered before or after a substitute reports.

ENFORCEMENT
SPOT FOR
ILLEGAL SUB

(2) If it is not discovered until the end of a down but prior to the start of next one that a player had returned illegally, enforcement is from the previous spot when definitely known. Otherwise, enforcement is from succeeding spot as a foul between downs (14-5).

Section 2   Substitutes

LEGAL
SUBSTITUTION

Article 1   Substitutes may not enter the field while the ball is in play. Any entering offensive substitute who participates in a play must enter while the ball is dead and must move onto the field as far as the inside of the field numerals; in addition, the player or players replaced must have cleared the field on their own side (between end lines) prior to the snap or free kick. There can never be 12 or more players in the offensive huddle.

QUICK SNAP
FOLLOWING
SUBSTITUTION

NOTE: WHILE IN THE PROCESS OF SUBSTITUTION OR SIMULATED SUBSTITUTION, THE OFFENSE IS PROHIBITED FROM RUSHING QUICKLY TO THE LINE AND SNAPPING THE BALL WITH THE OBVIOUS ATTEMPT TO CAUSE A DEFENSIVE FOUL; I.E., TOO MANY MEN ON THE FIELD. IF IN THE JUDGMENT OF THE OFFICIALS THIS TAKES PLACE, THE FOLLOWING PROCEDURE WILL BE APPLIED:

(1) If the play takes place and a defensive foul results, the flag will be picked up and the down replayed. At this time, the referee will notify the head coach that any further use of this tactic will result in an unsportsmanlike penalty being assessed.

NOTE: COVERING OFFICIAL(S) WILL EXTEND BOTH ARMS HORIZONTALLY TO INDICATE THAT SUBSTITUTIONS HAVE BEEN MADE. ALSO, THE SAME QUICK-SNAP RULE WILL NOT BE APPLICABLE IN THE LAST TWO MINUTES OF EITHER HALF.

(2) On a fourth down punting situation, the Referee and the Umpire will not allow a quick snap which would prevent the defense from having a reasonable time to complete their substitutions. This will apply throughout the entire game.

PENALTY: FOR ILLEGAL SUBSTITUTION: LOSS OF FIVE YARDS (FOR DELAY) FROM PREVIOUS SPOT AND NUMBER OF DOWN AND NECESSARY LINE REMAIN THE SAME FOR:

(A) ENTRY DURING PLAY;

(B) WITHDRAWN PLAYER ON FIELD AT SNAP OR FREE-KICK; OR

(C) CLEARING FIELD ON OPPONENTS' SIDE OR ACROSS END LINE (WHETHER VIOLATION IS DISCOVERED DURING DOWN, OR AT END OF DOWN).

Interference with play during (a) to (c) is a palpably unfair act (12-3-3).

SUPPLEMENTAL NOTES

(1) See 5-1-5, for illegal return or withdrawal.

(2) If a substitute enters during dead ball with time in or after Referee's whistle following a time out, no Official is to signal his entry and Field Judge continues his timing of 40/25 seconds, if and when it has been started (4-3-10-S.N. 1).

Exception: On an illegal return, ball remains dead if discovered prior to snap.

(3) Under no circumstances is Referee to delay start of neutral zone because of an incoming substitute.

SUBSTITUTE
BECOMES
PLAYER

(4) A substitute is not to report to an Official. He becomes a player when:

    a) he informs a teammate that he is replacing him;

    b) he participates in at least one play after communicating with a teammate;

    c) a teammate voluntarily withdraws upon his entering; or

    d) in the absence of any of the above a, b, or c, he is on the field at snap or free kick.

(5) A player is legally in the game when he has participated in at least one play.

(6) A player is legally substituted for when he leaves the game for at least one play.

(7) If a player enters field of play, communicates with teammate(s) and then leaves without participating in one play, it shall be ruled Unsportsmanlike Conduct (12-3-1-f) and so penalized, unless one of his teammates leaves the field of play. If this occurs, any teammate may replace him provided all other prescribed game rules are adhered to. Use of players who have not qualified either as legal players or substitutes for ulterior purposes defeats the purpose of the game.

(8) Referee shall sound his whistle for play to start immediately upon completion of a penalty for an illegal substitution, return, or withdrawal. Game clock will start as appropriate. See 4-3-10.

CONSERVING
TIME

Article 2 After the two-minute warning of either half, a violation of the substitution rule occurs while ball is dead with time in by the team in possession.

(a) If the act is designed to conserve time, Referee stops play, penalizes, and will run off 10 seconds prior to allowing ball to be put in play. Clock starts when Umpire lowers his arm and gives wind-the-clock signal. See 4-3-10.

(b) Repeated violations of substitution rule to conserve time are unsportsmanlike conduct (12-3-1-h).

Section 3   Equipment, Uniforms, Player Appearance

GENERAL
POLICY

Article 1 Throughout the game-day period while in view of the stadium and television audience, including during pregame warm-ups, all players must dress in a professional manner under the uniform standards specified in this Section 3. They must wear equipment offering reasonable protection to themselves while reasonably avoiding risk of injury to other players. And they generally must present an appearance that is appropriate to representing their individual clubs and the National Football League. The term uniform, as used in this section, applies to every piece of equipment worn by a player, including helmet, shoulder pads, thigh pads, knee pads, and any other item of protective gear, and to every visible item of apparel, including but not limited to pants, jerseys, wristbands, gloves, stockings, shoes, visible undergarments, and accessories such as head coverings worn under helmets and hand towels. All visible items worn on game-day by players must be issued by the club or the League, or, if from outside sources, must have approval in advance by the League.

TEAM
COLORS

Article 2 Pursuant to the official colors established for each NFL club in the League Constitution and Bylaws, playing squads are permitted to wear only those colors or a combination of those colors for helmets, jerseys, pants, and stockings; provided that white is also an available color for jerseys and mandatory color for the lower portion of stockings [see 5-3-3-(i), "Stockings", below]. Each player on a given team must wear the same colors on his uniform as all other players on his team in the same game. Before July 1 each year, home clubs are required to report to the League office their choice of jersey color (either white or official team color) for their home games of that forthcoming season (including postseason, in the event that the club should become a host for such a game), and visiting clubs must wear the opposite. For preseason or postseason games, the two competing teams may wear jerseys in their official colors (non-white), provided the Commissioner determines that such colors are of sufficient contrast.

MANDATORY EQUIPMENT, APPAREL

Article 3 All players must wear the equipment and uniform apparel listed below, which must be of a suitably protective nature, must be designed and produced by a professional manufacturer, and must not be cut, reduced in size, or otherwise altered unless for medical reasons approved in advance by the Commissioner; provided, however, that during pregame warm-ups players may omit certain protective equipment at their option, except that helmets must be worn. Where additional rules are applicable to specific categories of mandatory equipment or apparel, or where related equipment is optional, such provisions are also spelled out below.

HELMETS, FACE PROTECTORS

(a) Helmet with chin-strap fastened and face mask attached. Face masks must not be more than ⅝-inch in diameter and must be made of rounded material; transparent materials are prohibited. Clear (transparent) plastic face shields for eye protection are optional, provided the League office is supplied in advance with appropriate medical documentation that the shield is needed. No visible identification of a manufacturer's name or logo on the exterior of a helmet or on any attachment to a helmet is permitted unless provided for under a commercial arrangement between the League and manufacturer; in no event is identification of any helmet manufacturer permitted on the visible surface of a rear cervical pad. All helmets must carry a small NFL shield logo on the rear lower-left exterior, which logo will be provided in quantity by the League. All helmets must carry on the rear lower right exterior, an approved warning label (such labels will be supplied in quantity by the League).

JERSEYS

(b) Jersey that covers all pads and other protective equipment worn on the torso and upper arms, and that is appropriately tailored to remain tucked into the uniform pants throughout the game. Tearaway jerseys are prohibited. Mesh jerseys with large fish-net material (commonly referred to as "bullet-hole" or "port-hole" mesh) are also prohibited. Surnames of players in letters a minimum of 2½-inches high must be affixed to the exterior of jerseys across the upper back above the numerals; nicknames are prohibited; and in cases of duplicate surnames, the first initial of the given name must be used. All jerseys must carry a small NFL shield logo at the middle of the yoke of the neck on the front of the garment, which logo will be provided in quantity by the League.

NUMERALS

(c) Numerals on the back and front of jerseys in accordance with Rule 5, Section 1, Article 4. Such numerals must be a minimum of 8 inches high and 4 inches wide, and their color must be in sharp contrast with the color of the jersey. Smaller numerals should be worn on the tops of the shoulders or upper arms of the jersey. Small numerals on the back of the helmet or on the uniform pants are optional.

PANTS

(d) Pants that are worn over the entire knee area; pants shortened or rolled up to meet the stockings above the knee are prohibited. No part of the pants may be cut away unless an appropriate gusset or other device is used to replace the removed material. All pants must carry a small NFL shield logo on the front left groin area of the pants, midway between the fly opening and side seam, and ½-inch below the belt. The logo will be provided in quantity by the League.

SHOULDER PADS

(e) Shoulder pads that are completely covered by the uniform jersey.

STOCKINGS

(f) Stockings that cover the entire area from the shoe to the bottom of the pants, and that meet the pants below the knee. Players are permitted to wear as many layers of stockings and tape on the lower leg as they prefer, provided the exterior is a one-piece stocking that includes solid white from the top of the shoe to the mid-point of the lower leg, and approved team color or colors (non- white) from that point to the top of the stocking. Uniform stockings may not be altered (e.g., over-stretched, or cut at the toes, or sewn short) in order to bring the line between solid white and team colors lower or higher than the mid-point of the lower leg. No other stockings and/or opaque tape may be worn over the one-piece, two-color uniform stocking. Barefoot punters and placekickers may omit the stocking of the kicking foot in preparation for and during kicking plays.

SHOES

(g) Shoes that are of a standard football design, including "sneaker" type shoes such as basketball shoes, cross-training shoes, etc. League-approved tri-colored shoes are permitted with black, white, and one team color. Each team must select a dominant color for its shoes, either black or white (with a conforming selection of either all-black or all-white shoelaces). The selection of dominant color must be reported by each team to the League Office no later than July 1 each year. Each player may select among shoe styles previously approved by the League Office and NFL Properties. All players on the same team must wear shoes with the same dominant color. Approved shoe styles will contain one team color which must be the same for all players on a given team. A player may wear an unapproved standard football shoe style as long as the player tapes over the entire shoe to conform to his team's selected dominant color. Logos, names, or other commercial identification on shoes are not permitted to be visible unless advance approval is granted by the League Office (see Article 7). Size and location of logos and names on shoes must be approved by NFL Properties. When a shoe logo or a name approved by both League Office and NFL Properties is covered with an appropriate use of tape (see Article 4(f)), players will be allowed to cut out the tape covering the original logo or name, provided the cut is clean and is the exact size of the logo or name. The logo or name of the shoe manufacturer must not be reapplied to the exterior of the taped shoes unless advance approval is granted by the League Office. Kicking shoes must not be modified (including using a shoelace wrapped around the bottom of the shoe), and any shoe that is worn by a player with an artificial limb on his kicking leg must have a kicking surface which conforms to that of a normal kicking shoe. Punters and placekickers may omit the shoe from the kicking foot in preparation for and during kicking plays. Punters and placekickers may wear any combination of tri-colored shoes provided that the colors are consistent with those selected by the team and with the policy listed above.

OTHER PROHIBITED EQUIPMENT, APPAREL

Article 4 In addition to the several prohibited items of equipment and apparel specified in Article 3 above, the following are also prohibited:

PROJECTING OBJECTS

(a) Metal or other hard objects that project from a player's person or uniform, including from his shoes.

UNCOVERED HARD OBJECTS, SUBSTANCES

(b) Hard objects and substances, including but not limited to casts, guards or braces for hand, wrist, forearm, elbow, hip, thigh, knee, shin, unless such items are appropriately covered on all edges and surfaces by a minimum of ⅜-inch foam rubber or similar soft material. Any such item worn to protect an injury must be reported by the applicable coaching staff to the Umpire in advance of the game, and a description of the injury must be provided. If the Umpire determines that an item in question, including tape or bandages on hands or forearms, may present undue risk to other players, he may prevent its use at any time before or during a game until the item is removed or appropriately corrected.

DETACHABLE TOE

(c) Detachable kicking toe.

TORN ITEMS

(d) Torn or improperly fitting equipment creating a risk of injury to other players, e.g., the hard surfaces of shoulder pads exposed by a damaged jersey.

IMPROPER CLEATS

(e) Shoe cleats made of aluminum or other material that may chip, fracture, or develop a cutting edge. Conical cleats with concave sides or points which measure less than ⅜-inch in diameter at the tips, or cleats with oblong ends which measure less than ¼ by ¾-inch at the end tips are also prohibited. Nylon cleats with flat steel tips are permitted.

IMPROPER TAPE

(f) Opaque, contrasting-color tape that covers any part of the helmet, jersey, pants, stockings, or shoes; transparent tape or tape of the same color as the background material is permissible for use on these items of apparel. Players may use opaque white tape on hands and arms, provided it conforms to 5-3-4(b) above ("Uncovered Hard Objects, Substances") and 5-3-4(h) below ("Approved Glove Color on Linemen"). Opaque tape on shoes is permitted, provided it is the same color as the shoe, and provided it does not carry up into the stocking area.

ITEMS COLORED LIKE FOOTBALL

(g) Headgear or any other equipment or apparel which, in the opinion of the Referee, may confuse an opponent because of its similarity in color to that of the game football. If such color is worn, it must be broken by stripes or other patterns of sharply contrasting color or colors.

APPROVED GLOVE COLOR

(h) Gloves, wrappings, elbow pads, and other items worn on the arms below or over the jersey sleeves by interior offensive linemen (excluding tight ends) which are of a color different from that which is mandatorily reported to the League office by the club before July 1 each year. Such reported color must be white or other official color of the applicable team, and, once reported, must not be changed throughout that same season. Players at other positions (non-interior linemen) also may wear gloves provided they are NFL Properties-licensed items approved by the League office for wear on the field, and provided they are solid white or a solid color that is an official color of the applicable club. Clubs are not required to designate to the League office by July 1, the color of gloves that will be worn by their non-interior linemen.

ADHESIVE, SLIPPERY SUBSTANCES

(i) Adhesive or slippery substances on the body, equipment, or uniform of any player; provided, however, that players may wear gloves with a tackified surface if such tacky substance does not adhere to the football or otherwise cause handling problems for players.

GARMENTS UNDER JERSEYS

(j) Quarterbacks will be allowed to wear under the game jersey a solid color T-shirt, turtleneck, or sweatshirt (consistent with team undergarment color) with sleeves cut to any length, as long as both sleeves are evenly trimmed and the edges are sewn and hemmed. All other players may wear garments under game jerseys only if the undergarment sleeves either (a) do not extend below the sleeves of the jersey; or (b) are full length to the wrist. No other sleeve lengths for garments under jerseys are permitted for players other than quarterbacks. Any garments under jerseys that are exposed at the neck or sleeve area and that carry an exposed logo or commercial name must be licensed by NFL Properties and approved by the League Office for wear on the field (see Article 7). All members of the same team who wear approved undergarments with exposed necks or sleeves must wear the same color on a given day, which color must be white or a solid color that is an official team color ("solid" means that sleeves must not carry stripes, designs, or team names).

RECOMMENDED EQUIPMENT

Article 5   It is recommended that all players wear hip pads, thigh pads, and knee pads which reasonable avoid the risk of injury. Unless otherwise provided by individual team policy, it is the players' responsibility and decision whether to follow this recommendation and use such pads. If worn, all three forms of pads listed above must be covered by the outer uniform. Basketball-type knee pads are permitted but must also be covered by the outer uniform.

OPTIONAL EQUIPMENT

Article 6   Among the types of optional equipment that are permitted to be worn by players are the following:

RIB PROTECTORS

(a) Rib protectors ("flak jackets") under the jersey.

WRIST BANDS

(b) Wrist bands, provided they are white or in official team colors.

TOWELS

(c) Towels, provided they are white NFL Properties-licensed towels approved by the League Office for use on the playing field. Players are prohibited from adding to these towels personal messages, logos, names, symbols, or illustrations. Such towels also must be attached to or tucked into the front waist of the pants, and must be no larger than 6x8 inches (slightly larger size may be issued to quarterbacks, or may be folded to these limits for wearing in games). A player may wear no more than one towel. Players are prohibited from discarding on the playing field any loose towels or other materials used for wiping hands and the football. Streamers or ribbons, regardless of length, hanging from any part of the uniform, including the helmet, are prohibited.

HEAD COVERINGS

(d) Head coverings worn under the helmet, e.g., sweat bands and bandannas, are permissible and may be visible in the bench area, provided that they are of a solid color (official team color) and issued by the club, and further provided that no portion hangs from or is otherwise visible outside the helmet during play. Baseball-type caps may be worn in the bench area, provided they are in official team colors and issued by the club.

LOGOS AND COMMERCIAL IDENTIFICATION

Article 7   Throughout the period on game-day that a player is visible to the stadium and television audience (including in pregame warm-ups, in the bench area, and during postgame interviews in the locker room or on the field), players are prohibited from wearing, displaying, or orally promoting equipment, apparel, or other items that carry commercial names or logos of companies, unless such commercial identification has been approved in advance by the League Office. The size of any approved logo or other commercial identification involved in an agreement between a manufacturer and the League will be modest and unobtrusive, and there is no assurance that it will be visible to the television audience. Subject to any future approved arrangements with a manufacturer and subject to any decision by the Commissioner to suspend enforcement temporarily of this provision governing shoes, visible logos and names of shoes are prohibited, including on the sole of the shoe that may be seen from time to time during the game.

PERSONAL MESSAGES

Article 8   Throughout the period on game-day that a player is visible to the stadium and television audience (including in pregame warm-ups, in the bench area, and during postgame interviews in the locker room or on the field), players are prohibited from wearing, displaying, or otherwise conveying personal messages either in writing or illustration, unless such message has been approved in advance by the League Office. Items such as armbands and jersey patches worn to celebrate anniversaries of events, to promote charities, to recognize causes and campaigns, or to honor or commemorate personages are also prohibited unless approved in advance by the League Office. Further, such armbands and jersey patches must be modest in size, tasteful, non-commercial, and non-controversial; must not be worn for more than one football season; and if approved for use by a specific team, must not be worn by players on other teams in the League.

GENERAL
APPEARANCE

Article 9 Consistent with the equipment and uniform rules of this Section 3, players must otherwise present a professional and appropriate appearance while before the public on game-day. Among the types of activity that are prohibited are use of tobacco products (smokeless included) while in the bench area and use of facial makeup. The Referee is authorized to use his judgment in determining whether any other unusual appearance or behavior is in violation of this Article 9.

PENALTIES:

(A) FOR VIOLATION OF THIS SECTION 3 DISCOVERED DURING PREGAME WARMUPS OR AT OTHER TIMES PRIOR TO THE GAME, PLAYER WILL BE ADVISED TO MAKE APPROPRIATE CORRECTION; IF THE VIOLATION IS NOT CORRECTED, PLAYER WILL NOT BE PERMITTED TO ENTER THE GAME.

(B) FOR VIOLATION OF THIS SECTION 3 DISCOVERED WHILE PLAYER IS IN GAME, PLAYER WILL BE ADVISED TO MAKE APPROPRIATE CORRECTION AT THE NEXT CHANGE OF POSSESSION; IF VIOLATION IS NOT CORRECTED, PLAYER WILL NOT BE PERMITTED TO ENTER THE GAME. PROVIDED, HOWEVER, IF THE VIOLATION INVOLVES THE COMPETITIVE ASPECTS OF THE GAME (E.G. ILLEGAL KICKING TOE OF SHOE, AN ADHESIVE OR SLIPPERY SUBSTANCE) PLAYER WILL BE SUSPENDED IMMEDIATELY UPON DISCOVERY.

(C) FOR REPEAT VIOLATION: DISQUALIFICATION FROM GAME.

(D) FOR ILLEGAL ENTRY OR RETURN OF A PLAYER SUSPENDED UNDER THIS SECTION 3: LOSS OF 5 YARDS FROM SUCCEEDING SPOT AND REMOVAL UNTIL PROPERLY EQUIPPED AFTER ONE DOWN.

(E) FOR VIOLATION OF THIS SECTION 3 DETECTED IN THE BENCH AREA: PLAYER AND HEAD COACH WILL BE ASKED TO REMOVE THE OBJECTIONABLE ITEM, PROPERLY EQUIP THE PLAYER, OR OTHERWISE CORRECT THE VIOLATION. THE INVOLVED PLAYER OR PLAYERS WILL BE DISQUALIFIED FROM THE GAME IF CORRECTION NOT MADE PROMPTLY.

SUPPLEMENTAL NOTE

In addition to the game-day penalties specified above, the Commissioner may subsequently impose independent disciplinary action on the involved player, up to and including suspension from the team's next succeeding game—preseason, regular season, or postseason, whichever is applicable.

CHAPTER 6
FREE KICK

There are actually three types of free kicks: a kickoff, a safety kick, and a fair catch kick. Many fans are not aware of a fair catch kick. It allows the receiving team, after a fair catch, to attempt a kick which scores three points, just like a field goal.

Jerry Seeman
NFL DIRECTOR OF OFFICIATING

Section 1   Putting Ball in Play

KICKOFF

Article 1   A free kick called a kickoff (3-16) puts the ball in play:

(a) at the start of each half;

(b) after a Try; and

(c) after a successful field goal.

FREE KICK

Article 2   A free kick also puts the ball in play:

(a) after a safety (see 3-12-1b);

(b) following a fair catch when this method is chosen (10-1-6) (11-5-3);

(c) when there is a replay for a short free kick (6-2-1); and

(d) when enforcement for a foul during a free kick is from the previous spot (6-2-5).

NOTE: THE BALL IS PUT IN PLAY BY A SNAP IN ALL OTHER CASES (7-3-1).

SPOT OF FREE KICKS

Article 3   A free kick may be made from any point on or behind the offensive team's free kick line and between inbounds lines. A dropkick, placekick, or punt may be used.

Exceptions:

1) A punt may not be used on a kickoff.

2) During a placekick at the kickoff, the kicking team may use a manufactured tee that is 1-inch in height and approved by the league.

3) A fair catch-kick must be made on or behind the mark of the catch (3-9-1 and 10-1-6) without the use of a "tee".

NOTE: WHEN THE MARK OF A FAIR CATCH IS IN A SIDE ZONE, IT IS CONSIDERED TO BE ON THE INBOUNDS LINE.

PENALTY: FOR ILLEGAL KICK AT FREE KICK: NEW FREE KICK LINES ARE SET FIVE YARDS NEARER A'S GOAL LINE.

INITIAL FREE-KICK LINES

Article 4   The initial free kick lines during a given free kick shall be as follows (plus or minus any distance they might be moved because of a distance penalty enforced prior to the kick):

For the kicking team:

(a) Kickoff—offensive 30

(b) Safety kick—offensive 20

(c) Fair catch kick—the yard line through the mark of the catch.

For the receiving team:

A yard line 10 yards in advance of the offensive team's free-kick line.

NOTE: KICKING TEAM'S FINAL FREE-KICK LINE IS A YARD LINE THROUGH THE SPOT OF THE BALL WHEN KICKED.

PLAY 1 The Raiders' Tim Brown makes a fair catch attempt with three seconds remaining and the score tied. The ball slips through his hands and touches the ground as he falls on the ball.

PLAY 2 During the continuing action after a safety scored against the Giants, the Bears' defensive end punches an opponent.

PLAY 3 The Jacksonville Jaguars are called offsides as they kick off following a field goal. The penalty is accepted.

Ruling 1: No fair catch allowed, as the ball has to be caught (3-9-1). No fair catch option. The ball is in play with the snap if time remains.

Ruling 2: Disqualify the Bears' player. The initial free-kick line for the Giants is the 35 yard line (20 plus 15) and for the Bears it is the Giants' 45 yard line. No tee is allowed, but a punt is permitted.

Ruling 3: New free kick lines are set. The Jaguars' new free kick line is their 25 and the receiving team's is the Jacksonville 35. No punt is allowed, but a tee is permitted.

WHISTLE
PRIOR TO A
FREE KICK

Article 5 After the referee's whistle prior to a free kick:

    (a) All receiving players (Team B) must be inbounds and behind their line until the kick.

FREE-KICK
VIOLATION

    (b) All kicking players (Team A) must be inbounds and behind the ball when kicked except the holder of the placekick (3-23) may be beyond the line, and the kicker may be beyond the line but his kicking foot may not be.

PENALTY: FOR VIOLATION OF FREE KICK FORMATION: THE FREE KICK IS MADE AGAIN. NEW FREE KICK LINES ARE SET FIVE YARDS NEARER THE OFFENDER'S END LINE UNLESS A HALF-DISTANCE PENALTY IS BEING ENFORCED (14-2-1).

PLAY 1 On a kickoff after a Try, the kicker (soccer-type) places his non-kicking foot beyond the ball with his kicking foot kicking the ball on the free kick line.

PLAY 2 On a kickoff from the Cardinals' 30, the ball bounces to the Ravens' 35 and then goes backwards out of bounds at the Raven's 42.

Ruling 1: Legal. (Kicking foot may not be beyond the line.)

Ruling 2: Ravens' ball first-and-10 on Ravens' 42. Not a short free kick.

Section 2   Ball in Play After Free Kick

SHORT FREE
KICK

Article 1   A free kick is short when it does not go to or across the receiving team's free kick line unless, before doing so, it is first touched by a player of the receiving team, or goes out of bounds. See 11-5-3-Exception.

PENALTIES:

(A) FOR THE FIRST SHORT FREE KICK: LOSS OF FIVE YARDS FROM THE PREVIOUS SPOT.

(B) FOR THE SECOND (OR MORE) CONSECUTIVE SHORT FREE KICK ILLEGALLY TOUCHED : THE RECEIVING TEAM TAKES POSSESSION OF THE BALL AT THE SPOT OF ILLEGAL TOUCH OR RECOVERY. IF A RE-KICK IS TO BE MADE, NEW FREE KICK LINES ARE SET. SEE 6-3-1-NOTE.

PLAY **1**   On a kickoff after a field goal, the Browns' kicking team player Chris Spielman is first to touch the ball on his own 38-yard line (before it goes to or across the Jets' free kick line). The ball rolls to the Browns' 42-yard line where the Jets' Bryan Cox falls on it and is downed there.

PLAY **2**   On a kickoff after a field goal, the Browns' kicking team player Chris Spielman is first to touch the ball on his 38-yard line (before it goes to or across the Jets' restraining line). The ball rolls to his own 43-yard line where the Jets' Bryan Cox picks it up, takes a few steps and fumbles. The Browns recover at their 40.

PLAY **3**   The Jets' receiving team player Bryan Cox first touches a free kick after a Try on the Browns' 39. The Browns recover on their own 38.

PLAY **4**   A kickoff after a Try is caught in the air by a kicking team player on the his 41-yard line:
(a) before any touching by the receiving team. A receiving team player could have caught the ball.
(b) before any touching by the receiving team. No receiving team player was near enough to have caught the ball.

PLAY **5**   A kickoff from the 49ers' 30 bounces on their 38 and is in the air when 49ers' Merton Hanks leaps from his 39 and catches the ball on the 41.

Ruling 1: Jets' ball on the Browns' 42-yard line. (Jets have option to play or rekick from Browns' 25-yard line.)

Ruling 2: Browns rekick from their 25. A five-yard penalty from the previous spot for a short free kick (if the Jets didn't fumble and kept possession, they have the option to keep the ball when it is dead).

Ruling 3: Browns' ball on their own 38. No foul as the ball was touched first by Cox. The ball is dead where it is recovered by the Browns if it is muffed (no possession) by the Jets.

Ruling 4a: Interference with the opportunity to make a catch. 15-yard penalty from spot of foul, snap only (10-1-4).

Ruling 4b: Legal play. Kicking team's ball first-and-10 on their 41.

Ruling 5: Legal recovery. Not a short free kick, as the ball hit ground and ball was recovered after going 10 yards. The 49ers' ball, first-and-10 on their 41.

FREE KICK RECOVERY

Article 2 Free Kick Recovery

    (a) If a free kick is recovered by the receiving team it may advance.

    (b) If a free kick (legal or illegal) is recovered by the kicking team, the ball is dead. If the recovery is legal, the kicking team next puts the ball in play at the spot of recovery. Undue advance by the kicking team recovering (legal or illegal) is delay of game (4-3-9, 11-5-3).

    (c) If a free kick is simultaneously recovered by two opposing players, the ball is awarded to the receiving team.

PLAY 1 A Kickoff after a Try is first touched by the receiving team on the kicker's 38-yard line before it reached the receiving team's restraining line. A member of the kicking team recovers, takes one step, is tackled, fumbles and the receiving team recovers on their own 38.

PLAY 2 Kickoff after a Try goes to the kicking team's own 39 and no one attempts to recover.

Ruling 1: No short free kick as ball touched by receiving team. Kicking team's ball on their 43. The ball is dead when recovered.

Ruling 2: Rekick from kicking team's 25. Penalize five yards.

AFTER FREE KICK ENDS

Article 3 All general rules apply when play continues after a free kick (loose ball) ends.

PLAYER OUT OF BOUNDS DURING A FREE KICK

Article 4 No player of the kicking team may touch or recover a kickoff or safety kick before:

    (a) it is touched by the receiving team (B) if that kicking team player has been out of bounds during the kick; or

    (b) it has crossed the receiving team's restraining line, unless before doing so, it has first been touched by the receiving team.

 PENALTY: FOR ILLEGAL TOUCHING OF A FREE KICK BY THE KICKING TEAM: LOSS OF FIVE YARDS FROM THE PREVIOUS SPOT. NEW FREE-KICK LINES ARE SET IF ENFORCED.

PLAY 1 During a kickoff the Chiefs' Andre Rison is blocked out of bounds (or steps out of bounds). The Chargers' Charlie Jones muffs the kick and Rison re-enters and recovers the ball on the Chargers' 48.

PLAY 2 During a kickoff the Chiefs' Andre Rison avoids a block and steps out of bounds (or is blocked out). He re-enters and uses his hands in a personal attempt to recover a muff by the Chargers' Charlie Jones. Rison recovers the ball on the Chargers' 36.

Ruling 1: Legal recovery—Chiefs' ball first-and-10 on the Chargers' 48.

Ruling 2: Legal recovery—Chiefs' ball first-and-10 on the Chargers' 36.

FOUL DURING
A FREE KICK

Article 5 If there is a foul other than a personal foul (blocking) after a fair-catch signal, fair-catch interference or an invalid fair-catch signal during a free kick, any enforcement, if made, is from the previous spot and the free kick must be made again (10-1-3, 10-1-4, 10-1-1).

PLAY **1** During a Carolina Panthers' kickoff, a Panthers' player bats or kicks a ball muffed by the Dolphins towards the Miami goal line. The ball is recovered by the Dolphins on their own 5-yard line.

PLAY **2** During a kickoff the Raiders' kicking team player Kenny Shedd is offside. The Eagles return the ball to their 15-yard line.

Ruling 1: Previous spot foul. Loss of 10 yards (12-1-6, 7). New free-kick lines are set. Rekick—Carolina 20. Option for receivers, but they would take the penalty.

Ruling 2: Option for the Eagles. Rekick—5-yard penalty or Eagles' ball on their 15. New free-kick lines are set if rekicked.

ILLEGAL USE
OF HANDS

SUPPLEMENTAL NOTES

(1) During a free kick, a kicking team player may not block or use his hands or arms on an opponent within the first ten yards, or until the ball has touched a receiving team player (6-2-1). After the ball touches a receiver, any player may use his hands or arms on an opponent in an actual legal attempt to recover the ball (12-1-2-Exc 2)

RUNNING INTO
FREE KICKER

(2) Running into the kicker by the receiving team before he recovers his balance is a 5-yard penalty.

PLAY **1** On a kickoff after a Try prior to the ball going 10 yards the Rams' Todd Lyght blocks the Vikings' Robert Smith above the waist on the Rams' 38. The Rams' Ricky Proehl falls on the ball on his 41.

Ruling 1: Rekick from the Rams' 20. The Rams may not use hands, arms, or body prior to the ball going 10 yards unless ball was first touched by the Vikings. See 6-2-5, S.N. 1.

Section 3   Free Kick Out of Bounds or In Touch

FREE KICK
OUT OF
BOUNDS

Article 1 The kicking team may not kick a free kick out of bounds between the goal lines.

RECEIVING
TEAM LAST TO
TOUCH

Exception: If the receiving team is the last one to touch the kick before it goes out of bounds, it is not a foul by the kicking team, and the receiving team next puts the ball in play at the inbounds spot.

PENALTIES:

(A) RECEIVER'S BALL 30 YARDS FROM THE SPOT OF THE KICK OR THE TEAM MAY ELECT THE OPTION OF TAKING POSSESSION OF THE BALL AT THE OUT-OF-BOUNDS SPOT.

Exception: If the ball goes out of bounds the first time an onside kick is attempted, the kicking team is to be penalized five yards and rekick must be made (no declinations). New free-kick lines are set.

While the receiving team may not waive the kicking team's obligations to rekick, it is not deprived of a choice of distance penalties in case of a multiple foul.

(B) FOR THE SECOND (OR MORE) CONSECUTIVE ONSIDE KICK OUT OF BOUNDS: RECEIVING TEAM TAKES POSSESSION OF THE BALL AT THE OUT-OF-BOUNDS SPOT.

FREE-KICK
TIMING, LAST
TWO MINUTES

NOTE: TIME IS IN DURING THE LAST 2 MINUTES OF A HALF AFTER LEGAL TOUCHING OR RECOVERY OF A KICKOFF OR SAFETY KICK:

    A)   WHEN THE RECEIVING TEAM TOUCHES IN FIELD OF PLAY;

    B)   WHEN THE RECEIVING TEAM RECOVERS IN FIELD OF PLAY;

    C)   WHEN THE RECEIVING TEAM RECOVERS IN END ZONE AND IMMEDIATELY PROCEEDS INTO FIELD OF PLAY; AND

    D)   WHEN THE KICKING TEAM LEGALLY TOUCHES IN FIELD OF PLAY.

TIME IS NOT IN IF:

    A)   THE RECEIVING TEAM RECOVERS IN THE END ZONE AND MAKES NO ATTEMPT TO ENTER THE FIELD OF PLAY (INCLUDING RUNNING LATERALLY IN END ZONE);

    B)   THE KICKING TEAM RECOVERS IN THE FIELD OF PLAY. (REFEREE'S TIME OUT UNDER CHANGE OF POSSESSION RULE (4-3-7-S.N. 1); OR

    C)   THE RECEIVING TEAM SIGNALS FOR AND MAKES A FAIR CATCH.

PLAY ❶ A free kick goes 12 yards and is first touched by a receiving team player. A kicking team player then touches the ball before it goes out of bounds on the 50.

PLAY ❷ A free kick is first touched by a kicking team player before it goes 10 yards. A receiving team player touches the ball before it rolls out of bounds on the kicking team's 43.

PLAY ❸ A kickoff crosses the receiver's goal line and a receiving team player muffs the ball in the end zone. The kick is out of bounds on the receiving team's 2-yard line after last touching a kicking team player who tried to recover.

PLAY ❹ A kickoff crosses the receiving team's goal line, and a receiving team player muffs the ball in the end zone. The kick rolls out of bounds on the receiving team's 2-yard line without any other player touching the ball.

Ruling 1: Kicking team player last one to touch ball. Receiver's ball on the 50.

Ruling 2: Option for the receiving team. Receiver's ball on the kicking team's 43 or rekick—5-yard penalty for a short free kick (6-2-1).

Ruling 3: Receiving team's ball 30 yards from spot of kick. See 6-3-1.

Ruling 4: Receiving team's ball on its 2-yard line. (No rekick as the receiving team player was the last one to touch the ball).

FREE KICK
BEHIND GOAL
LINE

Article 2   Rule 11 governs if a free kick:

(a)   goes out of bounds behind the receiving team's goal line;

(b)   kickoff or safety kick becomes dead because the ball strikes the receiving team's goal post; or

(c)   is downed in the end zone.

MAKE THE RIGHT CALL

PLAY **1**   A free kick is muffed by a receiving team player and the ball then rolls into the goal posts. A kicking team player then falls on it in the end zone.

PLAY **2**   A free kick is caught in the end zone by a receiving team player who goes to his 1-yard line, is tackled and fumbles, and the ball rolls into the end zone and hits the goal post. A kicking team player falls on it in the end zone.

Ruling 1: Touchback (11-6-1). A ball hitting the goal post is out of bounds.

Ruling 2: (11-4-1-b). Safety. Ball was out of bounds when it hit the goal post.

CHAPTER 7
SCRIMMAGE

There are various types of scrimmage infraction that may occur when the ball is snapped including offside, illegal motion, and illegal formation.

Jerry Seeman
NFL DIRECTOR OF OFFICIATING

Section 1   Necessary Gain on Downs

NEW SERIES, FIRST-AND-10

Article 1   A new series (first-and-10) is awarded to the offensive team when the following conditions exist; subject, however, to the specific rules of enforcement (Rule 12).

NECESSARY GAIN

(a) When, during a given series, the ball is declared dead in possession of offensive team while it is on, above, or across the necessary line, or unless a penalty places it there, or unless a touchback for them results.

CHANGE OF POSSESSION

(b) When the ball is dead in the field of play in the offense's possession, after having been in the defensive team's possession during the same down.

DEFENSIVE FOULS

(c) When a foul is made by the defense, except as otherwise specified (14-8-5), or when an impetus by them results in a touchback for offensive team.

KICK RECOVERED AFTER TOUCH

(d) When the kicking team recovers a scrimmage kick anywhere in the field of play after it *first* has been touched *beyond* the line by the receivers. See 9-1-6-Note.

FORWARD PART OF BALL DETERMINES GAIN

Article 2   The *forward part of the ball* in its position when declared dead in the field of play shall be taken as the determining point in measuring any distance gained. *The ball shall not be rotated when measuring.*

ENTIRE BALL OUT OF END ZONE

NOTE: A BALL IN THE END ZONE WHICH IS CARRIED TOWARD THE FIELD OF PLAY IS STILL IN TOUCH. IT IS A SAFETY OR TOUCHBACK IF ANY PART OF THE BALL IS ON, ABOVE, OR BEHIND THE GOAL LINE (PLANE) WHEN DEAD. IN SUCH A CASE, THE BALL MUST BE ENTIRELY IN THE FIELD OF PLAY IN ORDER NOT TO BE IN TOUCH.

MAKE THE RIGHT CALL

PLAY 1   Second-and-10 on the Jets' 30. The Cowboys' Chris Warren goes to the Jets' 25 where he is tackled, fumbles, and the Jets' Bryan Cox recovers and runs to his 28. Cox then fumbles and the Cowboys' Michael Irvin recovers on the Jets' 28 where he is downed.

PLAY 2   Second-and-10 on Seahawks' 30. Charger quarterback Ryan Leaf throws an incomplete pass. Defensive tackle held tight end Freddie Jones on the line of scrimmage.

PLAY 3   Fourth-and-10 on 49ers' 30. A punted ball is muffed by the Falcons' Jessie Tuggle on his own 35. The 49ers' Lee Woodall recovers on the Falcons' 30.

PLAY 4   Fourth-and-10 on 49ers' 30. Punt is first touched by 49ers' kicking team player Lee Woodall on Chargers' 35 and then muffed by the Chargers' Junior Seau. The 49ers' Tim McDonald recovers on the Chargers' 30.

PLAY 5   Fourth-and-10 on the Bills' 30. A punt is blocked and rolls beyond line to the Bills' 35 where Raiders' defensive player Darrell Russell tries to recover but muffs it back to the Bills' 28 where punter Chris Mohr falls on it.

Ruling 1: Cowboys' ball first-and-10 on Jets' 28. The ball is dead in Cowboys' possession after having been in the Jets' possession during same down.

Ruling 2: Chargers' ball first-and-10 on Seahawks' 25. Foul by defense is automatic first down for Chargers unless otherwise specified in 14-8-5.

Ruling 3: 49ers' ball first-and-10 on the Falcons' 30. The 49ers recover kick first touched by Falcons beyond line. The ball is dead when recovered by 49ers' (9-1-6-Note).

Ruling 4: Chargers' ball first-and-10 on their own 35. Illegal touch. It was first touched by the 49ers and not the Chargers (9-1-4).

Ruling 5: Bills' ball first-and-10 on their 28. Ball first touched beyond line by Raiders (9-1-6- Note).

NO FIRST
DOWN FOR
OFFENSE

Article 3   If offensive team fails to advance ball to necessary line during a given series, it is awarded to defensive team for a new series at the spot:

(a) where dead at end of fourth down; or

(b) where it is placed because of a combination penalty (14-8-2) *or* a touchback for defensive team.

Exceptions: Ball is not awarded to defensive team when fourth down results either in:

(a) a safety by the offensive team; or

(b) a touchback for the offensive team.

Section 2   Position of Players at Snap

SEVEN MEN
ON LINE

Article 1   The offensive team must have:

(a) seven or more players on its line (3-17) at the snap.

(b) all players who are *not* on line, other than the snap receiver under center, must be at least 1-yard behind it at snap, except as provided in 7-2-4.

NOTE: OFFENSIVE LINEMAN MAY LOCK LEGS.

PENALTY: FOR VIOLATION OF SNAP FORMATION: LOSS OF FIVE YARDS FROM PREVIOUS SPOT.

MAKE THE RIGHT CALL   PLAY **1**   Fourth-and-10 on Patriots' 35. On a field goal attempt Chiefs' offensive tackle Marcus Spears and offensive guard Will Shields lock their legs as they line up. The field goal is good.

Ruling 1: Field goal good, no foul.

ENCROACH-
MENT, OFFSIDE,
NEUTRAL ZONE
INFRACTION

Article 2   After the neutral zone starts, no player of either team at snap may:

(a) encroach upon it (3-18); or

(b) be offside (3-19).

NOTE 1: OFFICIALS ARE TO BLOW THEIR WHISTLES IMMEDIATELY WHENEVER A DEFENDER PENETRATES BEYOND THE NEUTRAL ZONE PRIOR TO THE SNAP AND CONTINUES UNABATED TOWARD THE QUARTERBACK (INCLUDING KICKER) EVEN THOUGH NO CONTACT IS MADE BY A BLOCKER.

NOTE 2: OFFICIALS ARE TO IMMEDIATELY BLOW THEIR WHISTLES WHENEVER A DEFENDER ENTERS THE NEUTRAL ZONE CAUSING THE OFFENSIVE PLAYER(S) DIRECTLY OPPOSITE TO IMMEDIATELY REACT (MOVE). THIS IS CONSIDERED A FOUL (NEUTRAL ZONE INFRACTION) BY THE DEFENSE. IF THERE IS NO IMMEDIATE REACTIONAL MOVEMENT BY THE OFFENSIVE PLAYER(S) DIRECTLY OPPOSITE, THERE IS NO FOUL.

PENALTY: FOR ENCROACHMENT, OFFSIDE, OR A NEUTRAL ZONE INFRACTION: LOSS OF FIVE YARDS FROM PREVIOUS SPOT. NUMBER OF DOWN AND NECESSARY LINE REMAIN THE SAME.

SUPPLEMENTAL NOTES

WHISTLE ON CONTACT

INITIAL ACTION RESPONSIBLE

(1) Unless both teams charge simultaneously, there cannot be a double foul.

(2) If any player crosses his line and contacts an opponent, it is encroaching. *Blow whistle* immediately on contact.

(3) If a defensive player charges into the neutral zone, and the action draws an immediate charge forward by an offensive player directly opposite, the action by the defense is a neutral-zone infraction.

(4) If a player charges into neutral zone without violating items (2) and (3), and returns to a legal position prior to the snap, it is not encroaching unless it is a repeated act after a warning.

PLAY 1 Second-and-10 on Raiders' 30. Raiders' defensive tackle Russell Maryland's initial charge into neutral zone makes the Steelers' offensive guard Brendan Stai directly across from him flinch and draw back.

PLAY 2 Second-and-10 on the Patriots' 30. Raiders' defensive back Russell Maryland runs toward the line of scrimmage as if he is going right over the Steelers' guard Brendan Stai. He stops on the defensive side of the neutral zone but guard Stai in a three-point stance picks up.

PLAY 3 Second-and-10 on the Saints' 30. The Packers LeRoy Butler jumps across the line and contacts the Saints' William Roaf prior to the snap.

PLAY 4 Second-and-10 on the Chargers' 35. The 49ers use a double shift (first, second, or third time during the game). At the start of the second shift, the Chargers' Junior Seau charges into the neutral zone and is in the neutral zone at the snap.

PLAY 5 Second-and-5 on the Chargers' 50. The 49ers use a double shift. At the start of the second shift, Chargers' Junior Seau charges into the neutral zone and makes contact.

PLAY 6 Third-and-7 on the Chargers' 25. The 49ers' Garrison Hearst moves abruptly (simulating the snap) when he goes in motion prior to the snap.

Ruling 1: Blow the whistle immediately. Penalize Maryland for a neutral-zone infraction. Steelers' ball second-and-5 on Raiders' 25.

Ruling 2: Penalize Stai for false start. Steelers' ball second-and-15 on Raiders' 35. Blow the whistle immediately.

Ruling 3: Blow whistle immediately and kill play. Saints' ball second-and-five on their 35.

Ruling 4: 49ers' ball second-and-5 from Chargers' 30. Defense offside.

Ruling 5: 49ers' ball first-and-10 on Chargers' 45. Encroachment.

Ruling 6: 49ers' ball third-and-12 on Chargers' 30. Blow whistle immediately. False start.

REPORTING CHANGE OF POSITION

Article 3 An offensive player who comes into game wearing an illegal number for the position he takes must report to the referee who in turn will report same to the defensive captain. The clock shall not be stopped and the ball may not be put in play until the referee takes his normal position.

FAILURE TO REPORT

PENALTIES:

A) FIVE YARDS FOR ILLEGAL SUBSTITUTION IF PLAYER IN ABOVE CATEGORY ENTERS THE GAME AND/OR HIS TEAM'S HUDDLE WITHOUT REPORTING AND LATER REPORTS HIS PLAYER POSITION STATUS TO THE REFEREE PRIOR TO SNAP. IN SUCH CASES THE CLOCK SHALL START WITH THE REFEREE'S WHISTLE (CLOCK SIGNAL) IMMEDIATELY UPON ENFORCEMENT OF PENALTY, IF CLOCK HAD PREVIOUSLY BEEN RUNNING.

B) FOR FAILURE TO NOTIFY REFEREE OF CHANGE IN ELIGIBILITY OR INELIGIBILITY STATUS (WHEN REQUIRED) PRIOR TO SNAP: LOSS OF FIVE YARDS FOR ILLEGAL SUBSTITUTION.

SUPPLEMENTAL NOTES

(1) It is not necessary for entering substitutes or players legally in the game to report to the Referee under the following conditions:

LEGAL POSITION CHANGES

   a) players wearing eligible pass receiver number playing in eligible pass receiver positions; or

   b) players wearing ineligible pass receiver numbers playing in ineligible pass receiver positions.

(2) When a player is legally designated (Referee informed) as being eligible or ineligible (Article 3), he must participate in such a position until legally withdrawn. If the player remains in this position, he must report on every play.

PLAYER RETURNING TO ORIGINAL POSITION

Exception: If the change in playing position status is followed by: 1) a touchdown; 2) a completed kick from scrimmage (a punt, drop kick, or place kick); 3) a foul; 4) a team time out; 5) the end of a quarter; or 6) time out for the two-minute warning, the said player may return to his originally eligible or ineligible playing position without restriction. However, if the kick is not completed or a touchdown not made, the said player must remain in his new position until legally withdrawn (5-1-5). If withdrawn, he is to re-enter to the position indicated by his number unless he again informs the Referee that he is assuming a position other than that designated by his number.

NOTIFY REFEREE ON POSITION CHANGE

(3) Coaches must instruct those players wearing numbers not qualifying them for designated positions to report to the Referee, *prior to the huddle*, their change in eligibility or ineligibility status. This rule prevails whether player is already in the game or is an entering substitute and whether it is a play from scrimmage; an attempted field goal; or a Try after touchdown.

(4) The Referee especially must be alert to the above situation at all times and be certain that the defensive captain is notified of the change of any player position status.

Article 4 At the snap, a center, guard, or tackle of the offensive team may be anywhere on his line, but he may not be behind it unless he is at least 1-yard behind it and has informed the Referee of his change of position to that of an eligible receiver (7-2-3).

PENALTY: FOR CENTER, GUARD, OR TACKLE NOT ON THE LINE AT THE SNAP: LOSS OF FIVE YARDS FROM THE PREVIOUS SPOT.

PLAY 1 Bears' offensive tackle Andy Heck is legally shifted to the backfield and is then withdrawn. He returns before the next snap to a tackle position.

Ruling 1: *Illegal. Heck must stay out one play, or have his team request a team time out. See 5-2-1-S.N.6 and 7-2-3 Exception.*

PLAYER
MOVEMENT
AT SNAP

Article 5 At the snap, all offensive players must be stationary in their positions:

  (a) without any movement of feet, head, or arms;

  (b) without swaying of body; and

  (c) without moving directly forward *except that one* player only and he, playing in a backfield position, may be in motion provided he is moving, parallel to, obliquely backward from, *or* directly backward from the line of scrimmage at snap.

ILLEGAL
MOTION

NOTE 1: NO PLAYER IS EVER PERMITTED TO BE MOVING OBLIQUELY OR DIRECTLY FORWARD TOWARD HIS OPPONENT'S GOAL LINE AT SNAP.

NOTE 2: NON-ABRUPT MOVEMENT OF HEAD AND/OR SHOULDERS BY OFFENSIVE PLAYERS PRIOR TO THE SNAP IS LEGAL. PLAYERS MUST COME TO A STOP BEFORE BALL IS SNAPPED. IF OFFICIALS JUDGE THE ACTION OF THE OFFENSIVE PLAYERS TO BE ABRUPT, FALSE START FOUL IS TO BE CALLED.

PENALTY: FOR PLAYER ILLEGALLY IN MOTION AT SNAP: LOSS OF FIVE YARDS FROM PREVIOUS SPOT. IN CASE OF DOUBT, THIS PENALTY SHALL BE ENFORCED.

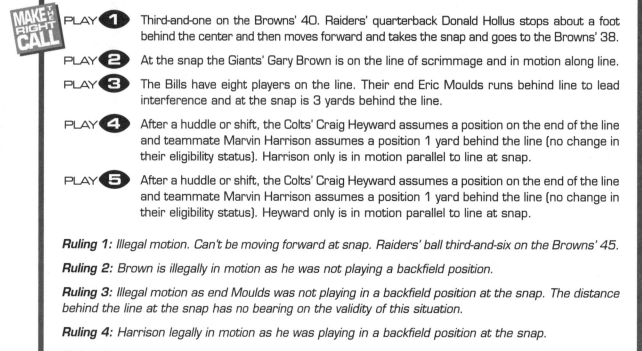

PLAY 1 Third-and-one on the Browns' 40. Raiders' quarterback Donald Hollus stops about a foot behind the center and then moves forward and takes the snap and goes to the Browns' 38.

PLAY 2 At the snap the Giants' Gary Brown is on the line of scrimmage and in motion along line.

PLAY 3 The Bills have eight players on the line. Their end Eric Moulds runs behind line to lead interference and at the snap is 3 yards behind the line.

PLAY 4 After a huddle or shift, the Colts' Craig Heyward assumes a position on the end of the line and teammate Marvin Harrison assumes a position 1 yard behind the line (no change in their eligibility status). Harrison only is in motion parallel to line at snap.

PLAY 5 After a huddle or shift, the Colts' Craig Heyward assumes a position on the end of the line and teammate Marvin Harrison assumes a position 1 yard behind the line (no change in their eligibility status). Heyward only is in motion parallel to line at snap.

Ruling 1: *Illegal motion. Can't be moving forward at snap. Raiders' ball third-and-six on the Browns' 45.*

Ruling 2: *Brown is illegally in motion as he was not playing a backfield position.*

Ruling 3: *Illegal motion as end Moulds was not playing in a backfield position at the snap. The distance behind the line at the snap has no bearing on the validity of this situation.*

Ruling 4: *Harrison legally in motion as he was playing in a backfield position at the snap.*

Ruling 5: *Heyward illegally in motion as he was not playing in a backfield position at the snap.*

COMPLETE
STOP ONE
SECOND

Article 6 After a shift or huddle all offensive players after assuming a set position must come to an absolute stop. They also must remain stationary in their position without any movement of their feet, head or arms, or swaying of their body for a period of at least one second before snap.

PENALTY: FOR ILLEGAL PAUSE OR MOTION AFTER A SHIFT: LOSS OF FIVE YARDS FROM PREVIOUS SPOT. IN CASE OF DOUBT THE PENALTY IS TO BE ENFORCED.

SUPPLEMENTAL NOTES

(1) A single man in motion is not a shift, but if he is moving directly forward at the snap, it is illegal motion (7-2-5-c).

(2) After a shift, if all players come to a legal stop and then one or more men start again before snap, the play may result in encroaching (7-2-2), illegal motion (7-2-5), a second shift (7-2-6), or a false start (7-3-4).

PLAY **1** The Colts shift and come to a stop for one second. The Colts' Marvin Harrison then goes out along his line and stops. Teammate Craig Heyward then moves backward and the ball is snapped less than one second after Harrison stops.

PLAY **2** After a shift or a huddle, the Colts' offensive players come to a stop and remain stationary. Before the lapse of 1 second the Colts' Craig Heyward, who did not shift or huddle, starts and is in motion backward at snap.

PLAY **3** After a legal pause following a shift:
(a) The Colts' running backs Craig Heyward and Edgerin James move forward just prior to snap. They regain their positions and are stationary at the snap.
(b) The Vikings' offensive back Robert Smith charges forward just prior to snap. He regains his position at snap but the Bears' Barry Minter contacts Vikings' guard Randall McDaniel as a result of the movement of Allen.

PLAY **4** Following a shift or huddle all Steelers' offensive players except tackle Mark Bruener make a legal pause prior to snap. Bruener moves into the neutral zone but regains a stationary position less than 1 second prior to snap.

Ruling 1: *Legal play. Movement of Harrison and Heyward are not simultaneous.*

Ruling 2: *Illegal shift. All eleven players must come to an absolute stop for 1 second.*

Ruling 3a: *A second shift and 1 second rule again applies.*

Ruling 3b: *Loss of five yards from previous spot against Smith for false start. Blow whistle on contact.*

Ruling 4: *Illegal shift unless Bruener is penalized for false start.*

OUT OF
BOUNDS AT
SNAP

Article 7 No player may be out of bounds at the snap.

PENALTY: FOR PLAYER OUT OF BOUNDS AT SNAP: LOSS OF FIVE YARDS FROM THE PREVIOUS SPOT.

Section 3   Putting the Ball in Play

PUT BALL IN
PLAY

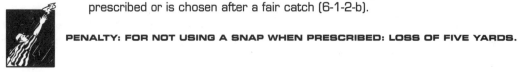

Article 1   The offensive team must put the ball in play by a snap at the spot where previous down ended, unless otherwise specifically provided for, *unless* a free kick is prescribed or is chosen after a fair catch (6-1-2-b).

PENALTY: FOR NOT USING A SNAP WHEN PRESCRIBED: LOSS OF FIVE YARDS.

NO SNAP
UNTIL
ENFORCEMENT

Article 2

When a foul occurs, the ball shall *not* be put in play again until the penalty (Rule 14):

(a) has been enforced;

(b) declined;

(c) offset;

(d) been annulled by a choice; or

(e) disregarded.

SNAP
PROVISIONS

Article 3   The snap (3-31) may be made by any offensive player who is on the line but must conform to the following provisions:

(a) The snap must start with ball on ground with its long axis horizontal and at right angles to line, and

(b) The impulse must be given by one quick and continuous motion of hand or hands of snapper. The ball must actually leave or be taken from his hands during this motion.

(c) The snapper may *not:*

SNAPPER
RESTRICTIONS

(1) move his feet abruptly from the start of snap until the ball has left his hands;

(2) have quick plays after the neutral zone starts if the Referee has not had a reasonable time to assume his normal stance. The ball remains dead. No penalty unless for a repeated act after a warning (delay of game).

PENALTY: FOR ILLEGALLY SNAPPING BALL: LOSS OF FIVE YARDS FROM SPOT OF SNAP FOR FALSE START.

FALSE START

Article 4   From the start of the neutral zone until the snap, no offensive player, if he assumed a set position, shall charge or move in such a way as to simulate the start of a play (false start).

PENALTY: FOR FALSE START: LOSS OF FIVE YARDS FROM SPOT OF SNAP.

SUPPLEMENTAL NOTES

MOVEMENT OF
INTERIOR
LINEMEN

(1) When interior lineman of the offensive team (tackle to tackle) takes or simulates a three-point stance and then moves after taking that stance, the offensive team shall be penalized for a false start. The official *must* blow his whistle immediately.

(2) The penalty for a false start (Article 4) shall be enforced regardless of whether snap is made. The distance penalty for the false start may be declined.

NO OFFENSIVE
MOVEMENT

(3) Any quick, abrupt movement by a single offensive player or by several offensive players in unison, which simulates the start of the snap is a false start.

Exception: This does not apply to an offensive player under the center who turns his head or shoulders (only) provided he receives a hand to hand snap. Any obvious attempt by the quarterback to draw an opponent offside is to be penalized as a false start.

EXTENSION
OF HANDS

(4) Any extension of hands by a player under center as if to receive the snap is a false start unless he receives the snap. This includes any player under or behind the center placing his hands on his knees or on the body of the center.

(5) Any offensive backfield player, not under center, including a kicker or a place kick holder who extends his hands, does not have to receive the snap, nor must he retract them prior to the snap.

PLAY **1** Second-and-10 on the Titans' 40. Broncos' quarterback Bubby Brister bobs his head in an exaggerated manner prior to the snap and draws the Titans into the neutral zone.

PLAY **2** Second-and-10 on the Jets' 30. Jets' offensive interior lineman Erik Norgard simulates a three-point stance after a huddle. He then moves to a regular three-point stance. Defensive player charges and contacts player not directly opposite him.

PLAY **3** Second-and-10 on the Patriots' 30. The Patriots break from huddle and all linemen except tackle Edward Ellis assume a three-point stance. Ellis rests his elbows on his knees in a crouched position. After a second, Ellis assumes a three-point stance. When he started his move to a three-point stance the Raiders' Darrell Russell charges across line and contacts Ellis.

PLAY **4** Second-and-10 on the Jets' 30. Jets' offensive interior lineman Erik Norgard moves his feet abruptly after taking a three-point stance to make himself more comfortable. The ball is then snapped and the Raiders' Charles Woodson gets Jets' quarterback Vinny Testaverde to fumble and Woodson recovers on the Jets' 25.

PLAY **5** Third-and-10 on the Jets' 30. Jets' quarterback Vinny Testaverde places his hands on side of snapper. Ball goes through Testaverde 's legs to Jets' back Curtis Martin who completes a pass to their 40.

PLAY **6** The Jets come out of a huddle into a T formation. Jets' quarterback Vinny Testaverde extends his hands under the center, after which the Jets shift into a spread formation, with Testaverde assuming a blocking halfback position. Jets' back Curtis Martin assumes a tailback position with hands extended for the snap. During the shift into the spread formation by the Jets, the Raiders' Darrell Russell is drawn offside.

Ruling 1: Penalize five yards for false start. Blow the whistle immediately.

Ruling 2: False start against the Jets. Blow whistle immediately to kill play. Defensive action ignored. Jets' ball second-and-15 on their 25.

Ruling 3: Penalize Russell for encroachment. Harlow's move was legal. Blow the whistle immediately. Patriots' ball second-and-five on their 35.

Ruling 4: False start. Blow whistle immediately on Norgard's movement.

Ruling 5: False start. Five-yard penalty. Snap must go to Testaverde. Jets' ball third- and-15 on their 25. Blow whistle immediately.

Ruling 6: False start against the Jets. Blow whistle immediately. Loss of five yards. If the Raiders were not offside, it would be a legal play.

DEFENSE
CAN'T TOUCH
BALL

Article 5 Prior to the snap no defensive player shall enter the neutral zone and touch the ball.

PENALTY: FOR ACTIONS INTERFERING WITH THE BALL PRIOR TO OR DURING THE SNAP: LOSS OF FIVE YARDS FOR DELAY FROM THE SPOT OF THE SNAP. BLOW WHISTLE IMMEDIATELY ON CONTACT.

LEGAL SNAP

Article 6 The snap must be to a player who was *not* on his line at the snap, unless it has first struck the ground. The play continues as after any other backward pass 8-4-1-Exception) if the snap either:

(a) first touches the ground; or

(b) first touched or is caught by an eligible backfield receiver.

PENALTY: FOR SNAPPING TO INELIGIBLE SNAP RECEIVER: BLOW WHISTLE. LOSS OF FIVE YARDS FROM THE SPOT OF SNAP.

PLAY **1** Fourth-and-10 on the Titans' 30. The snap first touches the ground and goes off Titans' kicker Al Del Greco's hands. A defensive player picks it up on the Titans' 20 and scores.

PLAY **2** Fourth-and-10 on Cardinals' 30. Snap is high and Cardinals punter Scott Player jumps high and muffs the ball, which rolls to his 20. The Bengals' Corey Sawyer picks up the ball on the Cardinals' 20 and scores.

Ruling 1: Touchdown (8-4-1).

Ruling 2: Touchdown. (8-4-1).

SNAP AT
INBOUNDS
SPOT

Article 7 Ball is next put in play (snap) at inbounds spot by the team entitled to possession (7-1-1 and 3) when:

(a) a loose ball is out of bounds between goal lines;

(b) a runner is out of bounds between goal lines;

(c) the ball is dead in a side zone;

(d) the ball is placed there as the result of an enforcement; or

(e) the mark of a fair catch is in a side zone (6-1-3-Note).

Exceptions: The ball is next put in play at the previous spot if:

(a) a forward pass goes out of bounds;

(b) a forward pass falls incomplete; or

(c) a foul by the defense occurs in a side zone during an unsuccessful try.

Section 4 Dead Ball

DEAD BALL
DECLARED

Article 1 An official shall declare dead ball and the down ended:

(a) when a runner is out of bounds, cries "down," or falls to the ground and makes no effort to advance.

QUARTERBACK KNEEL

(b) any time a quarterback immediately drops his knee (or simulates dropping his knee) to the ground behind the line of scrimmage during the last two minutes of a half. The game clock will not stop during this action.

RUNNER SLIDE FEET FIRST

(c) whenever a runner declares himself down by sliding feet first on the ground. The ball is dead at the spot of the ball at the instant the runner so touches the ground.

(d) when a runner is so held or otherwise restrained that his forward progress ends.

CONTACTED BY DEFENSE

(e) when a runner is contacted by a defensive player and he touches the ground with any part of his body except his hands or feet, ball shall be declared dead immediately. The contact by the defensive player must be the cause of runner going down.

NOTES THE BALL IS DEAD AT THE SPOT OF THE BALL AT THE INSTANT THE RUNNER SO TOUCHES THE GROUND, IRRESPECTIVE OF THE CONDITION OF THE FIELD. A RUNNER TOUCHING THE GROUND WITH HIS HANDS OR FEET WHILE IN THE GRASP OF AN OPPONENT MAY CONTINUE TO ADVANCE.

GRABBING OF BALL FROM PLAYER

(f) when an opponent takes a ball (hand in hand) in possession of a runner who is down on the ground.

(g) when any forward pass (legal or illegal) is incomplete (8-1-5).

(h) when any legal kick touches receivers' goal posts or crossbar unless it later scores a goal from field (9-1-14).

(i) when any scrimmage kick crosses receivers' goal line from the impetus of kick and no attempt is made to run it out, or if it is lying loose in the end zone from the impetus of the kick.

(j) when any legal kick or a short free kick is recovered by the kickers, except one kicked from behind line which is recovered behind line (not a Try-kick). See 9-1-4-Note for exception.

(k) when defense gains possession during a Try, or a Try-kick ceases to be in play.

(l) when a touchdown, touchback, safety, field goal, or Try has been made.

(m) when any receiver catches after a fair catch signal (valid or invalid) before kick is touched in flight by an opponent.

(n) when any official sounds his whistle, even if inadvertently.

(o) when any fourth down fumble by offensive team is recovered by any offensive player other than the fumbling player. See 8-4-2-Exception and S.N.

NOTE: AN OPPONENT MAY TAKE OR GRAB A BALL (HAND TO HAND) IN POSSESSION OF A RUNNER PROVIDED THE RUNNER IS ON HIS FEET OR IS AIRBORNE.

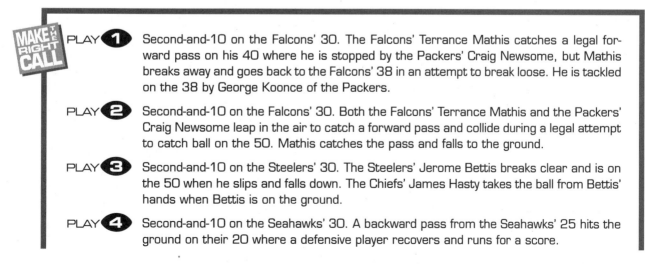

MAKE THE RIGHT CALL

PLAY 1 Second-and-10 on the Falcons' 30. The Falcons' Terrance Mathis catches a legal forward pass on his 40 where he is stopped by the Packers' Craig Newsome, but Mathis breaks away and goes back to the Falcons' 38 in an attempt to break loose. He is tackled on the 38 by George Koonce of the Packers.

PLAY 2 Second-and-10 on the Falcons' 30. Both the Falcons' Terrance Mathis and the Packers' Craig Newsome leap in the air to catch a forward pass and collide during a legal attempt to catch ball on the 50. Mathis catches the pass and falls to the ground.

PLAY 3 Second-and-10 on the Steelers' 30. The Steelers' Jerome Bettis breaks clear and is on the 50 when he slips and falls down. The Chiefs' James Hasty takes the ball from Bettis' hands when Bettis is on the ground.

PLAY 4 Second-and-10 on the Seahawks' 30. A backward pass from the Seahawks' 25 hits the ground on their 20 where a defensive player recovers and runs for a score.

PLAY Second-and-goal on the Chiefs' 4. The Steelers' Jerome Bettis gets to the goal line and ball touches goal line when he is tackled. He fumbles and the Chiefs' James Hasty recovers in end zone.

Ruling 1: Falcons' ball third-and-two on their 38. No forward progress is given as Mathis was not stopped. He broke away before he was downed.

Ruling 2: Ball is dead at spot. Falcons' ball first-and-10 on the 50.

Ruling 3: Blow whistle to kill play. May not take ball unless runner is on his feet. Steelers' ball first-and-10 on the 50.

Ruling 4: Touchdown (8-4-1).

Ruling 5: Touchdown. Ball dead as soon as ball touches goal line in player possession (11-2-1-a).

LOOSE BALL
BECOMES
DEAD

Article 2 If a loose ball comes to rest anywhere in field and no player attempts to recover, official covering the play should pause momentarily before signaling dead ball (official's time out). Any legal kick is awarded to receivers and any other ball to team last in possession. When awarded to a team behind the goal line, the ball is placed on its 1-yard line. See 7-4-5 and Note.

PLAY Second-and-goal on the Chiefs' 2. The Steelers' Jerome Bettis goes to the line of scrimmage where he is tackled and fumbles. The ball rolls into the end zone when the Referee inadvertently blows his whistle as the ball is loose in the end zone. The Chiefs then fall on the ball.

PLAY ② A player recovers a loose ball in play by falling on it. He then arises and advances.

Ruling 1: Ball dead when whistle blew. Steelers' ball third-and-one on Chiefs' 1. Place ball on 1-yard line.

Ruling 2: Legal advance unless he has recovered a legal kick made by his team.

INADVERTENT
WHISTLE

Article 3 If an official inadvertently sounds his whistle during a play, the ball becomes dead immediately:

WHISTLE
DURING RUN

(a) If during a run, it is the offensive team's ball at the spot of the ball at the time of the whistle.

WHISTLE
DURING
BACKWARDS
PASS OR
FUMBLE

(b) If during a backward pass or fumble, it is the offensive team's ball at the spot of the ball at the time of the whistle. Exception: The ball is placed on the 1-yard line if the whistle sounds when the ball is loose in either end zone.

WHISTLE
DURING KICK

(c) If during a kick, it is the receivers' ball at the spot of the ball at the time of the whistle.

WHISTLE
DURING
FORWARD
PASS

(d) If during a forward pass from behind the line, the ball reverts to the passers at the previous spot. It is an incomplete pass.

(e) If during a forward pass from beyond the line, the ball reverts to the passers at the spot of the pass. It is an illegal pass. The penalty is assessed from the spot of the pass.

(f) If during a forward pass not from scrimmage, the ball reverts to the passers at the spot of the pass. The penalty is assessed from the spot of the pass.

NOTE: PENALTY ENFORCEMENT FOLLOWING PLAY BLOWN DEAD BY AN INADVERTANT WHISTLE IS AS ORDINARY FOR FOULS DURING RUNS, PASSES, KICKS, FUMBLES, AND BACKWARDS PASSES.

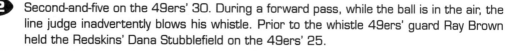

PLAY 1 Second-and-10 on the Seahawks' 30. The Seahawks' Ricky Watters fumbles a handoff from quarterback John Kitna on their 25. The ball is on the 49ers' 22 when the Referee inadvertently blows his whistle.

PLAY 2 Second-and-five on the 49ers' 30. During a forward pass, while the ball is in the air, the line judge inadvertently blows his whistle. Prior to the whistle 49ers' guard Ray Brown held the Redskins' Dana Stubblefield on the 49ers' 25.

PLAY 3 A forward pass first touches Raiders' ineligible receiver Steve Wisniewski beyond line. While the pass is still in flight, a whistle sounds. The pass is incomplete.

Ruling 1: Seahawks' ball third-and-18 on their 22. Seahawks' ball at the spot of the ball at whistle.

Ruling 2: Option for the Redskins. Either an incomplete pass (49ers' ball third-and-five on their 30) or foul for holding against the 49ers (second-and-15 on 49ers' 20). Any enforcement is as ordinary.

Ruling 3: Loss of down or 10 yards from previous spot. See 8-1-5-(e).

BALL PUT IN PLAY

Article 4 When the ball is dead, it is next put in play (7-3-1) at spot designated by official so declaring it. This is usually the spot of the ball when his whistle sounded, but may be some other spot, in case Referee is informed by an official that the ball should have been dead at another spot or in case the rules prescribe otherwise (15-2-3).

BALL TOUCHES OFFICIAL

Article 5 The ball is not dead because of touching an official who is inbounds or because of a signal by an official other than a whistle.

NOTE: WHEN A FOUL OCCURS, ANY OFFICIAL OBSERVING IT IMMEDIATELY SOUNDS HIS WHISTLE IF IT IS ONE FOR WHICH BALL REMAINS DEAD OR IS DEAD IMMEDIATELY. OTHERWISE HE SIGNALS IT BY MEANS OF DROPPING HIS FLAG (15-1-4-NOTE) AT THE SPOT OF THE FOUL UNLESS DISTANCE PRECLUDES IT. IN SUCH CASE, HE STILL INDICATES THE FOUL IN THE SAME MANNER, BUT APPROXIMATES SPOT, AND NOTES ANY PERTINENT CIRCUMSTANCES. UNLESS A WHISTLE SOUNDS, BALL CONTINUES IN PLAY UNTIL OTHERWISE DEAD (7-4-1).

Section 5   Possession of Ball After Out of Bounds

KICK OUT OF BOUNDS

Article 1 If any legal kick, except for a free kick, is out of bounds between the goal lines, ball is next put in play at inbounds spot by the receivers, *unless* there is a spot of illegal touching nearer kickers' goal line. For free kick out of bounds, see 6-3-1.

FOURTH DOWN OUT OF BOUNDS

Article 2 If it is a play from scrimmage, any possession by offensive team after an out of bounds during fourth down is governed by the location of the necessary line (7-1-3).

RUNNER OUT OF BOUNDS

Article 3 If a runner (3-27) is out of bounds between goal lines, the ball is next put in play by his team at inbounds spot.

FORWARD PASS OUT OF BOUNDS

Article 4

If a forward pass is out of bounds between the goal lines, the ball is next put in play by passing team as provided for an incompletion or for an illegal pass. See 8-1-5.

BACKWARD PASS OUT OF BOUNDS

Article 5
If a backward pass is out of bounds between the goal lines, the ball is next in play at the inbounds spot by the team last in possession.

FUMBLE NOT RECOVERED

Article 6
A fumble by the offensive team cannot result in an advance by that team if the ball is not recovered in the field of play or end zone.

(a) A fumble that goes forward and out of bounds is to return to that team at the spot of the fumble.

FUMBLE OUT OF BOUNDS AND CLOCK

NOTE: IF, ON A PLAY FROM SCRIMMAGE, A FUMBLE GOES OUT OF BOUNDS FORWARD, THE GAME CLOCK IS TO BE STOPPED BUT IS TO BE RESTARTED WHEN THE BALL CAN BE MADE READY FOR PLAY AT THE SPOT OF THE FUMBLE. IF THE BALL GOES OUT OF BOUNDS BEHIND THE SPOT OF THE FUMBLE, GAME CLOCK IS TO BE STOPPED AND IS TO BE RESTARTED WHEN THE BALL IS SNAPPED FOR THE NEXT DOWN.

(b) A fumble in the field of play that goes backward and out of bounds belongs to the offense at the out-of-bounds spot.

FUMBLE OUT OF BOUNDS IN END ZONE

(c) A fumble in the field of play that goes forward into the opponent's end zone and over the end line or sideline results in the ball being given over to the defensive team and a touchback awarded.

(d) A fumble which occurs in a team's own end zone and goes forward into the field of play and out of bounds will result in a safety *if that team provided the impetus that put the ball into the end zone. If the impetus was provided by the opponent, the play will result in a touchback.*

(e) A fumble which occurs in a team's own end zone or in the field of play and the ball goes out of bounds in the end zone will result in a safety *if that team provided the impetus that put the ball into the end zone. If the impetus was provided by the opponent, the play will result in a touchback.*

PLAY **1** Second-and-goal on the Patriots' 4. The Cowboys' Emmitt Smith fumbles at line of scrimmage where ball rolls out of bounds:
a) at 1-yard line.
b) over end line.

PLAY **2** Second-and-14 on the Cowboys' 2. The Cowboys' Emmitt Smith fumbles in end zone. Ball rolls out of bounds.
a) at 1-yard line.
b) in end zone.

PLAY **3** Second-and-14 on the Dolphins' 2. The Broncos' Tyrone Braxton intercepts a forward pass on the Dolphins' 20, runs to the Dolphins' 3, and fumbles. The ball rolls into the end zone. The Dolphins' John Avery picks up the ball in the end zone, is tackled there, and fumbles ball in end zone. The ball rolls out of bounds over the end line.

PLAY **4** Third-and-12 on the Broncos' 22. The Broncos' Tyrone Braxton intercepts forward pass in end zone. Tries to run it out and fumbles in end zone. Ball rolls out of bounds:
a) on Broncos' 3-yard line.
b) over the end line.

Ruling 1a: Cowboys' ball third-and-goal on the Patriots' 4.

Ruling 1b: Patriots' ball first-and-10 on the Patriots' 20.

Ruling 2a: Safety.

Ruling 2b: Safety.

Ruling 3: Touchback; Dolphins' ball—first-and-10 on their 20. (See 7-5-6-(e)).

Ruling 4a: Touchback (see 7-5-6-(d)).

Ruling 4b: Touchback (see 7-5-6-(d)).

OUT OF BOUNDS BEHIND GOAL LINE

Article 7 If a pass, kick, or fumble is out of bounds behind a goal line, Rule 11 governs.

MAKE THE RIGHT CALL

CHAPTER 8

FORWARD PASS, BACKWARD PASS, FUMBLE

Sometimes fans are not sure what constitutes illegal contact downfield. This infraction refers to overt contact by a defender on a receiver that occurs downfield with the quarterback in the pocket with the ball.

If the quarterback has rolled out of the pocket or made a backward pass or handed off to someone, then the illegal contact rules are off.

Jerry Seeman
NFL DIRECTOR OF OFFICIATING

Section 1   Forward Pass

ONE
FORWARD
PASS LEGAL

Article 1   The offensive team may make *one* forward pass from behind the line during each play from scrimmage provided the ball does not cross the line and return behind line prior to the pass.

ILLEGAL PASS

(a) Any other forward pass by either team is illegal and is a foul by the passing team.

ILLEGAL PASS
INTERCEPTED

(b) When any illegal pass is intercepted, the ball may be advanced and the penalty declined.

(c) When illegal pass is caught by an offensive player, the ball is dead immediately and the pass is considered incomplete, in addition to a penalty.

PENALTIES:

A) **FOR A FORWARD PASS NOT FROM SCRIMMAGE: LOSS OF FIVE YARDS FROM THE SPOT OF THE PASS. IT IS A SAFETY WHEN THE SPOT OF THE PASS IS BEHIND THE PASSER'S GOAL LINE.**

B) **FOR A SECOND FORWARD PASS FROM BEHIND LINE, OR FOR A PASS· THAT WAS THROWN *AFTER* THE BALL RETURNED BEHIND THE LINE: LOSS OF 5 YARDS FROM THE PREVIOUS SPOT.**

NOTE: SEE 8-3-1 FOR INTENTIONAL GROUNDING.

C) **FOR A FORWARD PASS FROM BEYOND THE LINE: LOSS OF DOWN AND FIVE YARDS FROM THE SPOT OF THE PASS (COMBINATION PENALTY). SEE 14-8-2. SEE S.N. 3 BELOW.**

ILLEGAL
PASSES AND
PASS
INTERFERENCE

SUPPLEMENTAL NOTES

(1) Eligibility and pass interference rules apply to a second pass from behind the line or a forward pass that was thrown from behind the line after the ball returned behind the line. On all other illegal passes, eligibility rules do not apply.

(2) Intentional grounding also can occur on a second forward pass, or a pass after the ball had crossed the line of scrimmage.

SPOT OF
ENFORCEMENT
OF ILLEGAL
PASSES

(3) The penalty for a forward pass beyond the line is to be enforced from the spot where any part of the passer's body is beyond the line of scrimmage when the ball is released.

NECESSARY
YARDAGE

(4) When a distance penalty in Penalty c) leaves the ball in advance of the necessary line, it is first-and-10 for the offensive team.

INTENTIONAL
FUMBLE
FORWARD

(5) An intentional fumble forward is a forward pass. See 8-4-2, Exception 1.

(6) For when any legal or illegal pass becomes incomplete, see 8-1-5.

INCOMPLETE
ILLEGAL PASSES

(7) For team possession during a forward pass (loose ball) or when it ends, see 3-2-3.

PLAY **1**   Second-and-10 on the Saints' 40. A forward pass is batted back by a Bengals' player. The ball goes back in the air to the Saints' quarterback Billy Joe Tolliver behind his line. He throws it again to wide receiver Andre Hastings who catches it on the Saints' 40, goes for a score.

PLAY **2**   Second-and-18 on the Saints' 4. A second forward pass from behind the line is caught by Saints' wide receiver Andre Hastings in his end zone. He is downed in his end zone.

PLAY **3**   Second-and-10 on the Saints' 40. A second forward pass from behind the line is intercepted by the defensive team at midfield. A defensive player returns it for a touchdown.

PLAY **4**   A punt is caught on the receiving team's 20-yard line. The player who caught the ball attempts to throw a backward pass, but the ball goes forward and hits the ground. The kicking team falls on it.

PLAY 5 A forward pass is intercepted by a defensive player in his end zone. While in the end zone, he attempts to pass backward. The pass goes forward, hits the ground on the 1-yard line and is recovered by the first passing team.

PLAY 6 Third-and-10 on the Chargers' 35. A second forward pass is thrown from behind the line to Buccaneers' wide receiver Reidel Anthony. The Chargers' Junior Seau interferes with Anthony on the Chargers' 20, but Anthony catches it anyway and is downed on the Chargers' 20.

PLAY 7 Third-and-15 on the Buccaneers' 30. During a forward pass from beyond the line on the Buccaneers' 40, Buccaneers' wide receiver Reidel Anthony clips on his 40. The pass is incomplete.

PLAY 8 Third-and-15 on Buccaneers' 30. During a forward pass from beyond the line on the Buccaneers' 40, Chargers' linebacker Junior Seau clips on the Buccaneers' 40. The ball falls incomplete.

Ruling 1: *No score. Loss of down. Third-and-10 on Bengals' 40.*

Ruling 2: *The ball is dead when Hastings catches it. Loss of down at the previous spot. Not a safety. Saints' ball third-and-18 on their 4.*

Ruling 3: *Touchdown. Illegal passes may be intercepted.*

Ruling 4: *Incomplete pass. The ball is dead when it hits the ground. Penalize from the spot of the pass as it was an illegal pass (8-1-1, Pen. a). Defense's ball first-and-10 on their 15.*

Ruling 5: *Safety. Forward pass not from scrimmage in the end zone.*

Ruling 6: *Double foul. Illegal pass by the Buccaneers and interference by the Chargers. Interference rules apply on the second forward pass from behind the line (14-3-1). Buccaneers' ball third-and-10 on the Chargers' 35 (replay).*

Ruling 7: *Choice for defensive team. Loss of down and five from the spot of the pass or loss of 15 from the spot of the pass (unless offensive player fouls behind the spot of pass). Buccaneers' ball fourth-and-10 on their 35 or third-and-20 on their 25.*

Ruling 8: *Double foul (14-3-1). Replay at the previous spot. Buccaneers' ball third-and-15 on their 30.*

LEGAL TOUCHING OF FORWARD PASS

ELIGIBLE RECEIVERS

Article 2 A forward pass from behind the line may be touched or caught by any eligible player. (Pass in flight may be tipped, batted, or deflected in any direction by any eligible player at any time. See 12-1-6-Exception and Note).

(a) Defensive players are eligible at all times.

(b) Offensive players who are on either end of the line (other than a center, guard, or tackle) are eligible. See 5-1-4, 7-2-4.

(c) Offensive players who are at least (legally) one yard behind the line at the snap are eligible, except T-formation quarterbacks. See 7-2-4.

ELIGIBILITY LOST

Article 3 An eligible receiver becomes ineligible if he:

(a) goes out of bounds (prior to or during a pass) and remains ineligible until an eligible receiver or any defensive player touches the pass.

Exception: If the eligible receiver is forced out of bounds because of a foul by a defender, including illegal contact, defensive holding, or defensive pass interference, he will become eligible to legally touch the pass (without prior touching by another eligible receiver or defender) as soon as he legally returns in bounds.

ELIGIBILITY REGAINED

NOTE: ALL OFFENSIVE PLAYERS BECOME ELIGIBLE ONCE A PASS IS TOUCHED BY AN ELIGIBLE RECEIVER OR ANY DEFENSIVE PLAYERS.

INELIGIBLE RECEIVERS

Article 4   An ineligible offensive player is one who:

(a) was originally ineligible;

(b) loses his eligibility by going out of bounds (8-1-5, Note 2);

FAILURE TO REPORT ELIGIBILITY

(c) fails to notify the referee of being eligible when indicated (7-2-3, Pen.); or

(d) is a T-formation quarterback who, takes his stance behind center,

(1) receives a hand-to-hand pass or snap from him while moving backward;

(2) does not receive a hand-to-hand pass or snap from him and is not legally one yard behind the line of scrimmage; or

(3) ever receives a forward pass (handed or thrown) from a teammate during a play from scrimmage.

ELIGIBILITY FOR T-FORMATION QUARTERBACK

NOTE: TO BECOME AN ELIGIBLE PASS RECEIVER, A T-FORMATION QUARTERBACK MUST ASSUME THE POSITION OF A BACKFIELD PLAYER (AS IN A SINGLE WING, DOUBLE WING, BOX OR SPREAD FORMATION) AT LEAST ONE YARD BEHIND HIS LINE AT THE SNAP. IN CASE OF DOUBT, THE PENALTY FOR AN INELIGIBLE PLAYER RECEIVING A FORWARD PASS SHALL BE ENFORCED.

INCOMPLETE PASS

Article 5   Any forward pass (legal or illegal) becomes incomplete and the ball is dead immediately if the pass strikes the ground, goes out of bounds, or is caught by any offensive player after it has touched an ineligible player before any touching by any eligible receiver.

ILLEGAL TOUCHING FORWARD PASS

It is a foul for illegal touching, if a forward pass (legal or illegal):

(a) first touches or is caught by an ineligible offensive player behind, on, or beyond the Forward Pass line of scrimmage, or

(b) if an eligible receiver goes out of bounds or is legally forced out of bounds by a defender and returns to first touch or catch a pass inbounds.

PENALTY: LOSS OF FIVE YARDS FROM THE PREVIOUS SPOT.

NOTE 1: *SEE 8-3-1 FOR INTENTIONAL GROUNDING.*

NOTE 2: IF AFTER A FORWARD PASS (LEGAL OR ILLEGAL) IS ILLEGALLY TOUCHED AND THEN IS INTERCEPTED BY B. THE INTERCEPTION IS LEGAL. 8-1-2-A.

COMPLETED PASSES

Article 6 A legal forward pass thrown from behind the line is complete and may be advanced if it is:

(a) caught by an eligible offensive player before any illegal touching by a teammate;

(b) caught by any offensive player after it is first touched by any eligible player; or

(c) intercepted by the defense (defense may also intercept and advance an illegal forward pass).

MUFFED FORWARD HANDOFF

SUPPLEMENTAL NOTES

(1) A ball handed forward (no daylight) to an eligible receiver behind the line is treated as a fumble if he muffs it (3-21-2, Exception). A ball handed forward (no daylight) to an ineligible receiver behind the line is treated as a forward pass and is incomplete when caught or muffed (unless intercepted by B in which case the play continues). See 8-1-5 Pen.

(2) The penalty for an incompletion may not be declined unless there was another foul by the passing team. This does not preclude the ball being dead (14-4).

(3) The bat of a pass in flight by any player (even when illegal touching) does not end a pass nor does it change the impetus if the act sends it in touch.

SIMULTANEOUS CATCH

(4) If a pass is caught simultaneously by two eligible opposing players who both retain it, the ball belongs to the passers. It is not a simultaneous catch if a player gains control first and retains control, regardless of subsequent joint control with an opponent. If the ball is muffed after simultaneous touching by two such players, all the players of the passing team become eligible to catch the loose ball.

BOTH FEET INBOUNDS

(5) A pass is completed or intercepted if the player has both feet or any other part of his body, except his hands, inbounds prior to and after the catch.

FORCED OUT OF BOUNDS

(6) A pass is completed or intercepted, or a loose ball recovered, if the player inbounds would have landed inbounds with both feet but is carried or pushed out of bounds while in possession of the ball in the air or before the second foot touches the ground inbounds by an opponent.

(7) A pass is not intercepted if the defensive player does not have both feet inbounds prior to the interception (as well as after the interception).

NOTE: SEE 11-4-1-EXC FOR INTERCEPTING MOMENTUM.

PLAY **1** Third-and-10 on the Browns' 40. A forward pass from behind the line goes off Cowboys' eligible wide receiver Michael Irvin's hands and teammate Raghib Ismail catches it in the end zone.

PLAY **2** While in midair, a receiver firmly takes hold of a pass, but loses possession of the ball when his shoulder lands on the ground with or without being contacted by an opponent.

PLAY **3** A runner (in full possession of the ball) is contacted by an opponent while he is attempting to gain yardage. The contact causes the runner to hit the ground, at which time the ball comes loose.

PLAY **4** Second-and-15 on the Cowboys' 4. A second forward pass from behind the line is caught by the Cowboys' eligible wide receiver Raghib Ismail after the ball had touched a Cowboys' eligible wide receiver Michael Irvin. He is downed in the end zone.

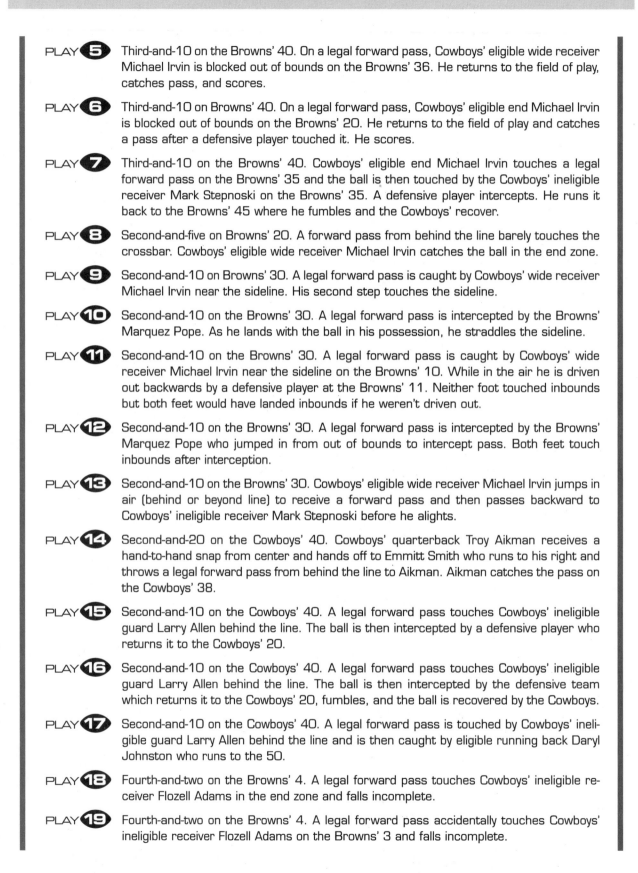

PLAY **5** Third-and-10 on the Browns' 40. On a legal forward pass, Cowboys' eligible wide receiver Michael Irvin is blocked out of bounds on the Browns' 36. He returns to the field of play, catches pass, and scores.

PLAY **6** Third-and-10 on Browns' 40. On a legal forward pass, Cowboys' eligible end Michael Irvin is blocked out of bounds on the Browns' 20. He returns to the field of play and catches a pass after a defensive player touched it. He scores.

PLAY **7** Third-and-10 on the Browns' 40. Cowboys' eligible end Michael Irvin touches a legal forward pass on the Browns' 35 and the ball is then touched by the Cowboys' ineligible receiver Mark Stepnoski on the Browns' 35. A defensive player intercepts. He runs it back to the Browns' 45 where he fumbles and the Cowboys' recover.

PLAY **8** Second-and-five on Browns' 20. A forward pass from behind the line barely touches the crossbar. Cowboys' eligible wide receiver Michael Irvin catches the ball in the end zone.

PLAY **9** Second-and-10 on Browns' 30. A legal forward pass is caught by Cowboys' wide receiver Michael Irvin near the sideline. His second step touches the sideline.

PLAY **10** Second-and-10 on the Browns' 30. A legal forward pass is intercepted by the Browns' Marquez Pope. As he lands with the ball in his possession, he straddles the sideline.

PLAY **11** Second-and-10 on the Browns' 30. A legal forward pass is caught by Cowboys' wide receiver Michael Irvin near the sideline on the Browns' 10. While in the air he is driven out backwards by a defensive player at the Browns' 11. Neither foot touched inbounds but both feet would have landed inbounds if he weren't driven out.

PLAY **12** Second-and-10 on the Browns' 30. A legal forward pass is intercepted by the Browns' Marquez Pope who jumped in from out of bounds to intercept pass. Both feet touch inbounds after interception.

PLAY **13** Second-and-10 on the Browns' 30. Cowboys' eligible wide receiver Michael Irvin jumps in air (behind or beyond line) to receive a forward pass and then passes backward to Cowboys' ineligible receiver Mark Stepnoski before he alights.

PLAY **14** Second-and-20 on the Cowboys' 40. Cowboys' quarterback Troy Aikman receives a hand-to-hand snap from center and hands off to Emmitt Smith who runs to his right and throws a legal forward pass from behind the line to Aikman. Aikman catches the pass on the Cowboys' 38.

PLAY **15** Second-and-10 on the Cowboys' 40. A legal forward pass touches Cowboys' ineligible guard Larry Allen behind the line. The ball is then intercepted by a defensive player who returns it to the Cowboys' 20.

PLAY **16** Second-and-10 on the Cowboys' 40. A legal forward pass touches Cowboys' ineligible guard Larry Allen behind the line. The ball is then intercepted by the defensive team which returns it to the Cowboys' 20, fumbles, and the ball is recovered by the Cowboys.

PLAY **17** Second-and-10 on the Cowboys' 40. A legal forward pass is touched by Cowboys' ineligible guard Larry Allen behind the line and is then caught by eligible running back Daryl Johnston who runs to the 50.

PLAY **18** Fourth-and-two on the Browns' 4. A legal forward pass touches Cowboys' ineligible receiver Flozell Adams in the end zone and falls incomplete.

PLAY **19** Fourth-and-two on the Browns' 4. A legal forward pass accidentally touches Cowboys' ineligible receiver Flozell Adams on the Browns' 3 and falls incomplete.

PLAY **20** Second-and-15 on the Cowboys' 8. A legal forward pass is batted back by a defensive player and the ball lands in the end zone. A defensive player falls on it in the end zone.

PLAY **21** First-and-10 on the Cowboys' 30. A legal forward pass is touched simultaneously by two opposing eligible players, the Cowboys' Raghib Ismail and the Browns' Marquez Pope. The pass goes in the air where Cowboys' ineligible receiver Flozell Adams catches it on the Cowboys' 40 and runs to midfield.

Ruling 1: Touchdown.

Ruling 2: Incomplete pass. Receiver must hold onto the ball when he alights on the ground in order to complete the reception.

Ruling 3: Play is dead when the impact jars the ball loose. No fumble.

Ruling 4: The ball is dead when Ismail caught it. No safety (8-1-5-Pen. 1). Loss of down from the previous spot. Cowboys' ball third-and-15 on their 4.

Ruling 5: No score. Loss of down as Irvin became an ineligible receiver by going out of bounds. Cowboys' ball fourth-and-10 on Browns' 40.

Ruling 6: Touchdown. Legal play as all ineligible receivers become eligible after the defense touches the ball.

Ruling 7: Legal touch. Cowboys' ball first-and-10 on the Browns' 45.

Ruling 8: No score. The ball is dead immediately upon touching the crossbar (or goal posts). Loss of down from the previous spot. Cowboys' ball third-and-five on Browns' 20.

Ruling 9: Incomplete pass. Both feet have to alight inbounds. Cowboys' ball third-and-10 on the Browns' 30.

Ruling 10: Incomplete pass. Both feet have to touch inbounds. Cowboys' ball third-and-10 on the Browns' 30.

Ruling 11: Completed pass. Cowboys' ball first-and-goal on the Browns' 10, wind clock.

Ruling 12: Incomplete pass. Both feet have to be inbounds prior to interception. Cowboys' ball third-and-10 on the Browns' 30. See 8-1-6-S.N. 7.

Ruling 13: Legal catch.

Ruling 14: The ball is dead when caught by Aikman. T-quarterback is an ineligible receiver. Loss of down at previous spot. Third-and-20 on the Cowboys' 40.

Ruling 15: Pass not incomplete when Allen touched by ball. Pass continues in play. Browns' ball first-and-10 on the Cowboys' 20.

Ruling 16: Loss of down penalty for touching ineligible receiver behind the line. Pass not incomplete when ineligible receiver touches it. Cowboys' ball third-and-10 on their 40.

Ruling 17: The ball is dead when caught. A pass touched by an ineligible player behind the line is loss of down. Cowboys' ball third-and-10 on their 40.

Ruling 18: The Browns will accept option of loss of down at previous spot rather than loss of 10 yards. Browns' ball first-and-10 on their 4.

Ruling 19: Loss of down penalty as touching was beyond the line. Browns' ball first-and-10 on their 4. See 8-1-5-e.

Ruling 20: Incomplete pass. Cowboys' ball third-and-15 on their 8.

Ruling 21: Legal completion.

Section 2   Pass Interference/Ineligible Player Downfield

PASS INTERFERENCE NOT ALLOWED

Article 1   There shall be *no pass interference* beyond line of scrimmage when there is a forward pass thrown from behind the line. This applies regardless of whether the pass crosses the line.

PASS RESTRICTIONS

(a) The restriction for the offensive team begins with the snap.

(b) The restriction for the defensive team begins when the ball leaves the passer's hands.

INELIGIBLE PLAYER DOWNFIELD

Article 2   It is a foul when an ineligible offensive player (including a T-formation quarterback), prior to a legal forward pass:

(a) advances beyond his line, after losing contact with an opponent at the line of scrimmage;

(b) loses contact with an opponent downfield after the initial charge and then continues to advance or move laterally; or

(c) moves downfield without contacting an opponent at the line of scrimmage.

The above restrictions end when the ball leaves the passer's hand.

PENALTY: INELIGIBLE OFFENSIVE PLAYER DOWNFIELD: LOSS OF 5 YARDS FROM PREVIOUS SPOT.

NOT INELIGIBLE PLAYER DOWNFIELD

Article 3   It is *not* a foul for an ineligible receiver downfield when ineligible receivers:

(a) immediately retreat voluntarily behind the line after legally crossing the line;

(b) are forced behind their line;

(c) move laterally behind their line (before or after contact of their initial charge) provided they do not advance *beyond* their line until the ball leaves the passer's hands; or

(d) have legally crossed their line in blocking an opponent (eligible offensive player A1 may complete a pass between them and the offensive line).

INELIGIBLES LEGALLY DOWNFIELD

Article 4   *After* the ball leaves the passer's hand, ineligible forward pass receivers can advance:

(a) from behind their line;

(b) from their own line; or

(c) from their initial charge position, provided they do *not* block or contact a defensive player(s) *until* the ball is touched by a player of either team. *Such prior blocking and/or contact is forward pass interference.*

When an ineligible lineman, who has legally crossed his line in blocking an opponent or a T-formation quarterback, is touched by a forward pass while beyond his line, enforcement is for Penalty (e) under 8-1-5 (loss of down or 10 yards).

PASS INTERFERENCE BY EITHER TEAM

Article 5   It is pass interference by either team when any player movement beyond the line of scrimmage significantly hinders the progress of an eligible player of such player's opportunity to catch the ball. Offensive pass interference rules apply from the time the ball is snapped until the ball is touched. Defensive pass interference rules apply from the time the ball is thrown until the ball is touched.

DEFENSIVE PASS INTERFERENCE

Actions that constitute defensive pass interference include but are not limited to:

(a) Contact by a defender who is not playing the ball and such contact restricts the receiver's opportunity to make the catch.

(b) Playing through the back of a receiver in an attempt to make a play on the ball.

(c) Grabbing a receiver's arm(s) in such a manner that restricts his opportunity to catch a pass.

(d) Extending an arm across the body of a receiver thus restricting his ability to catch a pass, regardless of whether the defender is playing the ball.

(e) Cutting off the path of a receiver by making contact with him without playing the ball.

(f) Hooking a receiver in an attempt to get to the ball in such a manner that it causes the receiver's body to turn prior to the ball arriving.

NOT DEFENSIVE PASS INTERFERENCE

Actions that do not constitute pass interference include but are not limited to:

(a) Incidental contact by a defender's hands, arms or body when both players are competing for the ball, or neither player is looking for the ball. If there is any question whether contact is incidental, the ruling shall be no interference.

(b) Inadvertent tangling of feet when both players are playing the ball or neither player is playing the ball.

(c) Contact that would normally be considered pass interference, but the pass is clearly uncatchable by the involved players.

(d) Laying a hand on a receiver that does not restrict the receiver in an attempt to make a play on the ball.

(e) Contact by a defender who has gained position on a receiver in an attempt to catch the ball.

OFFENSIVE PASS INTERFERENCE

Actions that constitute offensive pass interference include but are not limited to:

(a) Blocking downfield by an offensive player prior to the ball being touched.

(b) Initiating contact with a defender by shoving or pushing off thus creating a separation in an attempt to catch a pass.

(c) Driving through a defender who has established a position on the field.

NOT OFFENSIVE PASS INTERFERENCE

Actions that do not constitute offensive pass interference include but are not limited to:

(a) Incidental contact by a receiver's hands, arms, or body when both players are competing for the ball or neither player is looking for the ball.

(b) Inadvertent touching of feet when both players are playing the ball or neither player is playing the ball.

(c) Contact that would normally be considered pass interference, but the ball is clearly uncatchable by involved players.

PASS INTERFERENCE NOTES

NOTE 1: IF THERE IS ANY QUESTION WHETHER PLAYER CONTACT IS INCIDENTAL, THE RULING SHOULD BE NO INTERFERENCE.

NOTE 2: DEFENSIVE PLAYERS HAVE AS MUCH RIGHT TO THE PATH OF THE BALL AS ELIGIBLE OFFENSIVE PLAYERS.

NOTE 3: PASS INTERFERENCE FOR BOTH TEAMS ENDS WHEN THE PASS IS TOUCHED.

NOTE 4: THERE CAN BE NO PASS INTERFERENCE AT OR BEHIND THE LINE OF SCRIMMAGE, BUT DEFENSIVE ACTIONS SUCH AS TACKLING A RECEIVER CAN STILL RESULT IN A 5-YARD PENALTY FOR DEFENSIVE HOLDING, IF ACCEPTED.

NOTE 5: WHENEVER A TEAM PRESENTS AN APPARENT PUNTING FORMATION, DEFENSIVE PASS INTERFERENCE IS NOT TO BE CALLED FOR ACTION ON THE END MAN ON THE LINE OF SCRIMMAGE, OR AN ELIGIBLE RECEIVER BEHIND THE LINE OF SCRIMMAGE WHO IS ALIGNED OR IN MOTION MORE THAN ONE YARD OUTSIDE THE END MAN ON THE LINE. DEFENSIVE HOLDING, SUCH AS TACKLING A RECEIVER, STILL CAN BE CALLED AND RESULT IN A 5-YARD PENALTY FROM THE PREVIOUS SPOT, IF ACCEPTED. OFFENSIVE PASS INTERFERENCE RULES STILL APPLY.

PASS INTERFERENCE PENALTIES

PENALTIES:

(A) PASS INTERFERENCE BY OFFENSE: LOSS OF 10 YARDS FROM PREVIOUS SPOT.

(B) PASS INTERFERENCE BY DEFENSE: FIRST DOWN FOR OFFENSIVE TEAM AT THE SPOT OF ANY SUCH FOUL. IF THE INTERFERENCE IS ALSO A PERSONAL FOUL (12-2), THE USUAL DISTANCE PENALTY FOR SUCH A FOUL (WHETHER THE PASS IS COMPLETE OR INCOMPLETE) IS ALSO ENFORCED (FROM SPOT TO FOUL). IF THE INTERFERENCE IS BEHIND THE DEFENSIVE GOAL LINE, IT IS

FIRST DOWN FOR THE OFFENSIVE TEAM ON THE DEFENSE'S 1-YARD LINE, OR, IF THE PREVIOUS SPOT WAS INSIDE THE 2-YARD LINE, THEN HALFWAY BETWEEN THE PREVIOUS SPOT AND THE GOAL LINE.

See 8-3-3 and 4 for optional penalty in case of a personal foul (12-2) by opponents prior to any completion or interception.

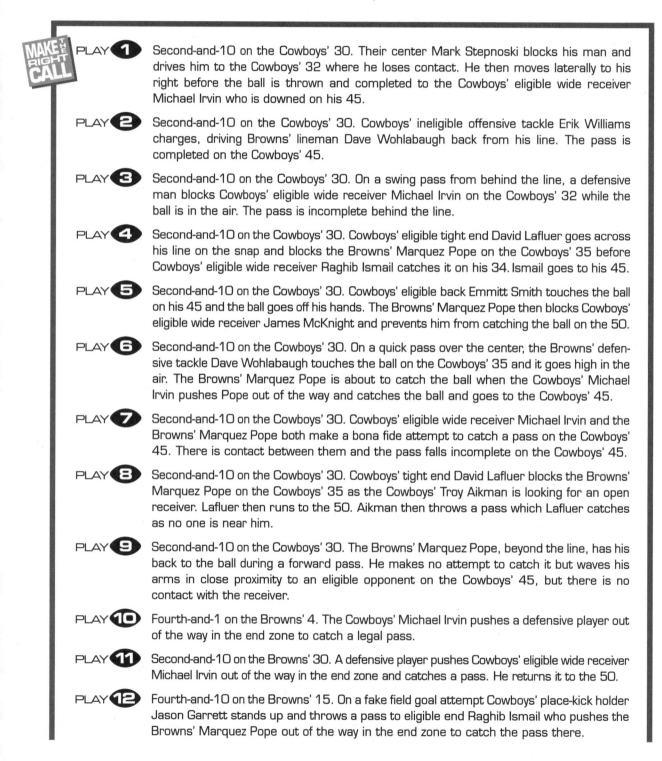

PLAY 1 Second-and-10 on the Cowboys' 30. Their center Mark Stepnoski blocks his man and drives him to the Cowboys' 32 where he loses contact. He then moves laterally to his right before the ball is thrown and completed to the Cowboys' eligible wide receiver Michael Irvin who is downed on his 45.

PLAY 2 Second-and-10 on the Cowboys' 30. Cowboys' ineligible offensive tackle Erik Williams charges, driving Browns' lineman Dave Wohlabaugh back from his line. The pass is completed on the Cowboys' 45.

PLAY 3 Second-and-10 on the Cowboys' 30. On a swing pass from behind the line, a defensive man blocks Cowboys' eligible wide receiver Michael Irvin on the Cowboys' 32 while the ball is in the air. The pass is incomplete behind the line.

PLAY 4 Second-and-10 on the Cowboys' 30. Cowboys' eligible tight end David Lafluer goes across his line on the snap and blocks the Browns' Marquez Pope on the Cowboys' 35 before Cowboys' eligible wide receiver Raghib Ismail catches it on his 34. Ismail goes to his 45.

PLAY 5 Second-and-10 on the Cowboys' 30. Cowboys' eligible back Emmitt Smith touches the ball on his 45 and the ball goes off his hands. The Browns' Marquez Pope then blocks Cowboys' eligible wide receiver James McKnight and prevents him from catching the ball on the 50.

PLAY 6 Second-and-10 on the Cowboys' 30. On a quick pass over the center, the Browns' defensive tackle Dave Wohlabaugh touches the ball on the Cowboys' 35 and it goes high in the air. The Browns' Marquez Pope is about to catch the ball when the Cowboys' Michael Irvin pushes Pope out of the way and catches the ball and goes to the Cowboys' 45.

PLAY 7 Second-and-10 on the Cowboys' 30. Cowboys' eligible wide receiver Michael Irvin and the Browns' Marquez Pope both make a bona fide attempt to catch a pass on the Cowboys' 45. There is contact between them and the pass falls incomplete on the Cowboys' 45.

PLAY 8 Second-and-10 on the Cowboys' 30. Cowboys' tight end David Lafluer blocks the Browns' Marquez Pope on the Cowboys' 35 as the Cowboys' Troy Aikman is looking for an open receiver. Lafluer then runs to the 50. Aikman then throws a pass which Lafluer catches as no one is near him.

PLAY 9 Second-and-10 on the Cowboys' 30. The Browns' Marquez Pope, beyond the line, has his back to the ball during a forward pass. He makes no attempt to catch it but waves his arms in close proximity to an eligible opponent on the Cowboys' 45, but there is no contact with the receiver.

PLAY 10 Fourth-and-1 on the Browns' 4. The Cowboys' Michael Irvin pushes a defensive player out of the way in the end zone to catch a legal pass.

PLAY 11 Second-and-10 on the Browns' 30. A defensive player pushes Cowboys' eligible wide receiver Michael Irvin out of the way in the end zone and catches a pass. He returns it to the 50.

PLAY 12 Fourth-and-10 on the Browns' 15. On a fake field goal attempt Cowboys' place-kick holder Jason Garrett stands up and throws a pass to eligible end Raghib Ismail who pushes the Browns' Marquez Pope out of the way in the end zone to catch the pass there.

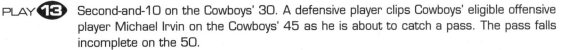

PLAY **13** Second-and-10 on the Cowboys' 30. A defensive player clips Cowboys' eligible offensive player Michael Irvin on the Cowboys' 45 as he is about to catch a pass. The pass falls incomplete on the 50.

PLAY **14** Second-and-10 on the Cowboys' 30. During a pass, a Browns' defensive back grabs the face mask of the Cowboys' Michael Irvin on the Cowboys' 35. The ball is thrown to the 50 where the Browns' Marquez Pope interferes with the Cowboys' Daryl Johnston. The pass falls incomplete.

PLAY **15** Second-and-10 on the Cowboys' 30. On a legal forward pass which is unintentionally thrown too high and too far for the Cowboys' Michael Irvin to catch, the Browns' Marquez Pope pushes Irvin as the ball is already beyond him and Irvin obviously couldn't reach the ball. Ball hits ground 12 yards away from Irvin.

Ruling 1: Ineligible man moved laterally beyond the line after losing contact. Loss of 5 yards. Cowboys' ball second-and-15 on their 25 (8-2-1).

Ruling 2: Not ineligible player downfield. Cowboys' ball first-and-10 on their 45 (8-2-1).

Ruling 3: Defensive pass interference. It is defensive pass interference regardless of whether the pass crosses the line once the ball is thrown. Cowboys' ball first-and-10 on their 32.

Ruling 4: Offensive pass interference. Can't block beyond the line prior to the ball being touched. Cowboys' ball second-and-20 on their 20.

Ruling 5: Legal block. The ball was touched. No pass interference. Cowboys' ball third-and-10 on their 30.

Ruling 6: Legal play as the ball was touched by the defense. Interference rules ended when defensive player touched the pass. Cowboys' ball first-and-10 on their 45.

Ruling 7: Incomplete pass. Legal play as it was a simultaneous and bona fide attempt by opposing players. Cowboys' ball third-and-10 on their 30.

Ruling 8: Offensive pass interference. Cowboys' ball second-and-20 on their 20.

Ruling 9: No foul. Legal action by defender.

Ruling 10: Loss of 10 yards from previous spot. Cowboys' ball fourth-and-11 on the Browns' 14.

Ruling 11: Defensive pass interference in the defensive end zone. Cowboys' ball first-and-goal on the Browns' 1.

Ruling 12: Offensive pass interference. Cowboys' ball fourth-and-20 on the Browns' 25.

Ruling 13: Interference is also a personal foul and penalize for both. Cowboys' ball first-and-10 on the Browns' 40.

Ruling 14: Additional yardage would have been tacked on if the personal foul (face mask) was the pass interference at the 50 (Pen. b) or if the pass had been completed (8-3-3). Cowboys' ball first-and-10 on 50.

Ruling 15: No pass interference. Ball wasn't catchable.

INTENTIONAL
GROUNDING

Section 3   Fouls on Passes and Enforcement

Article 1   Intentional grounding will be called when a passer, facing an imminent loss of yardage because of pressure from the defense, throws a forward pass without a realistic chance of completion.

> **NOTE 1:** THE PENALTY IS THE SOLE RESPONSIBILITY OF THE REFEREE AND THE PROTECTION OF THE QUARTERBACK IS HIS PRIMARY RESPONSIBILITY; THE FLIGHT OF THE BALL IS SECONDARY. IF THERE IS ANY QUESTION, THE REFEREE SHOULD NOT CALL INTENTIONAL GROUNDING.

> **NOTE 2:** INTENTIONAL GROUNDING WILL NOT BE CALLED WHEN A PASSER (THE QUARTERBACK), WHILE OUT OF THE POCKET AND FACING AN IMMINENT LOSS OF YARDAGE, THROWS A FORWARD PASS THAT LANDS NEAR OR BEYOND THE LINE OF SCRIMMAGE, EVEN IF NO OFFENSIVE PLAYER(S) HAVE A REALISTIC CHANCE TO CATCH THE BALL (INCLUDING IF THE BALL LANDS OUT OF BOUNDS OVER THE SIDELINE OR ENDLINE).

> **NOTE 3:** A PASSER, AFTER DELAYING HIS PASSING ACTION FOR STRATEGIC PURPOSES, IS PROHIBITED FROM THROWING THE BALL TO THE GROUND IN FRONT OF HIM, EVEN THOUGH HE IS UNDER NO PRESSURE FROM DEFENSIVE RUSHER(S).

> **NOTE 4:** A PASSER IS PERMITTED TO STOP THE CLOCK LEGALLY TO SAVE TIME IF IMMEDIATELY UPON RECEIVING THE SNAP HE BEGINS A CONTINUOUS THROWING MOTION AND THROWS THE BALL DIRECTLY FORWARD INTO THE GROUND.

PENALTY: FOR INTENTIONAL GROUNDING: LOSS OF DOWN AND 10 YARDS FROM THE PREVIOUS SPOT, OR IF FOUL OCCURS MORE THAN 10 YARDS FROM LINE OF SCRIMMAGE OR WHERE IT IS MORE ADVANTAGEOUS TO THE DEFENSE, LOSS OF DOWN AT SPOT OF FOUL, OR SAFETY IF PASSER IS IN HIS END ZONE WHEN BALL IS THROWN.

> **NOTE:** THE PENALTY FOR INTENTIONAL GROUNDING MAY BE DECLINED AND THE RESULT OF THE PLAY IS AN INCOMPLETE PASS.

PLAY 1   Second-and-20 on the Cowboys' 4. Their quarterback Troy Aikman drops back into his end zone. Just before he is tackled in his end zone, he intentionally grounds the ball by throwing a pass directly in front of him. A defensive player falls on it.

PLAY 2   Second-and-10 on the Cowboys' 30. Their quarterback Troy Aikman intentionally grounds ball forward as he stands on his 16 to keep from being tackled.

PLAY 3   Second-and-10 on the Browns' 20. Cowboys' quarterback Troy Aikman deliberately throws the ball out of bounds to stop the clock.

Ruling 1: Intentional grounding. Safety.

Ruling 2: Loss of down at spot of foul as Aikman is more than 10 yards behind the line. Third-and-24 on Cowboys' 16.

Ruling 3: The pass was not thrown away to prevent loss of yardage. Cowboys' ball third-and-10 on the Browns' 20. See 8-3-1-Note 4.

ENFORCEMENT
SPOT ON
FORWARD
PASS FOULS

Article 2   If there is a foul by either team from the time of the snap until a forward pass from behind the line ends, the penalty is enforced from the previous spot.

> **NOTE:** A FORWARD PASS IN FLIGHT THAT IS CONTROLLED OR CAUGHT MAY ONLY BE THROWN BACKWARDS. IF THROWN FORWARD IT IS CONSIDERED ILLEGALLY BATTING A LOOSE BALL AND THE PENALTY IS ENFORCED FROM THE PREVIOUS SPOT.

Exceptions:

1)   Pass interference by the defense is enforced from the spot of the foul.

2)   On a personal foul prior to interception or completion of a pass from behind the line, enforcement is from the spot chosen (8-3-3, 4).

3)   It is a safety when the offensive team commits a foul behind its own goal line.

PLAY **1** Third-and-10 on the Cowboys' 30. During a run prior to an incompleted pass, the Cowboys' Darryl Johnston holds a defensive player on the Cowboys' 25.

PLAY **2** Third-and-10 on the Cowboys' 30. During a run prior to an intended pass by Cowboys' quarterback Troy Aikman, the Browns' Marquez Pope holds the Cowboys' Ernie Mills on the Cowboys' 45. Aikman doesn't throw the ball and is downed on his 20.

Ruling 1: Choice for defense. Fourth-and-10 on the Cowboys' 30 or third-and-20 on the Cowboys' 20 (from previous spot).

Ruling 2: Enforce from the previous spot. Cowboys' ball first-and-10 on their 35.

PERSONAL FOUL PRIOR TO COMPLETION

Article 3 When the defense commits a personal foul **prior** to a completion of a legal forward pass from behind the line, the offense shall have the choice of either:

(a) the usual penalty—15 yards from the previous spot; or

(b) a 15-yard penalty enforced from the spot where the ball is dead.

Exception: If the passing team is fouled and loses possession after a completion, enforcement is from the previous spot and the ball will be retained by the offended team after enforcement of the personal foul.

PERSONAL FOUL PRIOR TO INTERCEPTION

Article 4 When the offense commits a personal foul prior to an interception of a legal forward pass from behind the line, the defense will have a 15-yard penalty enforced from the spot where the ball is dead.

Exception: If the intercepting team is fouled and loses possession after the interception, enforcement is from the spot where the interception occurred and the ball will be retained by the offended team after the enforcement of the personal foul.

NOTE: PERSONAL FOULS DO NOT INCLUDE HOLDING, ILLEGAL USE OF HANDS, ILLEGAL BATTING, KICKING THE BALL, OR TRIPPING. SEE RULE 12-2.

PLAY **1** Third-and-10 on the 49ers' 40. A Jets' defensive player roughs the passer prior to a pass completion to the 49ers' Jerry Rice on the Jets' 45. Rice runs to the Jets' 40 where he is downed.

PLAY **2** Third-and-10 on the 49ers' 40. A Jets' defensive player roughs 49ers' quarterback Steve Young as he throws a short swing pass to the 49ers' Garrison Hearst who is downed on his 35. The foul is prior to the completion of the pass.

PLAY **3** Third-and-10 on the 49ers' 40. 49ers' offensive guard Ray Brown clips the Jets' Bryan Cox as he tries to reach the passer. The Jets' Aaron Glenn intercepts the pass and returns it to the 49ers' 30.

PLAY **4** Third-and-10 on the 49ers' 40. The Jets' Bryan Cox roughs the passer prior to a completed pass to the 49ers' Jerry Rice on the 50. Rice runs to the Jets' 40 where he is tackled, fumbles and the Jets recover on their 35.

PLAY **5** Third-and-10 on the 49ers' 30. The Jets' Aaron Glenn intercepts forward pass at his 30, runs to his 35, fumbles and the 49ers recover. Prior to pass, the 49ers' J. J. Stokes crackbacks on his 26.

PLAY **6** Third-and-10 on the 49ers' 40. The Jets' Bryan Cox roughs the passer prior to a completion to the 49ers' Jerry Rice on the Jets' 40. Rice goes for a score.

Ruling 1: Personal foul prior to completion of a legal forward pass. Fifteen-yard penalty enforced from the spot where the ball is dead. 49ers' ball first-and-10 on the Jets' 25.

Ruling 2: Enforce from the previous spot as the usual penalty on a pass. 49ers' ball first-and-10 on the Jets' 45.

Ruling 3: Enforce from the spot where the ball is dead. Personal foul prior to interception. Jets' ball first-and-10 on the 49ers' 15.

Ruling 4: Personal foul prior to completion. Enforce from the previous spot and the ball reverts to the offended team. 49ers' ball first-and-10 on the Jets' 45.

Ruling 5: Jets' ball first-and-10 on their 45.

Ruling 6: Touchdown. Loss of 15 on the kickoff. Kick off on 45. See 14-1-14.

DEFENSIVE FOUL AND INCOMPLETE PASS

Article 5 If there is a foul by the defense from the start of the snap until a legal forward pass ends, it is *not* offset by an incompletion by the offensive team.

Exception: Any foul by the offensive team would offset a foul by the defensive team (14-3-1).

PLAY **1** Second-and-10 on the 49ers' 30. During a forward pass the ball goes off 49ers' eligible wide receiver Jerry Rice's fingers and teammate J. J. Stokes catches it on the Jets' 40. The Jets were offside.

PLAY **2** Second-and-10 on the 49ers' 30. A forward pass is caught by 49ers' ineligible tackle Derrick Deese on his 28. The Jets' Anthony Pleasant was offside.

PLAY **3** Second-and-10 on the 49ers' 30. A forward pass is caught by 49ers' ineligible receiver Derrick Deese beyond the line. Prior to or during the pass, a Jets' defensive player strikes the 49ers' Jerry Rice.

Ruling 1: 49ers' ball first-and-10 on the Jets' 40.

Ruling 2: Penalties offset. Second-and-10 on the 49ers' 30.

Ruling 3: Disqualify the Jets' player. Replay at previous spot.

Section 4   Backward Pass and Fumble

Article 1 A runner may pass backward at any time (3-21-4).

  (a) An offensive player may catch a backward pass or recover it after the pass touches the ground and advance.

  (b) A defensive player may catch a backward pass or recover it after the pass touches the ground and advance.

NOTE: A DIRECT SNAP FROM CENTER IS TREATED AS A BACKWARD PASS.

Exception: See actions to conserve time (4-3-10).

PLAY ❶ Third-and-10 for the 49ers on the Jets' 30. A backward pass hits the ground on the Jets' 35. A defensive player recovers it and runs to the Jets' 45.

Ruling: Legal recovery and advance. Defense's ball first-and-10 on the Jets' 45 (8-4-1-b).

FUMBLE
RECOVERY

Article 2   Any player of either team may recover or catch and advance a fumble:

(a) before the fumble strikes the ground; or

(b) after the fumble strikes the ground.

> NOTE: A FUMBLE IS LEGALLY RECOVERED OR CAUGHT IN BOUNDS BY A PLAYER IF THE PLAYER HAD BOTH FEET IN BOUNDS PRIOR TO THE RECOVERY OR CATCH. SEE 7-5-6 FOR FUMBLE OUT OF BOUNDS AND 11-4-1-EXCEPTION, FOR A FUMBLE IN END ZONE FOLLOWING INTERCEPTING MOMENTUM.

Exceptions:

INTENTIONAL
FUMBLE

1) If a runner *intentionally* fumbles forward, it is a forward pass (3-21-2-a and Note).

FOURTH DOWN
FUMBLE AND
LEGAL
ADVANCE

2) If a fourth down fumble occurs during a play from scrimmage and the fumbling player recovers the ball, he only:

a) may advance; or

b) hand and/or pass the ball forward or backward (as prescribed by rule).

DEAD BALL ON
FOURTH DOWN
FUMBLE

3) If a fourth down fumble occurs during a play from scrimmage and the recovery or catch is by another offensive player, the spot of the next snap is:

a) the spot of the fumble unless

b) the spot of recovery is behind the spot of the fumble and it is then at the spot of recovery. See 8-4-4.

4) If a fourth down fumble occurs during a play from scrimmage and the ball rolls out of bounds from field of play, the ball is next put in play at the spot of the fumble, unless the spot of out of bounds is behind the spot of the fumble, then it is at that spot (Rule 7-5-6). See 11-6-1.

SUPPLEMENTAL NOTE

FUMBLE AFTER
TWO-MINUTE
WARNING
APPLIES TO
BOTH TEAMS

After the two-minute warning, any fumble that occurs during a down (including Try), the fumbled ball may only be advanced by the offensive player who fumbled the ball, or any member of the defensive team. See 11-3-1-b.

PLAY ❶ Fourth-and-10 on the 49ers' 40. A high snap from center glances off the 49ers' kicker's hands as he muffs the ball on his 28. The ball rolls to the 49ers' 25. A defensive player picks it up and goes for a score.

PLAY ❷ 49ers' ball fourth-and-10 on the Jets' 20. Direct snap from center on an attempted field goal glances off 49ers' placekick holder's hands at the Jets' 27. Field goal kicker recovers the ball at the Jets' 30 and *runs for a touchdown.*

PLAY ❸ Second-and-10 on the Jets' 14. On last play of game the 49ers are behind by 4 points. 49ers' quarterback Steve Young falls back to pass, fumbles, and ball eventually winds up in the Jets' end zone. The 49ers' Garrison Hearst falls on it.

PLAY 4 Fourth-and-four on the Jets' 9. The 49ers' Garrison Hearst fumbles (forward unintentionally) on the Jets' 9. Hearst recovers and goes to the Jets' 4.

PLAY 5 Fourth-and-four on the Jets' 9. The 49ers' Garrison Hearst fumbles on the Jets' 9 (forward unintentionally). Teammate J. J. Stokes recovers on the Jets' 7 and goes to the Jets' 4.

PLAY 6 Fourth-and-four on the Jets' 9. The 49ers' Garrison Hearst fumbles on the Jets' 9 and teammate Jerry Rice recovers on the Jets' 12 and goes to the Jets' 4.

PLAY 7 Fourth-and-four on the Jets' 9. The 49ers' Garrison Hearst fumbles on the Jets' 9. The Jets' Bryan Cox touches the ball and then the 49ers' Jerry Rice recovers on the Jets' 7.

PLAY 8 Fourth-and-four on the Jets' 9. The 49ers' Garrison Hearst fumbles on the Jets' 9 and the ball rolls out of bounds on the Jets' 4 without any player touching it.

Ruling 1: Touchdown. (8-4-1-Note).

Ruling 2: Legal touchdown. See 8-4-1-Note.

Ruling 3: No score. Game over. See 8-4-2, S.N.

Ruling 4: Legal advance as the fumbling player recovered. 49ers' ball first-and-goal on the Jets' 4.

Ruling 5: Player other than the fumbling player recovered. The spot of the snap is the spot of the fumble (Jets' 9). Jets' ball first-and-10 on their 9.

Ruling 6: Other player than the fumbler recovered and spot of next snap is the spot of recovery as it is behind the spot of the fumble. Jets' ball first-and-10 on their 12.

Ruling 7: Ball is returned to spot of fumble (Jets' 9). Jets' ball first-and-10 on their 9.

Ruling 8: The ball is next put in play at the spot of the fumble. Jets' ball first-and-10 on their 9.

SIMULTANEOUS RECOVERY

NOTE: WHEN A BACKWARD PASS OR FUMBLE IS A SIMULTANEOUS OR HIDDEN BALL RECOVERY BY TWO OPPOSING PLAYERS, THE BALL IS AWARDED TO THE TEAM MAKING THE PASS OR FUMBLE.

BACKWARD PASS OUT OF BOUNDS

Article 3 If a backward pass goes out of bounds between the goal lines, the ball is next put in play at the inbounds spot by the team in last possession. The ball is dead (7-5-5). Rule 11 governs if a backward pass is declared dead behind the goal line.

ENFORCEMENT SPOT DURING BACKWARD PASS OR FUMBLE

Article 4 When a foul occurs during a backward pass or fumble, the basic spot of enforcement is the spot of the fumble or the spot of the backward pass. If the offensive team fouls behind the spot of the fumble or backward pass, the spot of enforcement is the spot of the foul (4-1-5).

Exceptions: When the spot of the backward pass or fumble is behind the line (including A's end zone) and either team fouls during the loose ball, the spot of enforcement is the previous spot, even if B's foul is in A's end zone. See 11-4-2 for safety (offensive foul in own end zone).

NOTE: WHEN THE SPOT OF THE FUMBLE OR BACKWARD PASS IS BEYOND THE LINE, A DEFENSIVE FOUL DURING THE BACKWARD PASS OR FUMBLE OCCURRING ANYWHERE IS ENFORCED FROM THE SPOT OF THE FUMBLE OR BACKWARD PASS.

SUPPLEMENTAL NOTES

BACKWARD
PASS OR
FUMBLE
TOUCHING
GOAL POSTS

USE OF
HANDS ON
BACKWARD
PASS OR
FUMBLE

(1) When a backward pass or fumble touches a goal post, ball is dead as it is out of bounds.

(2) For team possession during a backward pass or fumble (loose ball) or when it ends, see 3-2-3 and 3-21-2-Note.

(3) After a backward pass or fumble touches the ground, any player may legally block or otherwise use his hands or arms to push or pull an opponent out of the way, but only in an actual personal attempt to recover (12-1-2 and 3).

(4) A backward pass going out of bounds during the last two minutes of a half stops the clock (4-3-10-S.N. 5).

(5) For fumbles forward out of bounds or unrecovered in the field of play or in the end zone, see 7-5-6.

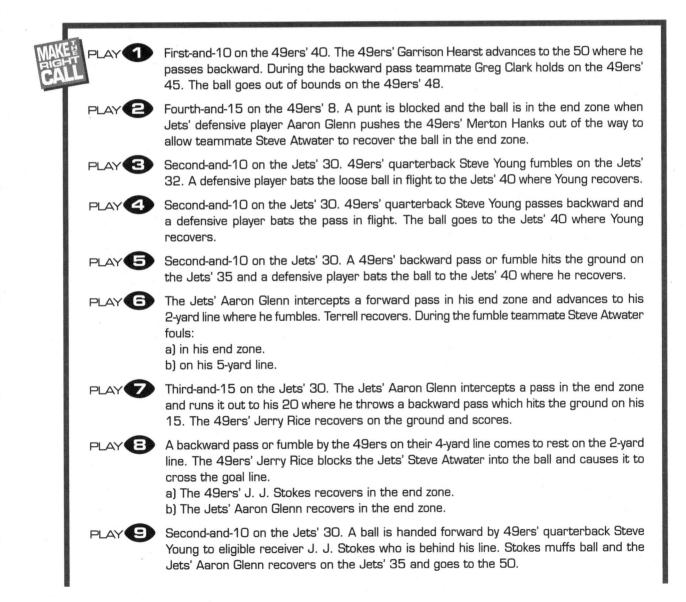

MAKE THE RIGHT CALL

PLAY 1 First-and-10 on the 49ers' 40. The 49ers' Garrison Hearst advances to the 50 where he passes backward. During the backward pass teammate Greg Clark holds on the 49ers' 45. The ball goes out of bounds on the 49ers' 48.

PLAY 2 Fourth-and-15 on the 49ers' 8. A punt is blocked and the ball is in the end zone when Jets' defensive player Aaron Glenn pushes the 49ers' Merton Hanks out of the way to allow teammate Steve Atwater to recover the ball in the end zone.

PLAY 3 Second-and-10 on the Jets' 30. 49ers' quarterback Steve Young fumbles on the Jets' 32. A defensive player bats the loose ball in flight to the Jets' 40 where Young recovers.

PLAY 4 Second-and-10 on the Jets' 30. 49ers' quarterback Steve Young passes backward and a defensive player bats the pass in flight. The ball goes to the Jets' 40 where Young recovers.

PLAY 5 Second-and-10 on the Jets' 30. A 49ers' backward pass or fumble hits the ground on the Jets' 35 and a defensive player bats the ball to the Jets' 40 where he recovers.

PLAY 6 The Jets' Aaron Glenn intercepts a forward pass in his end zone and advances to his 2-yard line where he fumbles. Terrell recovers. During the fumble teammate Steve Atwater fouls:
a) in his end zone.
b) on his 5-yard line.

PLAY 7 Third-and-15 on the Jets' 30. The Jets' Aaron Glenn intercepts a pass in the end zone and runs it out to his 20 where he throws a backward pass which hits the ground on his 15. The 49ers' Jerry Rice recovers on the ground and scores.

PLAY 8 A backward pass or fumble by the 49ers on their 4-yard line comes to rest on the 2-yard line. The 49ers' Jerry Rice blocks the Jets' Steve Atwater into the ball and causes it to cross the goal line.
a) The 49ers' J. J. Stokes recovers in the end zone.
b) The Jets' Aaron Glenn recovers in the end zone.

PLAY 9 Second-and-10 on the Jets' 30. A ball is handed forward by 49ers' quarterback Steve Young to eligible receiver J. J. Stokes who is behind his line. Stokes muffs ball and the Jets' Aaron Glenn recovers on the Jets' 35 and goes to the 50.

PLAY Second-and-10 on the Jets' 30. A ball is handed backward (no daylight) to 49ers' ineligible receiver Ray Brown on the Jets' 35. Brown muffs the ball and the Jets' Bryan Cox recovers and goes to the 50.

Ruling 1: *Enforcement is from the spot of the foul as it is behind the basic spot (14-1-5- d). 49ers' ball first-and-15 on their 35.*

Ruling 2: *The spot of enforcement is the previous spot as the foul by the defense occurred behind this line. 49ers' ball first-and-10 on their 13.*

Ruling 3: *The enforcement spot is the previous spot as the foul is behind the line. Illegal bat (12-1-6). 49ers' ball first-and-10 on the Jets' 20.*

Ruling 4: *Legal bat (12-1-6-Exc.). 49ers' ball third-and-20 on the Jets' 40.*

Ruling 5: *Illegal bat of a loose ball. Enforcement is from the previous spot as it is behind the line. 49ers' ball first-and-10 on the Jets' 20.*

Ruling 6a: *Safety. Enforcement is from the spot of the foul as it is not from scrimmage. See 11-4-2 and 14-1-11-b.*

Ruling 6b: *Jets' ball first-and-10 on their 1. Enforcement is from the spot of the fumble.*

Ruling 7: *Legal recovery and advance by Rice. Touchdown 49ers (8-4-1-b).*

Ruling 8a: *Safety if Stokes is downed in the end zone. May advance if he can (3-14-3, Note).*

Ruling 8b: *Touchdown.*

Ruling 9: *Legal advance. It is not a forward pass (3-21-2, Exception), and it is treated as a fumble. Jets' ball first-and-10 on 50.*

Ruling 10: *Legal recovery. A ball which is handed backward from one player to another (no daylight) and is dropped, shall be treated as a fumble. Either team may recover and advance. Jets' ball first-and-10 on 50.*

CHAPTER 9
SCRIMMAGE KICK

It is illegal for an offensive player to punt or drop kick the ball beyond the line of scrimmage.

Jerry Seeman
NFL DIRECTOR OF OFFICIATING

Section 1   Kick from Scrimmage

Article 1   The kicking team, behind the scrimmage line, may:

PUNT

(a) punt;

(b) dropkick; or

(c) placekick.

PENALTY: FOR A PUNT, DROPKICK, OR PLACEKICK NOT KICKED FROM BEHIND THE LINE OF SCRIMMAGE: 10 YARDS FROM THE SPOT OF THE KICK.

NOTE: THIS IS NOT CONSIDERED ILLEGALLY KICKING THE BALL.

PLAY **1**   The Raiders' punt is blocked and the Raiders' Leo Araguz picks up the ball behind the line of scrimmage and throws a forward pass to teammate James Jett.

PLAY **2**   A field goal attempt inside the defense's 20 is blocked and bounces back toward the kicker. The kicker then kicks the loose ball on the ground from behind the line of scrimmage. The ball goes over the crossbar.

Ruling 1: Legal play (8-1-1).

Ruling 2: No field goal. Illegal. Option of 10-yard penalty from the previous spot for kicking a loose ball (12-1-7 and 14-1-5, Exception 1), or touchback (11-6-1-b).

RECEIVERS RECOVER

Article 2   If the receivers recover any kick, they may advance. For fair catch exception, see 10-1-2.

NOTE: FOR TEAM POSSESSION DURING A SCRIMMAGE KICK (LOOSE BALL) OR WHEN IT ENDS, SEE 3-2-3.

PLAYERS ON LINE DURING KICK

Article 3   During a kick from scrimmage, only the end men as eligible receivers on the line of scrimmage at the time of the snap, are permitted to go beyond the line before the ball is kicked.

COVER MEN ON KICKS

Exception: An eligible receiver who, at the snap, is aligned or in motion behind the line and more than one yard outside the end man on his side of the line clearly making him the outside receiver, *replaces* that end man as the player eligible to go downfield after the snap. All other members of the kicking team must remain at the line of scrimmage until the ball has been kicked, unless kick is made from beyond the line.

PENALTY: LOSS OF FIVE YARDS FROM THE PREVIOUS SPOT FOR LEAVING BEFORE THE BALL IS KICKED.

PLAY 1 Fourth-and-12 on the Raiders' 40. On a poor snap from center, Raiders' punter Leo Araguz picks up the ball and gets the punt off. The Redskins' Skip Hicks catches the ball on his 10, and is tackled by the Raiders' Steve Wisniewski, who had crossed the line of scrimmage prior to the ball being kicked.

Ruling 1: *Fourth-and-17 on Raiders' 35. It is illegal for the center to cross the line prior to the ball being legally kicked. Five-yard penalty from the previous spot. The Redskins would have the option of the ball on their 10, but would decline that option and take the penalty.*

ILLEGAL
TOUCHING

LEGAL
TOUCHING BY
OFFENSE

Article 4 No player of the kickers may illegally touch a scrimmage kick before it has been touched by a receiver (first touching).

Exception: When a kick is from behind the line, any touching on or behind the line by any offensive player is legal and any player may recover and advance (See 3-2-27-2, S.N. 2).

PENALTY: FOR ILLEGAL TOUCHING OF A SCRIMMAGE KICK: RECEIVER'S BALL AT ANY SPOT OF ILLEGAL TOUCHING OR POSSESSION. OFFICIALS' TIME OUT WHEN THE BALL IS DECLARED DEAD. THIS ILLEGAL TOUCH DOES NOT OFFSET A FOUL BY THE RECEIVERS DURING THE DOWN. SEE 4-3-1, 4-3-7, AND 14-3-1-EXCEPTION 4.

NOTE: WHEN ANY PLAYER OF THE KICKING TEAM ILLEGALLY RECOVERS OR CATCHES A SCRIMMAGE KICK INSIDE THE DEFENSIVE 5-YARD LINE, CARRIES IT ACROSS THE DEFENSE'S GOAL LINE OR HIS BODY CONTACTS THE END ZONE, IT IS A TOUCHBACK. THERE IS NO PENALTY FOR DELAY. (THIS CREATES EXCEPTION TO 4-3-9-K AND 7-4-1-K)

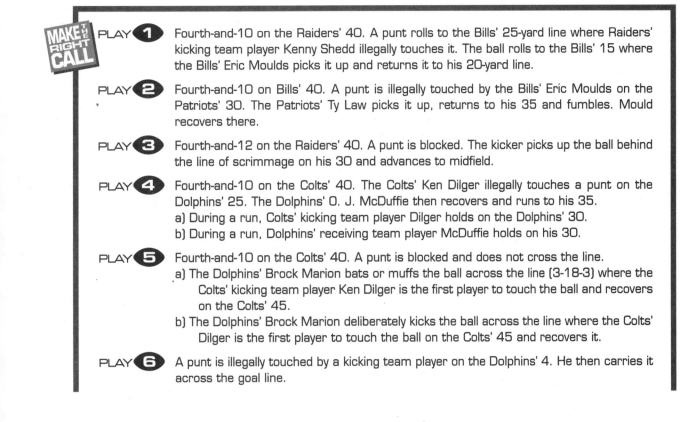

PLAY 1 Fourth-and-10 on the Raiders' 40. A punt rolls to the Bills' 25-yard line where Raiders' kicking team player Kenny Shedd illegally touches it. The ball rolls to the Bills' 15 where the Bills' Eric Moulds picks it up and returns it to his 20-yard line.

PLAY 2 Fourth-and-10 on Bills' 40. A punt is illegally touched by the Bills' Eric Moulds on the Patriots' 30. The Patriots' Ty Law picks it up, returns to his 35 and fumbles. Mould recovers there.

PLAY 3 Fourth-and-12 on the Raiders' 40. A punt is blocked. The kicker picks up the ball behind the line of scrimmage on his 30 and advances to midfield.

PLAY 4 Fourth-and-10 on the Colts' 40. The Colts' Ken Dilger illegally touches a punt on the Dolphins' 25. The Dolphins' O. J. McDuffie then recovers and runs to his 35.
a) During a run, Colts' kicking team player Dilger holds on the Dolphins' 30.
b) During a run, Dolphins' receiving team player McDuffie holds on his 30.

PLAY 5 Fourth-and-10 on the Colts' 40. A punt is blocked and does not cross the line.
a) The Dolphins' Brock Marion bats or muffs the ball across the line (3-18-3) where the Colts' kicking team player Ken Dilger is the first player to touch the ball and recovers on the Colts' 45.
b) The Dolphins' Brock Marion deliberately kicks the ball across the line where the Colts' Dilger is the first player to touch the ball on the Colts' 45 and recovers it.

PLAY 6 A punt is illegally touched by a kicking team player on the Dolphins' 4. He then carries it across the goal line.

PLAY **7** A punt is illegally touched by the Colts' Ken Dilger on the receiver's 4-yard line. The Dolphins' O. J. McDuffie tries to pick up the ball but muffs and the Colts' Marcus Pollard grabs it on the 3-yard line and carries it across the line.

PLAY **8** A punt is illegally touched on the Dolphins' 4 by Colts' kicking team player Ken Dilger. He carries it into the end zone. During his run to the end zone, the Dolphins' O. J. McDuffie clips in the end zone.

Ruling 1: Bills' ball on their 25-yard line where the Raiders illegally touched it.

Ruling 2: Patriots' ball on their 30 where the Bills illegally first touched.

Ruling 3: Legal recovery and advance. Didn't make yardage for a first down. Defense's ball at midfield. See 9-1-4, Exception.

Ruling 4a: Enforce from the end of the run (14-1-5-b). Dolphins' ball first-and-10 on their 40.

Ruling 4b: Enforce from the spot of the foul (14-1-5-d). Dolphins' ball first-and-10 on their 20.

Ruling 5a: Illegal touching of kick by Dilger. Dolphins' ball at the spot of illegal touching on the Colts' 45 (officials' time out).

Ruling 5b: Dolphins' loss of 10 from the previous spot. Illegal touching is not an offset foul (14-3-1-Exception 4). Colts' ball first-and-10 on the 50. See 9-1-4.

Ruling 6: Touchback.

Ruling 7: Illegal touching. No touchback as second touching by Pollard was not illegal touching. Dolphins' ball on their 4-yard line.

Ruling 8: Spot of enforcement is the Dolphins' 20. Dolphins' ball first-and-10 on their 10.

KICKER OUT OF BOUNDS

Article 5 No player of the kicker's team, who has been out of bounds, may touch or recover a scrimmage kick beyond the line until after it has been touched by a defensive player.

PENALTY: LOSS OF FIVE YARDS FROM THE PREVIOUS SPOT.

KICKERS RECOVER KICK MADE FROM BEHIND LINE

KICK RECOVERY BEYOND LINE

Article 6 A ball is dead if the kickers recover a kick made from behind the line (other than one recovered on or behind the line unless a Try-kick) (9-1-4, Exception).

NOTE: WHEN THE KICKERS RECOVER A LEGAL KICK FROM SCRIMMAGE AFTER IT HAS FIRST BEEN TOUCHED BY THE RECEIVING TEAM BEYOND THE LINE, IT IS FIRST-AND-10 FOR THE KICKER'S TEAM OR IF IT IS RECOVERED BY THE KICKERS IN THE RECEIVER'S END ZONE, IT IS A TOUCHDOWN FOR THE KICKERS. SEE 7-1-1-C-D AND 9-1-4, EXCEPTION.

PLAY 1 Fourth-and-five on the Eagles' 10. A punt crosses the line, touches the Cardinals' Aeneas Williams on the Eagles' 12, and rebounds behind the line where the Eagles' Jamie Asher picks it up and is downed on his 14.

Ruling 1: The ball had first touched the Cardinals beyond the line and wherever the Eagles recovered it would be a first down where the ball is finally dead. If the recovery by the Eagles is behind the line, the Eagles may advance. If the recovery is beyond the line, the ball is dead at the spot of recovery. First down for the Eagles in either situation. Eagles' ball first-and-10 on their 14.

KICK TOUCHED AT OR BEHIND LINE BY OFFENSE

Article 7 If a kick from behind the line is touched in the immediate vicinity of the neutral zone or behind the receiving team's line by the kicking team, such touching does not make the kicking team eligible to recover the kick beyond the line.

PLAY 1 Fourth-and-five on the Eagles' 10. A punt is partially blocked behind the line of scrimmage by the Cardinals' Aeneas Williams. The ball bounces around behind the line and then rolls beyond the line of scrimmage where the Eagles' Jamie Asher recovers on his 16.

Ruling 1: Though the Cardinals touched the ball, it was behind the line and legal. Asher illegally touched the ball beyond the line at his 16. Ball awarded to the Cardinals at that spot. Cardinals' ball first-and-10 on the Eagles' 16.

KICK REBOUNDS BEHIND LINE AND IS TOUCHED BY KICKERS

Article 8 Any touching behind the line by a kicking team player is legal, even if the kick crosses the line and returns behind the line before touching a receiver beyond the line.

KICK SIMULTANEOUSLY RECOVERED

Article 9 When a legal kick is simultaneously recovered anywhere by two eligible opposing players, or if it is lying on the field of play with no player attempting to recover, it is awarded to the receivers. See 7-4-2.

PLAY 1 Fourth-and-10 on the Packers' 40. A punt is first muffed by the Redskins' Matt Turk on his 20 and then simultaneously recovered by the Redskins' Darrell Green and the Packers' Leroy Butler on the Redskins' 15.

Ruling 1: Simultaneous recovery of a kick by two eligible opponents belongs to the receivers. Redskins' ball first-and-10 on their 15.

Article 10 Ordinarily there is no distinction between a player touching a ball or being touched by it.

BLOCKED INTO KICK

Exception: If he is pushed or blocked into a kick by an opponent, he is *NOT* considered to have touched it (3-14-3-Note).

PLAY 1 Fourth-and-five on Redskins' 30. A scrimmage kick comes to rest on the Packers' 45.

    a)   The Redskins' Fred Strickland blocks the Packers' Robert Brooks into the ball and the Redskins' Darrell Green recovers on the Packers' 40.

    b)   Strickland pushes Brooks into the ball and Green recovers on the Packers' 40.

Ruling 1a: Green illegally touched the ball as Brooks is not considered to have touched it. Packers' ball first-and-10 on their 40.

Ruling 1b: Illegal use of hands by kickers. Receiving team has option of taking illegal touch on the Packers' 40 or Redskins' ball fourth-and-15 on their 20.

OFFENSIVE
USE OF
HANDS
DURING KICK

Article 11 During a kick a kicking team player, after he has crossed his scrimmage line, may use his hands to ward off, push, or pull aside a receiver who is legally or illegally attempting to obstruct him. See 12-1-2-Exception 3, and Note.

> **NOTE:** SEE 12-2-12 FOR PROHIBITED LOW BLOCKS DURING KICKS.

KICK
RECOVERED
BEHIND LINE BY
OFFENSIVE
TEAM

Article 12 When a scrimmage kick from behind the line is recovered by the kicking team behind the line, the kicking team may advance (see 3-27-2, S. N. 2).

Exception: If the kicking team recovers a kick behind the line during a Try-kick the ball is dead immediately (11-3-1).

PLAY 1 Fourth-and-10 on the Jaguars' 30. A punt crosses the line and before being touched by the Raiders, the ball rebounds behind the line. The Jaguars' Leon Searcy recovers and advances to the 35.

PLAY 2 Fourth-and-10 on the Jaguars' 30. A punt crosses the line and is first touched by Raiders' receiver Tim Brown beyond the line at the Jaguars' 35. Jaguars' kicking team member Bryce Paup recovers beyond the line and advances.

Ruling 1: Legal recovery but necessary yardage for the first down for the Jaguars not made. Raiders' ball first-and-10 on the Jaguars' 35.

Ruling 2: The ball is dead where Paup recovered. First-and-10 for the Jaguars irrespective of the necessary line (9-6-1-Note). Jaguars' ball first-and-10 on their 35.

KICK CROSSES
RECEIVERS'
GOAL LINE

Article 13 When a kick from scrimmage, or unsuccessful field goal crosses the receivers' goal line from the impetus of the kick, it is a touchback *unless:*

    (a)   there is a spot of illegal touching by the kickers outside the receivers' 20-yard line; or

    (b)   the receivers, after gaining possession, advance with the ball into the field of play; or

    (c)   kickers recover in end zone after receivers first touch ball in field of play.

        Ruling: Touchdown for kickers; *or*

    (d)   kickers recover in end zone after receivers first touch ball in end zone.

        Ruling: Touchdown for kickers.

> **NOTE:** RECEIVING TEAM PLAYERS MAY ADVANCE ANY KICK (SCRIMMAGE OR UNSUCCESSFUL FIELD GOAL ATTEMPT) WHETHER THE BALL CROSSES THE RECEIVERS' GOAL LINE. RULE 9 (KICKS FROM SCRIMMAGE) APPLIES UNTIL THE RECEIVING TEAM HAS GAINED POSSESSION. SEE 11-5-2.

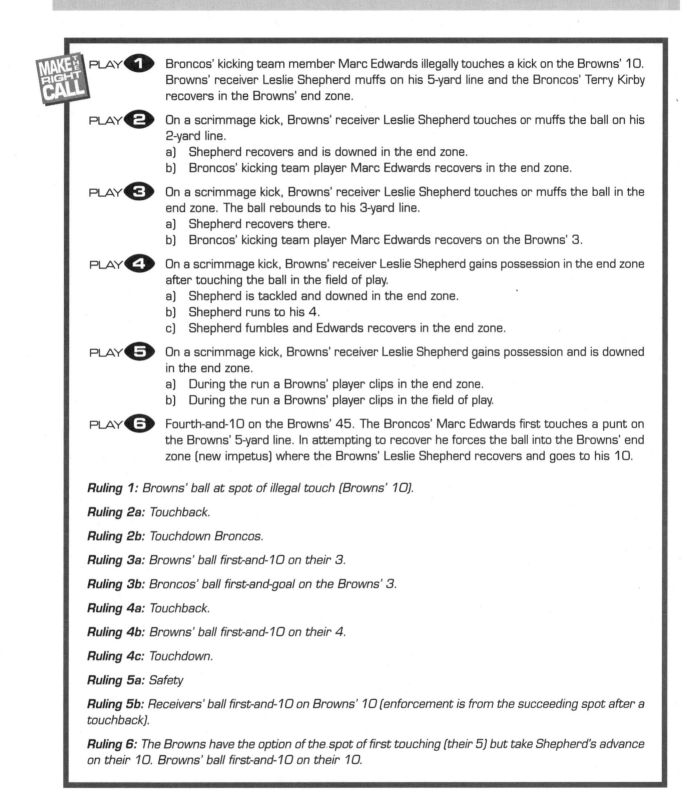

PLAY 1 Broncos' kicking team member Marc Edwards illegally touches a kick on the Browns' 10. Browns' receiver Leslie Shepherd muffs on his 5-yard line and the Broncos' Terry Kirby recovers in the Browns' end zone.

PLAY 2 On a scrimmage kick, Browns' receiver Leslie Shepherd touches or muffs the ball on his 2-yard line.
  a)   Shepherd recovers and is downed in the end zone.
  b)   Broncos' kicking team player Marc Edwards recovers in the end zone.

PLAY 3 On a scrimmage kick, Browns' receiver Leslie Shepherd touches or muffs the ball in the end zone. The ball rebounds to his 3-yard line.
  a)   Shepherd recovers there.
  b)   Broncos' kicking team player Marc Edwards recovers on the Browns' 3.

PLAY 4 On a scrimmage kick, Browns' receiver Leslie Shepherd gains possession in the end zone after touching the ball in the field of play.
  a)   Shepherd is tackled and downed in the end zone.
  b)   Shepherd runs to his 4.
  c)   Shepherd fumbles and Edwards recovers in the end zone.

PLAY 5 On a scrimmage kick, Browns' receiver Leslie Shepherd gains possession and is downed in the end zone.
  a)   During the run a Browns' player clips in the end zone.
  b)   During the run a Browns' player clips in the field of play.

PLAY 6 Fourth-and-10 on the Browns' 45. The Broncos' Marc Edwards first touches a punt on the Browns' 5-yard line. In attempting to recover he forces the ball into the Browns' end zone (new impetus) where the Browns' Leslie Shepherd recovers and goes to his 10.

Ruling 1: Browns' ball at spot of illegal touch (Browns' 10).

Ruling 2a: Touchback.

Ruling 2b: Touchdown Broncos.

Ruling 3a: Browns' ball first-and-10 on their 3.

Ruling 3b: Broncos' ball first-and-goal on the Browns' 3.

Ruling 4a: Touchback.

Ruling 4b: Browns' ball first-and-10 on their 4.

Ruling 4c: Touchdown.

Ruling 5a: Safety

Ruling 5b: Receivers' ball first-and-10 on Browns' 10 (enforcement is from the succeeding spot after a touchback).

Ruling 6: The Browns have the option of the spot of first touching (their 5) but take Shepherd's advance on their 10. Browns' ball first-and-10 on their 10.

KICK TOUCHING RECEIVERS' GOAL POSTS

Article 14 If a scrimmage kick *touches the receivers' goal posts or crossbar* either before or after touching a player of either team, it is a touchback unless it later scores a field goal. See 3-20-2 and 11-5-1.

PLAY **1** A kickoff to start the game hits the goal post before possession by the receivers.

Ruling 1: Touchback. Any legal kick (scrimmage or free kick) which touches the receivers' goal posts or crossbar other than one which scores a field goal is a touchback. See 11-6-1-d and 11-5-1.

KICK TOUCHING KICKERS' GOAL POSTS

Article 15 If a scrimmage kick *touches the kickers' goal post or crossbar* (irrespective of where it was made from, or how it occurred), it is a safety. Goal post is out of bounds. See 11-4-1-b.

PLAY **1** Fourth-and-10 on the Broncos' 10. A punt is blocked and the ball rebounds, hits the goal post, and rolls into the end zone where Titans' player Chris Sanders falls on it.

Ruling 1: Safety. Ball out of bounds.

KICK OUT OF BOUNDS

Article 16 For a scrimmage kick out of bounds between goal lines, see 7-5-1. If the kick becomes dead behind a goal line, Rule 11-6 governs.

SCRIMMAGE KICK SPOTS OF ENCROACHMENT

Article 17 If there is a foul from the time of the snap until a legal scrimmage kick ends, enforcement is from the previous spot. This includes a foul during a run prior to the legal kick (14-1-13-S.N. 1), and running into or roughing the kicker (12-2-6). If the offensive team commits a foul in its own end zone, it is a safety.

SPOT FOUL

Exception 1: Illegal touching of kick, fair catch interference, invalid fair catch signal, or personal foul (blocking) after fair catch signal are all enforced from the spot of the foul.

POST-POSSESION FOUL

Exception 2: If the receiving team commits a foul after the ball is kicked (ball crosses the scrimmage line) during a scrimmage down and the receivers possess and keep the kicked ball, the penalty for their infraction will be ruled as a foul after possession (post-possession) and must be assessed from:

1) The spot where possession was gained;

2) The spot where ball becomes dead; or

3) The spot of the foul.

NOTE: IF THERE IS A SPOT OF ILLEGAL TOUCH, IT IS NOT USED.

ILLEGAL TOUCH, RECEIVING TEAM FOUL DURING KICK, LOSS OF POSSESION

Exception 3: In cases of illegal touch by kicker and a foul by the receiving team during the kick, if the receiving team then loses possession, the ball reverts to the receivers and the spot of enforcement must be assessed from:

1) The spot where possession was gained;

2) The spot of the foul.

NOTE: THE SPOT OF ILLEGAL TOUCH IS NOT USED.

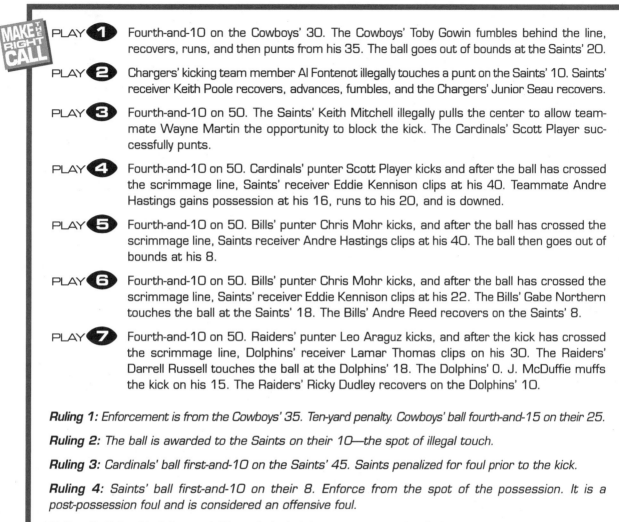

MAKE THE RIGHT CALL

PLAY 1 Fourth-and-10 on the Cowboys' 30. The Cowboys' Toby Gowin fumbles behind the line, recovers, runs, and then punts from his 35. The ball goes out of bounds at the Saints' 20.

PLAY 2 Chargers' kicking team member Al Fontenot illegally touches a punt on the Saints' 10. Saints' receiver Keith Poole recovers, advances, fumbles, and the Chargers' Junior Seau recovers.

PLAY 3 Fourth-and-10 on 50. The Saints' Keith Mitchell illegally pulls the center to allow teammate Wayne Martin the opportunity to block the kick. The Cardinals' Scott Player successfully punts.

PLAY 4 Fourth-and-10 on 50. Cardinals' punter Scott Player kicks and after the ball has crossed the scrimmage line, Saints' receiver Eddie Kennison clips at his 40. Teammate Andre Hastings gains possession at his 16, runs to his 20, and is downed.

PLAY 5 Fourth-and-10 on 50. Bills' punter Chris Mohr kicks, and after the ball has crossed the scrimmage line, Saints receiver Andre Hastings clips at his 40. The ball then goes out of bounds at his 8.

PLAY 6 Fourth-and-10 on 50. Bills' punter Chris Mohr kicks, and after the ball has crossed the scrimmage line, Saints' receiver Eddie Kennison clips at his 22. The Bills' Gabe Northern touches the ball at the Saints' 18. The Bills' Andre Reed recovers on the Saints' 8.

PLAY 7 Fourth-and-10 on 50. Raiders' punter Leo Araguz kicks, and after the kick has crossed the scrimmage line, Dolphins' receiver Lamar Thomas clips on his 30. The Raiders' Darrell Russell touches the ball at the Dolphins' 18. The Dolphins' O. J. McDuffie muffs the kick on his 15. The Raiders' Ricky Dudley recovers on the Dolphins' 10.

Ruling 1: Enforcement is from the Cowboys' 35. Ten-yard penalty. Cowboys' ball fourth-and-15 on their 25.

Ruling 2: The ball is awarded to the Saints on their 10—the spot of illegal touch.

Ruling 3: Cardinals' ball first-and-10 on the Saints' 45. Saints penalized for foul prior to the kick.

Ruling 4: Saints' ball first-and-10 on their 8. Enforce from the spot of the possession. It is a post-possession foul and is considered an offensive foul.

Ruling 5: Saints' ball first-and-10 on their 4. It is a post-possession foul.

Ruling 6: Saints' ball first-and-10 on their 4.

Ruling 7: Penalize the Dolphins 15 yards from the previous spot. Dolphins did not gain possession and recovery by Dudley was legal (touching by Russell was illegal). Not a post-possession foul.

KICKING TEAM PLAYER VOLUNTARILY OUT OF BOUNDS DURING A PUNT

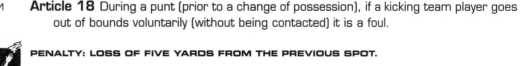

Article 18 During a punt (prior to a change of possession), if a kicking team player goes out of bounds voluntarily (without being contacted) it is a foul.

PENALTY: LOSS OF FIVE YARDS FROM THE PREVIOUS SPOT.

CHAPTER 10
FAIR CATCH

Here's a type of call where player safety is a key concern. It's important that the player give a valid fair catch signal — he <u>must</u> wave one arm above his head from side to side.

Not only is an invalid signal a foul, but the player doesn't get any protection after he catches the ball.

Jerry Seeman
NFL DIRECTOR OF OFFICIATING

Section 1   Fair Catch

VALID FAIR CATCH

Article 1   A fair catch signal is valid beyond the line while kick is in flight when one arm is fully extended above the head and waved from side to side.

SHIELDING EYES

NOTE: A RECEIVER MAY LEGALLY RAISE HIS HAND(S) TO HIS HELMET (BUT NOT ABOVE THE HELMET) IN ORDER TO SHIELD HIS EYES FROM THE SUN.

PENALTY: FOR INVALID FAIR CATCH SIGNAL: SNAP BY RECEIVERS FIVE YARDS BEHIND THE SPOT OF THE SIGNAL.

PLAY 1 The Raiders' Tim Brown gives a fair catch signal on his 30 and catches the ball on his 28.

a)   Brown's signal was arm fully extended straight up.

b)   Brown's signal was arm straight fully extended and waved from side to side.

Ruling 1a: Invalid signal. Raiders' ball first-and-10 on their 25 (five yards from signal).

Ruling 1b: Valid signal. Raiders' ball first-and-10 on their 28.

DEAD BALL ON FAIR CATCH

Article 2   If a receiver signals (valid or invalid) for a fair catch during any kick except one which does not cross the line, the ball is dead when caught by any receiver (Article 2, Exception). If the catcher did not signal, the ball is put in play by the receivers at the spot of the catch. See 10-1-6.

Exceptions: Any receiver may recover and advance after a fair catch signal if the kick either:

1)   touches the ground; or

2)   touches one of the kickers in flight.

DELAY PENALTY FOR UNDUE ADVANCE

NOTE: UNDUE ADVANCE BY ANY RECEIVER WHO CATCHES (EXCEPT AS PROVIDED IN ABOVE EXCEPTION) IS DELAY OF THE GAME BUT DOES NOT PRECLUDE THE FAIR CATCH. NO SPECIFIC DISTANCE IS SPECIFIED FOR UNDUE ADVANCE AS THE BALL IS DEAD AT THE SPOT OF THE CATCH (3-9-1) WHEN CAUGHT (TIME OUT). IF THE CATCHER COMES TO A REASONABLE STOP, THERE IS NO PENALTY FOR DELAY. ANY PENALTY IS ENFORCED FROM THE SPOT OF THE CATCH.

PLAY 1 The Lions' Johnnie Morton signals for a fair catch and then muffs. He recovers on the ground and then runs for a score.

PLAY 2 The Lions' Johnnie Morton and Herman Moore signal for a fair catch. Morton muffs. Moore catches and comes to a legal stop.

PLAY 3 The Lions' Johnnie Morton signals for a fair catch, muffs and Herman Moore who did not signal catches ball.

PLAY 4 The Lions' Johnnie Morton makes a valid fair catch signal on his 15. He catches on his 20, advances unduly and fumbles. The Packers' Robert Brooks recovers.

PLAY 5 The Lions' Johnnie Morton signals for a fair catch. The kick in flight strikes the Packers' Robert Brooks after which it is caught by Herman Moore who advances.

Ruling 1: Touchdown. Legal advance as the ball touched the ground. If the kicking team recovered after the muff, the ball is dead at the spot of recovery.

Ruling 2: Fair catch. Either man may catch but not advance.

Ruling 3: Not a fair catch. The ball is dead at the spot where it was caught. No option for fair catch and the ball is put in play by snap.

Ruling 4: Five-yard penalty for delay from the spot where the ball was caught. The ball is dead when caught. Lions' ball first-and-10 on their 15.

Ruling 5: Legal advance if any fair catch interference penalty is declined (choice).

ILLEGAL BLOCK AFTER FAIR CATCH SIGNAL

Article 3   If a player signals (valid or invalid) for a fair catch, he may not until the ball touches a player:

(a) block; or

(b) initiate contact with one of the kickers.

PENALTY: FOR ILLEGAL BLOCK AFTER A FAIR CATCH SIGNAL. SNAP BY RECEIVERS 15 YARDS FROM THE SPOT OF THE FOUL. (PERSONAL FOUL.)

PLAY 1   The Browns' Leslie Shepherd signals a fair catch on his 28. He disregards the ball and blocks the Seahawks' Sean Dawkins on the Browns' 30 as the ball goes over his head and, before touching any player, rolls out of bounds at the Browns' 18.

PLAY 2   The Browns' Leslie Shepherd signals a fair catch on his 12. He disregards the ball and blocks the Seahawks' Sean Dawkins on the Browns' 8 before or after the ball rolls into the end zone or out of bounds.

Ruling 1: Browns' ball first-and-10 on their 15.

Ruling 2: Browns' ball first-and-10 on their 4.

FAIR CATCH INTERFERENCE

Article 4   During any kick (except one which fails to cross the scrimmage line), if any receiver could reach the kick in flight, no player of the kickers shall interfere with either:

(a) the receiver;

(b) the ball; or

(c) the receiver's path to the ball.

PENALTY (A): FOR FAIR CATCH INTERFERENCE FOLLOWING A SIGNAL: LOSS OF 15 YARDS FROM THE SPOT OF THE FOUL. FAIR CATCH ALSO AWARDED IRRESPECTIVE OF A CATCH. SEE ARTICLE 5-NOTE, AND ARTICLE 6. (PERSONAL FOUL.)

PENALTY (B): FOR INTERFERENCE WITH THE OPPORTUNITY TO MAKE A CATCH (NO PRIOR SIGNAL MADE): LOSS OF 15 YARDS FROM THE SPOT OF THE FOUL AND OFFENDED TEAM IS ENTITLED TO PUT THE BALL IN PLAY BY A SNAP FROM SCRIMMAGE. SEE 4-3-11-F. (PERSONAL FOUL.)

SUPPLEMENTAL NOTES

RECEIVER'S
RIGHT TO
BALL

(1) A receiver running toward a kick in flight has the right of way and opponents must get out of his path to the ball. Otherwise it is interference irrespective of any contact or catch whether any signal (valid or invalid) is given or not.

FAIR CATCH
OPPORTUNITY

(2) After a valid fair catch signal, the opportunity to make a catch does not end when a kick is muffed. The player who signaled fair catch must have a reasonable opportunity to catch the ball before it hits the ground without being interfered with by the members of the kicking team.

INTENTIONAL
MUFF PRIOR TO
FAIR CATCH

(3) An intentional muff forward prior to a catch in order to gain ground is an illegal bat (see 12-1-6).

PLAY **1** The Redskins' Skip Hicks is about to catch a punt. Just before the ball reaches his hands, he is tackled by the Steelers' Jason Gildon on the Redskins' 30, but he catches the ball while falling.

PLAY **2** The Redskins' Skip Hicks does not signal for a fair catch and runs toward the punted ball in an attempt to catch it. The Steelers' Jason Gildon is in his way on the Redskins' 30 and Hicks can't get to the ball. The ball rolls to the Redskins' 20 where it is downed by the Redskins' Darrell Green.

PLAY **3** The Steelers' Jason Gildon goes downfield under a punt. He is struck by the kick in flight on the Redskins' 30 while standing in front of the Redskins' Darrell Green who is ready to catch. Woodson had signalled a fair catch.

PLAY **4** The Redskins' Skip Hicks signals for a fair catch and then muffs the ball on his 30. The Steelers' Jason Gildon catches at the Redskins' 30 and advances. Hicks could have caught the muffed ball.

Ruling 1: Interference with the opportunity to make a catch and fair catch awarded and 15 yards from the spot of the foul even though Hicks did not signal. Same ruling would apply if Hicks fumbles or muffs; however, the ball continues in play. Redskins' ball first-and-10 on their 45. Redskins did not signal, so they put the ball in play by snap from scrimmage. See S.N.

Ruling 2: A 15-yard penalty from the spot of the foul for interference with the opportunity to make a catch. No fair catch signal given. Redskins' ball first-and-10 on their 45. Ball in play by snap from scrimmage. See S.N.

Ruling 3: Fair catch interference and Redskins awarded whether the catch is made or not. Redskins can advance the ball if they get it and have option of yardage gained or penalty for fair catch interference. Redskins' ball first-and-10 on their 45. Green signalled fair catch and gets option of fair catch kick or putting ball in play by snap from scrimmage. See S.N.

Ruling 4: Fair catch interference as opportunity to make the catch does not end when the kick is muffed. The ball is dead when Hicks touches the ball. Redskins' ball first-and-10 on their 45. (See 10-1-4, S.N. 2).

RECEIVER'S RIGHT ON FAIR CATCH

Article 5   After a receiver has made a fair catch following a valid signal, an opponent:

(a) may not tackle him;

(b) may not block him; and

(c) must avoid contact with him.

PENALTY: FOR ILLEGAL CONTACT WITH THE MAKER OF A FAIR CATCH: LOSS OF 15 YARDS FROM THE MARK OF THE CATCH (SNAP OR FREE KICK). SEE 6-1-3-NOTE.

FAIR CATCH IN END ZONE

NOTE: FOLLOWING A SIGNAL A RECEIVER MAY MAKE OR BE AWARDED A FAIR CATCH (FOR INTERFERENCE) IN HIS END ZONE, BUT IT IS A TOUCHBACK. SEE ARTICLE 4, PENALTY (B) FOR INTERFERENCE WITH THE OPPORTUNITY TO MAKE A CATCH.

MAKE THE RIGHT CALL

PLAY ❶   Fourth-and-10 on the Chiefs' 20. The Bengals' James Hundon makes an invalid fair catch signal and catches on his 40. He comes to a legal stop on his 42 and is tackled by the Chiefs' James Hasty.

Ruling 1: Bengals' ball first-and-10 on their 35 (10-1-1).

CHOICES AFTER FAIR CATCH

Article 6   When a fair catch is declared for a team, the captain must choose (and his first choice is not revocable) either:

(a) A fair catch kick (punt, drop kick, or placekick without Tee); or

(b) A snap to next put the ball in play.

SUPPLEMENTAL NOTES

(1) If, with time remaining, receiver signals and makes a fair catch, receiver's captain has option of attempting a fair catch kick or putting ball in play by a snap from scrimmage.

(2) At the end of a period, if time expired when receiver signals and makes a fair catch, receiving team's only option is to fair catch kick.

(3) If, with time remaining, receiver signals for a fair catch and is interfered with, receiving team will be awarded a 15-yard penalty and has option of a fair catch kick or putting ball in play by a snap from scrimmage.

(4) At the end of a period, if time expired during a play in which receiver signalled for a fair catch and he was interfered with, receiving team will be awarded a 15-yard penalty and has option of a fair catch kick or putting ball in play by a snap from scrimmage.

(5) If, with time remaining, receiver does *not* signal for a fair catch and he is interfered with, receiving team will be awarded a 15-yard penalty, but must put the ball in play by a snap from scrimmage.

(6) At the end of a period, if time expires during a down and receiver does *not* signal for a fair catch but he is interfered with, receiving team will be awarded a 15-yard penalty, but must put the ball in play by a snap from scrimmage.

(7) If time expired, and receiver did not signal for a fair catch and there was no foul, the period is over.

MAKE THE RIGHT CALL

CHAPTER 11
SCORING

A *try will be put in play from the two-yard line, and in order to score two points, the team has to make what would normally be a touchdown.*

Jerry Seeman
NFL DIRECTOR OF OFFICIATING

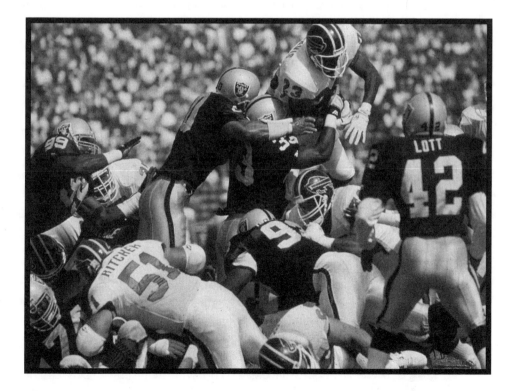

Section 1   Value of Scores

SCORES

Article 1   The team that scores the greater number of points during the entire game is the winner. Points are scored as follows:

(a) Touchdown .... 6 points

(b) Field Goal.. 3 points

(c) Safety .... 2 points

(d) Successful try after touchdown .... 1 or 2 points

> **NOTE:** IF A TEAM FORFEITS A GAME, THE OPPONENT WILL BE DECLARED THE WINNER BY A SCORE OF 2-0, BUT THE POINTS WILL NOT BE ADDED TO THE WINNING TEAM'S RECORD FOR PURPOSES OF OFFENSIVE PRODUCTION ON TIE-BREAKERS.

SUDDEN DEATH

Article 2   To insure a winner in all NFL games the sudden death method of deciding a tie game is Rule 16.

Section 2   Touchdown

TOUCHDOWN PLAYS

Article 1   It is a touchdown:

(a) when a runner (3-38) advances from the field of play and the ball touches the opponent's goal line (plane); or

(b) while inbounds, any player catches or recovers a loose ball (3-2-3) on or behind the opponent's goal line.

SUPPLEMENTAL NOTES

DEAD BALL

(1) The ball is automatically dead at the instant of legal player possession on, above, or behind the opponent's goal line.

PALPABLY UNFAIR ACT

(2) The referee may award a touchdown when a palpably unfair act deprives the offended team of one.

FOUL AFTER TOUCHDOWN

(3) For a foul after a touchdown (between downs), see 3-11-2-d and 14-5.

PLAY **1**   Third-and-goal on the Bears' 2. The Packers' Dorsey Levens goes to the goal line with the ball over the plane of the goal line. He is tackled and fumbles and the Bears recover in the end zone.

Ruling 1: Touchdown. The ball is automatically dead at the instant of legal player possession on the opponent's goal line.

Section 3   Try

TRY

Article 1   After a touchdown, the scoring team is allowed a Try. This Try is an attempt to score one or two additional points during one scrimmage down with the spot of snap:

(a) anywhere between the inbounds line *and*

(b) which is also two or more yards from the defensive team's goal line.

> **NOTE:** ALL GENERAL RULES FOR FOURTH-DOWN FUMBLES APPLY TO THE TRY (SEE 8-4-2-EXCEPTION 2), AND THE GAME CLOCK WILL NOT RUN.

During this try:

TRY-ONE POINT

(a) if a Try-kick is good, one point is scored. (The conditions of 11-5-1 must be met.) If a kick cannot score, the ball becomes dead as soon as failure is evident.

TRY-TWO POINTS

(b) if a Try results in what would ordinarily be a touchdown by the offense, two points are awarded. If a touchdown is not scored, the Try is over at the end of the play or if there is a change of possession.

TRY POINT AWARDED

(c) if there is no kick and the Try results in what would ordinarily be a safety by the defense, one point is awarded to the offensive team.

MAKE THE RIGHT CALL

PLAY 1 An attempted Try-kick is blocked. Offensive player recovers behind the line and advances across the goal line or recovers in defensive's end zone.

PLAY 2 During a Try, the Broncos' holder Bubby Brister fumbles. The Chiefs' Marvcus Patton kicks, bats, or muffs the loose ball (new impetus) on his 2 and it goes out of bounds behind the goal line.

Ruling 1: No score in either case. The ball is dead as soon as its failure as a kick to score a Try is evident.

Ruling 2: Ordinarily a safety (11-4-1). Award one point.

START OF TRY   **Article 2**   The Try begins when the referee sounds his whistle for play to start.

NOTE: SEE 3-11-1-D, EXCEPTION FOR A FOUL AFTER A TOUCHDOWN AND BEFORE THE WHISTLE.

MAKE THE RIGHT CALL

PLAY 1 The 49ers' J. J. Stokes clips after teammate Garrison Hearst had scored a touchdown.

Ruling 1: Penalty is enforced from the succeeding spot which is the spot of the next kickoff. Spot of ball for Try is from 2 or more yards from defense's goal line. Penalty is not enforced on Try.

Article 3   During a Try:

UNSUCCESSFUL TRY

(a) if any play or a foul by the offense would ordinarily result in a touchback or loss of down, the try is unsuccessful and there shall be no replay.

DEFENSIVE FOUL RESULTS IN SCORE

(b) if any play or a foul by the defense would ordinarily result in a safety, one point is awarded the offensive team.

REPLAY TRY

(c) if a foul by the defense does not permit the try to be attempted, the down is replayed and the offended team has the option to have the distance penalty assessed on the next try or on the ensuing kickoff.

DEFENSIVE FOUL ON UNSUCCESSFUL EXTRA POINT

(d) if the defensive team commits a foul and the try is attempted and is unsuccessful, the offensive team may either accept the penalty yardage to be assessed or decline the distance penalty before the down is replayed.

(e) all fouls committed by the defense on a successful try will result in the distance penalty being assessed on the ensuing kickoff or retry defensive player. See A.R. 14.27.

<table>
<tr><td>WHISTLE, PLAY DEAD</td><td>(f) if there is a false start, encroachment, or a neutral zone infraction which normally causes play to be whistled dead during ordinary scrimmage plays, they are to be handled the same way during Try situations. Blow whistle immediately. (See 7-2-2 and 7-3-4).</td></tr>
</table>

NOTE: SEE 12-3-1-J, K, L, N, O, THAT APPLY DURING A TRY.

PLAY 1 During a Try, the Steelers' Jerome Bettis is downed on the Lions' 2 in a side zone. During the run, the Lions' Mark Carrier commits a personal foul.

PLAY 2 During a Try which is unsuccessful, defensive player is offside.

PLAY 3 During a Try which is successful, defensive player is offside.

Ruling 1: Replay from the previous spot or from the spot after enforcement.

Ruling 2: Replay at previous spot or 1-yard line.

Ruling 3: Try good and loss of yardage on kickoff against defense, or retry from defense's 1-yard line.

DOUBLE FOUL REPLAYED

Article 4 If fouls are signalled against both teams during a Try, it must be replayed (14-3-1).

NO SCORE FOR DEFENSE

Article 5 During a Try the defensive team can never score. When it gains possession, the ball is dead immediately.

KICKOFF AFTER TRY

Article 6 After a Try the team on defense during the Try shall receive (6-1-1-b).

Section 4   Safety

SAFETY

Article 1 When an impetus by a team sends the ball in touch behind its own goal, it is a safety if the ball is either:

(a) dead in the end zone in its possession; or

(b) out of bounds behind the goal line.

INTERCEPTING MOMENTUM

Exception: If the intercepting momentum of a pass interception carries the defensive player and the ball into the end zone, the ball is next in play at the spot of the interception by the defense, unless the intercepting defensive player without fumbling the ball advances it into the field of play. This is irrespective of any other act (muff, fumble, pass, or recovery) by the intercepting team.

(a) If a player of the team which intercepts the ball commits a foul in the end zone, it is a safety.

(b) If a player who intercepts the ball throws an illegal forward pass in the end zone, it is a safety. If his opponent intercepts the illegal pass thrown from the end zone, the ball remains alive. If he scores, it is a touchdown.

(c) If a player of the team which intercepts the ball commits a foul in the field of play and the ball becomes dead in the end zone, the basic spot is the spot of the interception. See A.R. 11.15

(d) If spot of interception is inside the defense's 1-yard line, ball is to be spotted at the defense's 1.

SUPPLEMENTAL NOTES

IMPETUS

(1) The impetus is always attributed to the offense (team which passed, kicked, or fumbled) unless the defense creates a new momentum by a muff, bat, or illegal kick that sends it in touch (3-14-3).

(2) See 8-1-1-S.N.2 and Penalties under 8-1-2 to 5 for Exceptions to (b) of 11-4-1, when there is an incompletion or pass violation by the offense behind its goal line during a forward pass from behind the line.

PLAY 1 Second-and-10 on the Raiders' 6. Raiders' quarterback Donald Hollus throws a backward pass which is batted by the Bears' Jim Flanigan. The ball goes out of bounds behind the goal line.

PLAY 2 The Steelers' Hines Ward muffs a punt on his 5-yard line. In attempting to recover he forces the ball (new impetus) into his end zone. See 3-14-3.
a) where he recovers and is downed there.
b) where he recovers and advances.
c) where kicking team player recovers.

PLAY 3 The Steelers' Hines Ward catches a punt on his 4-yard line. He fumbles the ball on his 4 and the Bills' Eric Moulds bats the loose ball. The ball rolls over the end line.

PLAY 4 The Steelers' Hines Ward fumbles a punt on his 5 and it crosses his goal line. The Bills' Eric Moulds recovers while he is touching the sideline.

PLAY 5 Second-and-10 on the Lions' 20. The Lions' Mark Carrier intercepts a legal forward pass on his 2-yard line. His intercepting momentum carries him into the end zone where he is downed.

PLAY 6 Second-and-10 on the Lions' 20. The Lions' Mark Carrier intercepts a legal forward pass on his 4 and his intercepting momentum carries him into the end zone. He then runs it out to his 35.

PLAY 7 Second-and-10 on the Lions' 20. The Lions' Mark Carrier intercepts a pass on his 6 and the intercepting momentum carries him into the end zone where he is tackled, fumbles and the Vikings' Cris Carter recovers there.

PLAY 8 Second-and-10 on the Lions' 20. The Lions' Mark Carrier intercepts a legal forward pass on his 4 and his intercepting momentum carries him into the end zone where is is downed.
a) The Lions' Terry Fair clipped in the end zone.
b) The Lions' Terry Fair clipped on his 2.

Ruling 1: *Safety. Legal bat and no change of impetus.*

Ruling 2a: *Safety.*

Ruling 2b: *Legal advance.*

Ruling 2c: *Touchdown.*

Ruling 3: *Touchback. See 11-6-1 and 12-1-6.*

Ruling 4: *Safety. If it had been a muff (no new impetus or change of possession) and the same situation, it would be a touchback (11-6-1).*

Ruling 5: Lions' ball first-and-10 on their 2.

Ruling 6: He is the only one who can advance it. Lions' ball first-and-10 on their 35.

Ruling 7: Lions' ball first-and-10 on their 6.

Ruling 8a: Safety.

Ruling 8b: Lions' ball first-and-10 on their 1.

FOUL BEHIND
OFFENSIVE
GOAL

Article 2 It is a safety when the offense commits a foul (anywhere) and the spot of enforcement is behind its own goal line.

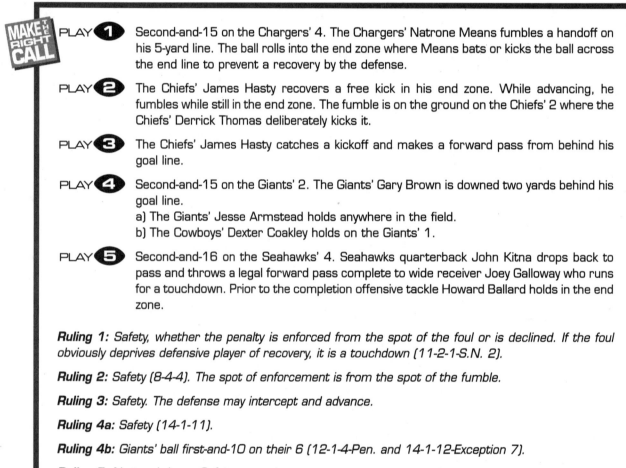

PLAY **1** Second-and-15 on the Chargers' 4. The Chargers' Natrone Means fumbles a handoff on his 5-yard line. The ball rolls into the end zone where Means bats or kicks the ball across the end line to prevent a recovery by the defense.

PLAY **2** The Chiefs' James Hasty recovers a free kick in his end zone. While advancing, he fumbles while still in the end zone. The fumble is on the ground on the Chiefs' 2 where the Chiefs' Derrick Thomas deliberately kicks it.

PLAY **3** The Chiefs' James Hasty catches a kickoff and makes a forward pass from behind his goal line.

PLAY **4** Second-and-15 on the Giants' 2. The Giants' Gary Brown is downed two yards behind his goal line.
a) The Giants' Jesse Armstead holds anywhere in the field.
b) The Cowboys' Dexter Coakley holds on the Giants' 1.

PLAY **5** Second-and-16 on the Seahawks' 4. Seahawks quarterback John Kitna drops back to pass and throws a legal forward pass complete to wide receiver Joey Galloway who runs for a touchdown. Prior to the completion offensive tackle Howard Ballard holds in the end zone.

Ruling 1: Safety, whether the penalty is enforced from the spot of the foul or is declined. If the foul obviously deprives defensive player of recovery, it is a touchdown (11-2-1-S.N. 2).

Ruling 2: Safety (8-4-4). The spot of enforcement is from the spot of the fumble.

Ruling 3: Safety. The defense may intercept and advance.

Ruling 4a: Safety (14-1-11).

Ruling 4b: Giants' ball first-and-10 on their 6 (12-1-4-Pen. and 14-1-12-Exception 7).

Ruling 5: No touchdown. Safety.

BALL IN PLAY
AFTER
SAFETY

Article 3 After a safety, the team scored upon must next put the ball in play by a free kick (punt, dropkick or placekick). No tee can be used. See 6-1-2 and 3.
Exception: Extension of period (4-3-11-Note h).

Section 5   Field Goal

LEGAL FIELD
GOAL

Article 1   A field goal is scored when all of the following conditions are met:

(a) The kick must be a placekick or dropkick made by the offense from behind the line of scrimmage or from the spot of a fair catch (fair catch kick).

(b) The ball must not touch the ground or any player of the offensive team before it passes through the goal.

ENTIRE BALL
THROUGH GOAL

(c) The entire ball must pass through the goal. In case wind or other forces cause it to return through the goal, it must have struck the ground or some object or person before returning.

MISSED FIELD
GOALS

Article 2   All field goals attempted and missed when the spot of the kick is beyond the 20-yard line will result in the defensive team taking possession of the ball at the spot of the kick. On any field goal attempted and missed when the spot of the kick is on or inside the 20-yard line, the ball will revert to the defensive team at the 20-yard line.

Exception 1: If a field goal attempt is missed and the ball is touched or possessed by the receivers beyond the line of scrimmage in the field of play, the ball will not come back to the spot of kick. All general rules for a kick from scrimmage will apply. If a foul occurs during the missed field goal attempt, Rule 9-1-17 governs.

Exception 2: If a blocked field goal attempted from anywhere on the field is recovered behind the line of scrimmage by a defensive player and is not advanced, or if the blocked field goal attempt goes out of bounds behind the line of scrimmage, it is the receiving team's ball at that spot.

SUPPLEMENTAL NOTES

(1) If a missed field goal is first touched by the receivers beyond the line in the field of play and the ball then goes out of bounds, it is the receiver's ball at the out of bounds spot.

(2) If a missed field goal does not touch a receiver in the end zone and the ball then bounces back into the field of play, it is the receivers' ball at the spot of the kick if they did not touch the ball in the field of play (touchback if kick is made from inside defense's 20).

(3) If on a missed field goal the ball first touches a receiver in the end zone and returns to the field of play where it is not covered and then declared dead, the ball belongs to the defense at the spot of the kick (touchback if kick is made from inside defense's 20).

(4) If the receivers first touch a missed field goal anywhere beyond the line of scrimmage and the kickers recover, the ball belongs to the kickers at the spot of the recovery. If in the end zone, it is a touchdown.

Exception: If a receiver is the first to touch a missed field goal in the field of play, and the ball then rolls into the end zone where it is declared dead (no new impetus) in possession of the defense, it is a touchback.

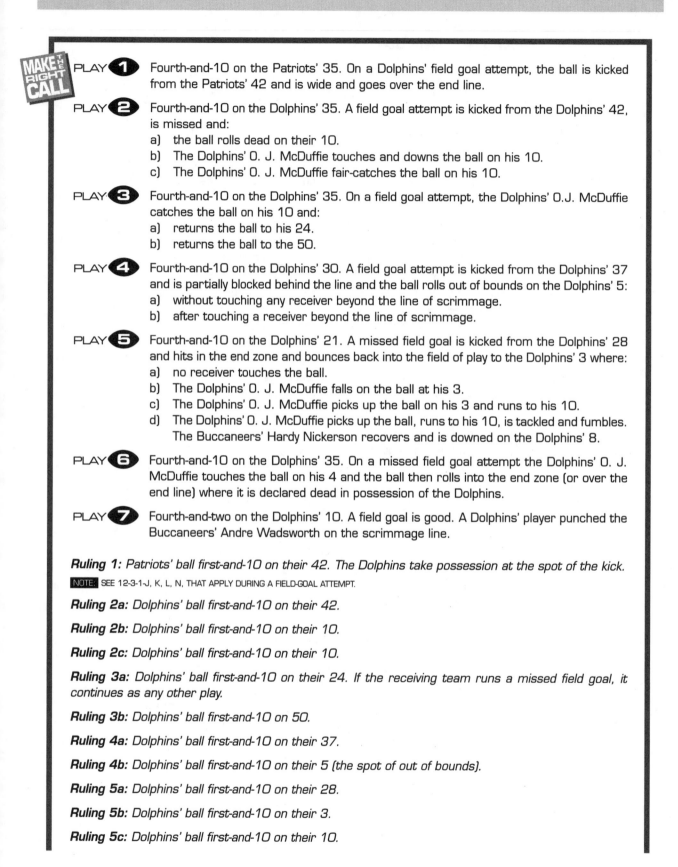

PLAY **1** Fourth-and-10 on the Patriots' 35. On a Dolphins' field goal attempt, the ball is kicked from the Patriots' 42 and is wide and goes over the end line.

PLAY **2** Fourth-and-10 on the Dolphins' 35. A field goal attempt is kicked from the Dolphins' 42, is missed and:
a) the ball rolls dead on their 10.
b) The Dolphins' O. J. McDuffie touches and downs the ball on his 10.
c) The Dolphins' O. J. McDuffie fair-catches the ball on his 10.

PLAY **3** Fourth-and-10 on the Dolphins' 35. On a field goal attempt, the Dolphins' O.J. McDuffie catches the ball on his 10 and:
a) returns the ball to his 24.
b) returns the ball to the 50.

PLAY **4** Fourth-and-10 on the Dolphins' 30. A field goal attempt is kicked from the Dolphins' 37 and is partially blocked behind the line and the ball rolls out of bounds on the Dolphins' 5:
a) without touching any receiver beyond the line of scrimmage.
b) after touching a receiver beyond the line of scrimmage.

PLAY **5** Fourth-and-10 on the Dolphins' 21. A missed field goal is kicked from the Dolphins' 28 and hits in the end zone and bounces back into the field of play to the Dolphins' 3 where:
a) no receiver touches the ball.
b) The Dolphins' O. J. McDuffie falls on the ball at his 3.
c) The Dolphins' O. J. McDuffie picks up the ball on his 3 and runs to his 10.
d) The Dolphins' O. J. McDuffie picks up the ball, runs to his 10, is tackled and fumbles. The Buccaneers' Hardy Nickerson recovers and is downed on the Dolphins' 8.

PLAY **6** Fourth-and-10 on the Dolphins' 35. On a missed field goal attempt the Dolphins' O. J. McDuffie touches the ball on his 4 and the ball then rolls into the end zone (or over the end line) where it is declared dead in possession of the Dolphins.

PLAY **7** Fourth-and-two on the Dolphins' 10. A field goal is good. A Dolphins' player punched the Buccaneers' Andre Wadsworth on the scrimmage line.

Ruling 1: Patriots' ball first-and-10 on their 42. The Dolphins take possession at the spot of the kick.
NOTE: SEE 12-3-1-J, K, L, N, THAT APPLY DURING A FIELD-GOAL ATTEMPT.

Ruling 2a: Dolphins' ball first-and-10 on their 42.

Ruling 2b: Dolphins' ball first-and-10 on their 10.

Ruling 2c: Dolphins' ball first-and-10 on their 10.

Ruling 3a: Dolphins' ball first-and-10 on their 24. If the receiving team runs a missed field goal, it continues as any other play.

Ruling 3b: Dolphins' ball first-and-10 on 50.

Ruling 4a: Dolphins' ball first-and-10 on their 37.

Ruling 4b: Dolphins' ball first-and-10 on their 5 (the spot of out of bounds).

Ruling 5a: Dolphins' ball first-and-10 on their 28.

Ruling 5b: Dolphins' ball first-and-10 on their 3.

Ruling 5c: Dolphins' ball first-and-10 on their 10.

Ruling 5d: Buccaneers ball first-and-goal on the Dolphins' 8.

Ruling 6: Touchback. Dolphins' ball first-and-10 on their 20.

Ruling 7: Option for the Buccaneers. Score for field goal or Buccaneers' ball first-and-goal on the Dolphins' 5. See 14-6. Disqualify Dolphins' player. If a score taken, it is 15-yard penalty against the Dolphins on kickoff (14-1-14).

FAIR CATCH
KICK

Article 3   On a free kick following a fair catch all general rules apply as for a field goal attempt from scrimmage. The clock starts when the ball is kicked.

Exception: The ball is no longer a free kick ball. The kicking team can't get the ball unless it had been first touched or possessed by the receivers.

PLAY **1**   On a fair catch kick from the Rams' 45, the Cardinals' Eric Swann touches and falls on the ball on the Rams' 33 without any Rams player touching the ball.

PLAY **2**   On a fair catch kick from the Cardinals' 45, the ball goes out of bounds on the Cardinals' 10:
a)   without touching any player.
b)   after touching any kicking team player.

Ruling 1: Rams' ball first-and-10 on their 45 (the previous spot). The clock is started when the ball is kicked.

Ruling 2a: Cardinals' ball first-and-10 on their 45. The clock starts when the ball is kicked.

Ruling 2b: Cardinals' ball first-and-10 on their 45. The clock starts when the ball is kicked.

NO ARTIFICIAL
MEDIA

Article 4   No artificial media shall be permitted to assist in the execution of a field goal and/or Try after touchdown attempt.

KICKOFF TEAM

Article 5   After a field goal, the team scored upon will receive. See 6-1-2 and 3.

Section 6   Touchback

NOTE: A TOUCHBACK, WHILE NOT A SCORE, IS INCLUDED IN THIS RULE BECAUSE, LIKE SCORING PLAYS, IT IS A CASE OF A BALL DEAD IN TOUCH (3-14-2).

TOUCHBACK
SITUATIONS

Article 1   When an impetus (3-14-3) by a team sends a ball in touch behind its opponent's goal line, it is a touchback:
(a)   if the ball is dead in the opponent's possession in their end zone;
(b)   if the ball is out of bounds behind the goal line (see 7-5-6-c);

    (c) if the impetus was a scrimmage kick, unless there is a spot of first touching by the kickers outside the receivers' 20-yard line or if the receivers after gaining possession advance with the ball into the field of play (9-1-13-b); or

    (d) if any legal kick touches the receivers' goal posts or crossbar other than one which scores a field goal.

NEW IMPETUS

> **NOTE:** THE IMPETUS IS NOT FROM A KICK IF A MUFF, BAT, JUGGLE, OR ILLEGAL KICK OF ANY KICKED BALL (BY A PLAYER OF EITHER TEAM) CREATES A NEW MOMENTUM WHICH SENDS IT IN TOUCH. SEE 3-14-1, NOTE, FOR A SPECIFIC BALL-IN-TOUCH RULING.

MAKE THE RIGHT CALL

PLAY 1 Broncos' quarterback Bubby Brister throws a legal pass which is intercepted in the end zone by the Cowboys' Deion Sanders. Sanders tries to run it out and is downed in the end zone.

PLAY 2 A punt is caught in end zone by the Saints' Andre Hastings who tries to run it out. He is tackled, fumbles and Eagles' kicking team player Torrence Small recovers in end zone.

Ruling 1: Touchback. Cowboys' ball first-and-10 on their 20.

Ruling 2: Touchdown for the Eagles.

FAIR CATCH INTERFERENCE IN END ZONE

Article 2   It is a touchback:

    (a) when the kickers interfere with a fair catch behind the receivers' goal line (10-1-5-Note); or

    (b) when the kickers first touch a scrimmage kick behind the receivers' goal line.

FIRST TOUCHING IN END ZONE

    (c) when a kicking team player illegally recovers or catches a punt inside the receivers' five-yard line and carries the ball across the defender's goal line or his body touches the end zone. (See 9-1-4-Note)

MAKE THE RIGHT CALL

PLAY 1 Fourth-and-10 on the Bengals' 35. The Buccaneers' Karl Williams is touching the goal line with his foot when he downs the punted ball on the 1-yard line in the field of play.

Ruling 1: Touchback.

DEFENSIVE FOUL BEHIND OFFENSIVE GOAL LINE

Article 3   When the spot of enforcement for a foul by the defense is behind the offensive goal line, the distance penalty is enforced from the goal line (14-1-11). See 8-4-4 for Exception.

PLAY ❶ The Bills' Andre Reed fumbles a punt and the ball rolls into his end zone where he recovers. Reed runs but is downed in the end zone. During Reeds' run the Chiefs' Will Shields commits a personal foul.

PLAY ❷ Second-and-15 on the Bears' 4. A backward pass or fumble by the Bears' Cade McNown on his 2 strikes ground. The Steelers' Jason Gildon deliberately bats or deliberately kicks the ball into the end zone.
a) where the Bears' Curtis Conway recovers.
b) where the Steelers' Levon Kirkland recovers.

Ruling 1: Bills' ball first-and-10 on their 15.

Ruling 2a: Touchback (or loss of 10 from previous spot). Bears' ball first-and-10 on their 20.

Ruling 2b: Loss of 10 from the previous spot. Bears' ball first-and-10 on their 14.

Article 4 After a touchback, the touchback team next snaps from its 20 (any point between the inbounds lines and the forward point of the ball on that line).

MAKE THE RIGHT CALL

CHAPTER 12
PLAYER CONDUCT

What we're concerned about here is avoiding any unsportsmanlike actions toward the other team. Taunting of opponents will not be tolerated.

Natural actions of exuberance will continue to be legal and a part of our game.

Jerry Seeman
NFL DIRECTOR OF OFFICIATING

Note—The spot of enforcement (when not stated), or the actual distance penalty, or both, are subordinate to the specific rules governing a foul during a fumble, pass, or kick, and these in turn are subordinate to the general provisions of Rule 14.

Section 1   Use of Hands, Arms, and Body

ASSISTING RUNNER

INTERLOCKED INTERFERENCE

PUSHING OR LIFTING RUNNER

Article 1   No offensive player may:

(a) assist the runner except by individually blocking opponents for him.

(b) use interlocking interference. Interlocked interference means the grasping of one another by encircling the body to any degree with the hands or arms; or

(c) push the runner or lift him to his feet.

PENALTY: FOR ASSISTING RUNNER OR INTERLOCKED INTERFERENCE: LOSS OF 10 YARDS.

MAKE THE RIGHT CALL   **PLAY 1**   Second-and-goal on the Chargers' 2. The Broncos' Howard Griffith gets to the line of scrimmage and is stopped but teammate Bubby Brister pushes him from behind and shoves him over the goal line.

Ruling 1: No score. Illegally assisting runner. Broncos' ball second-and-goal on Chargers' 12.

LEGAL USE OF HANDS

Article 2   A runner may ward off opponents with his hands and arms, but no other offensive player may use them to obstruct an opponent, by grasping with hands or encircling with arm in any degree any part of body, during a block.

Exceptions:

LEGAL BLOCK

1) During a legal block (3-3 and 12-1-5).

USE OF HANDS DURING LOOSE BALL

2) During a loose ball, an offensive player may use his hands/arms legally to block or otherwise push or pull an opponent out of the way in a ***personal legal*** attempt to recover. See specific fumble, pass or kick rules and especially 6-2-5-S-N. 1.

3) During a kick, a kicking team player may use his hands/arms to ward off or to push or pull aside a receiver who is legally or illegally attempting to obstruct him beyond the line.

4) A runner may lay his hand on a teammate or push him into an opponent but he may not grasp or hold on to him.

USE OF HANDS BEYOND LINE

NOTE: DURING A SCRIMMAGE KICK, A KICKING TEAM PLAYER MAY NOT USE HIS HANDS TO PUSH OR PULL ASIDE A RECEIVER WHO IS ATTEMPTING TO OBSTRUCT HIM **UNTIL** HE HAS CROSSED HIS LINE.

Article 3   No player on offense may push or throw his body against a teammate either:

(a) in such a way as to cause him to assist runner;

(b) to aid him in an attempt to obstruct an opponent or to recover a loose ball;

(c) to trip an opponent; or

(d) in charging, falling, or using hands on the body into the back from behind above the waist of an opponent.

PENALTY: FOR HOLDING, ILLEGAL USE OF HANDS, ARMS OR BODY OF OFFENSE: LOSS OF 10 YARDS.

NOTE: TRIPPING BY EITHER TEAM: LOSS OF 10 YARDS.

DEFENSIVE HOLDING

Article 4 A defensive player may not tackle or hold any opponent other than a runner. Otherwise, he may use his hands, arms, or body only to defend or protect himself against an obstructing opponent;

LEGAL CONTACT WITHIN FIVE YARDS OF LINE

Exception 1: An eligible receiver is considered to be an obstructing opponent only to a point five yards beyond the line of scrimmage unless the player who receives the snap demonstrates no further intention to pass the ball (including handing off the ball, pitching the ball or moving out of the pocket). Within this five-yard zone, a defensive player may chuck an eligible receiver in front of him. The defender is allowed to maintain continuous and unbroken contact within the five-yard zone, so long as the receiver has not moved beyond a point that is even with the defender.

ILLEGAL CONTACT WITHIN FIVE YARDS OF LINE

Within the five-yard zone, a defender may not make original contact in the back of a receiver, nor may he use his hands or arms to hang on to or encircle a receiver. The defender cannot extend an arm(s) to cut off or hook a receiver causing contact that impedes and restricts the receiver as the play develops, nor may he maintain contact after the receiver has moved beyond a point that is even with the defender.

ILLEGAL CONTACT BEYOND FIVE-YARD ZONE

Beyond the five-yard zone, if the player who receives the snap remains in the pocket with the ball, a defender may use his hands or arms only to defend or protect himself against impending contact caused by a receiver. If the receiver attempts to evade the defender, the defender cannot chuck him, or extend an arm(s) to cut off or hook him, causing contact that impedes and restricts the receiver as the play develops.

INCIDENTAL CONTACT BEYOND FIVE-YARD ZONE

Beyond the five-yard zone, incidental contact may exist between receiver and defender as long as it does not materially affect or significantly impede the receiver, creating a distinct advantage.

Exception 2: Eligible receivers lined up within two yards of the tackle, whether on or behind the line, may be blocked below the waist *at* or *behind* the line of scrimmage. *No* eligible receiver can be blocked below the waist after he goes beyond the line. (Illegal Cut.)

NOTE 1: ONCE THE QUARTERBACK HANDS OFF, IS TACKLED, PITCHES THE BALL TO A BACK, OR IF THE QUARTERBACK LEAVES THE POCKET AREA (SEE 3-24), THE RESTRICTIONS ON THE DEFENSIVE TEAM RELATIVE TO OFFENSIVE RECEIVERS (ILLEGAL CONTACT, ILLEGAL CUT) WILL END, PROVIDED THE BALL IS NOT IN THE AIR.

NOTE 2: WHENEVER A TEAM PRESENTS AN APPARENT PUNTING FORMATION, DEFENSIVE ACTION THAT WOULD NORMALLY CONSTITUTE ILLEGAL CONTACT (CHUCK BEYOND FIVE YARDS) WILL NO LONGER BE CONSIDERED A FOUL.

PENALTY: FOR ILLEGAL CONTACT, ILLEGAL CUT, OR HOLDING BY THE DEFENSE: LOSS OF FIVE YARDS AND AUTOMATIC FIRST DOWN.

SUPPLEMENTAL NOTES

(1) An eligible pass receiver who takes a position more than two yards outside of his own tackle (flexed receiver) may not be blocked below the waist (illegal cut), unless the quarterback hands off, is tackled, pitches the ball to a back, or if the quarterback leaves the pocket area.

(2) The unnecessary use of the hands by the defense, except as provided in Article 4, is illegal and is commonly used in lieu of a legal block (Article 5) (See 12-2-2).

(3) Any offensive player who pretends to possess the ball and/or one to whom a teammate pretends to give the ball, may be tackled provided he is crossing his scrimmage line between the offensive ends of a normal tight offensive line.

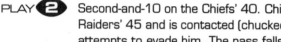

PLAY 1 Second-and-10 on the Cowboys' 40. The Cowboys' Kevin Smith holds Vikings' offensive end Cris Carter on the line of scrimmage. Vikings' quarterback Randall Cunningham can't throw the ball and is tackled at the 50.

PLAY 2 Second-and-10 on the Chiefs' 40. Chiefs' eligible end Andre Rison goes downfield to the Raiders' 45 and is contacted (chucked) by Raiders' defender Charles Woodson as Rison attempts to evade him. The pass falls incomplete.

PLAY 3 Second-and-10 on the Chiefs' 40. Chiefs' eligible receiver Andre Rison is chucked by the Raiders' Charles Woodson at the scrimmage line. Woodson then chucks Chiefs' back Bam Morris on the Chiefs' 44 prior to the pass. The pass then falls incomplete.

PLAY 4 Second-and-10 on the Chiefs' 30. Chiefs' eligible pass receiver Andre Rison takes a position three yards outside his own tackle and is blocked below the waist at line of scrimmage. The pass falls incomplete.

PLAY 5 Second-and-10 on the Chiefs' 30. Chiefs' eligible pass receiver Andre Rison lines up one yard outside of his own tackle and is blocked below the waist at the line of scrimmage. Pass falls incomplete.

PLAY 6 During a pass *behind* the line (forward or backward) Raiders' defender Charles Woodson uses his hands on potential Chiefs' receiver Andre Rison who is *behind* his line. Woodson is not using his hands to ward off Rison, to push or pull Rison out of the way in order to get to the runner (passer) or to push or pull him out of the way in an actual attempt to catch or recover a loose ball.

***Ruling 1** : Not a forward pass. Enforcement is from the previous spot. Vikings' ball first-and-10 on the Cowboys' 35.*

***Ruling 2:** Chiefs' ball first-and-10 on their 45. Illegal contact. Rison is not considered an obstructing player as he was more than five yards beyond line of scrimmage.*

***Ruling 3:** Legal use of hands as Rison and Morris were not the same player.*

***Ruling 4:** Illegal contact as Rison was more than two yards outside of his tackle. Five yard penalty. Chiefs' ball first-and-10 on their 35.*

***Ruling 5:** Legal block as Rison was lined up within two yards of the tackle. Chiefs' ball third-and-10 on their 30.*

***Ruling 6:** Illegal use of hands by the defense. Loss of five yards and first down for the Chiefs (14-8-5).*

LEGAL AND
ILLEGAL
BLOCK

Article 5   A player of either team may block at any time provided it is not:

(a) pass interference (8-2-1);

(b) fair catch interference (10-1-4);

(c) kicker (12-2-6) or passer interference (12-2-11);

(d) unnecessary roughness (12-2-8); or

(e) illegal cut (12-1-4-S.N.1); or

(f) illegal low block during free kick, scrimmage kick, or after change of possession (12-2-12).

MAKE THE RIGHT CALL **PLAY 1**   Rams' defensive tackle Demarco Farr blocks Buccaneers offensive tackle Paul Gruber which allows the Rams' June Henley to recover a loose ball.

Ruling 1: Legal block, although a player can only use hands in a personal attempt to recover (12-1-5).

ILLEGAL BAT

Article 6   A player may not bat or punch:

(a) a loose ball (in field of play) toward opponent's goal line;

(b) a loose ball in any direction if it is in either end zone;

(c) a ball in player possession;

(d) a backward pass in flight may not be batted forward by an offensive player.

NOTE: IF THERE IS ANY QUESTION AS TO WHETHER A DEFENDER IS STRIPPING OR BATTING A BALL IN PLAYER POSSESSION, THE OFFICIAL(S) WILL RULE THE ACTION AS A LEGAL ACT (STRIPPING THE BALL).

Exceptions: A forward pass in flight may be tipped, batted, or deflected in any direction by any player at any time.

PENALTY: FOR ILLEGAL BATTING OR PUNCHING THE BALL: LOSS OF 10 YARDS. FOR ENFORCEMENT, TREAT AS A FOUL DURING A BACKWARD PASS OR FUMBLE (SEE 8-4-4).

ILLEGALLY
KICKING BALL

Article 7   No player may deliberately kick any loose ball or ball in player's possession.

PENALTY: FOR ILLEGALLY KICKING THE BALL: LOSS OF 10 YARDS. FOR ENFORCEMENT, TREAT AS A FOUL DURING A BACKWARD PASS OR FUMBLE (SEE 8-4-4).

SUPPLEMENTAL NOTES

(1) If a loose ball is touched by any part of a player's leg (including knee), it is not considered kicking and is treated merely as touching.

(2) If the penalty for an illegal bat or kick is declined, procedure is the same as though the ball had been merely muffed. However, if the act (impetus) sends the ball in touch, 3-14-3 applies.

(3) The penalty for Article 6 and 7 does not preclude a penalty for a palpably unfair act, when a deliberate kick or illegal bat actually prevents an opponent from recovering. See Palpably Unfair Act (12-3-3).

(4) The ball is not dead when an illegal kick is recovered.

(5) The illegal kick or bat of a ball in player possession is treated as a foul during fumble (8-4-4).

PLAY **1** Second-and-15 on the Dolphins' 2, Dolphins' quarterback Dan Marino fumbles a snap in the end zone. While the ball is loose on the ground there, Marino deliberately kicks it. The ball is last touched by the Bills' Bruce Smith before going out of bounds on the Dolphins' 2-yard line.

Ruling 1: Safety. See 7-5-6-d; 11-4-2 and 12-1-7.

Section 2   Personal Fouls

STRIKING, KICKING OR KNEEING

Article 1   All players are prohibited from:

(a) striking with the fists;

(b) kicking or kneeing; or

(c) striking, swinging, or clubbing to the head, neck, or face with the heel, back, or side of the hand, wrist, forearm, elbow, or clasped hands. See 12-2-3.

NOTE: IT ALSO IS ILLEGAL FOR AN OPPONENT TO CLUB THE PASSER'S ARM.

PENALTY: FOR FOULS IN A, B, AND C: LOSS OF 15. IF ANY OF THE ABOVE ACTS IS JUDGED BY THE OFFICIAL(S) TO BE FLAGRANT, THE OFFENDER MAY BE DISQUALIFIED AS LONG AS THE ENTIRE ACTION IS OBSERVED BY THE OFFICIAL(S).

HEAD SLAP

Article 2   A defensive player shall not contact an opponent above the shoulders with the palm of his hands except to ward him off on the line. The exception applies only if it is not a repeated act against the same opponent during any one contact.

LEGAL CONTACT

Article 3   A defensive player may use the palm of his hands on an opponent's head, neck or face only to ward off or push him in an actual attempt to get at a loose ball.

NO STRIKING

Article 4   A player in blocking shall not strike an opponent below the shoulders with his forearm or elbows by turning the trunk of his body at the waist, pivoting or in any other way that is clearly unnecessary.

PENALTY: FOR ILLEGAL USE OF THE PALM OF THE HANDS OR FOR STRIKING AN OPPONENT BELOW THE SHOULDERS WITH THE FOREARM OR ELBOW: LOSS OF 15 YARDS.

NOTE: ANY IMPERMISSIBLE USE OF ELBOWS, FOREARMS, OR KNEES SHALL BE PENALIZED UNDER THE UNNECESSARY ROUGHNESS RULE; FLAGRANTLY UNNECESSARY ROUGHNESS SHALL BE PENALIZED UNDER THE SAME RULE AND THE PLAYER DISQUALIFIED.

 **PLAY 1** Second-and-10 on the Ravens' 30. A Bills' defensive player, on his initial charge, head slaps an offensive tackle on the helmet once with his open hand trying to get at the Ravens' Priest Holmes. Holmes is downed on his 35.

PLAY 2 Second-and-10 on the Ravens' 30. A Bills' defensive player, on his initial charge, head slaps an offensive tackle on his helmet repeatedly with his open hand in trying to get at the Ravens' Priest Holmes. Holmes is downed on his 35.

Ruling 1: Illegal. Ravens' ball first-and-10 on the 50.

Ruling 2: Illegal. Loss of 15 yards. Ravens' ball first-and-10 on the 50.

GRASPING
FACE MASK

Article 5 No player shall grasp the face mask of an opponent.

PENALTY: INCIDENTAL GRASPING OF THE MASK—FIVE YARDS. NOT A PERSONAL FOUL (IF BY THE DEFENSE THERE IS NO AUTOMATIC FIRST DOWN). TWISTING, TURNING, OR PULLING THE MASK—15 YARDS. A PERSONAL FOUL. THE PLAYER MAY BE DISQUALIFIED IF THE ACTION IS JUDGED BY THE OFFICIAL(S) TO BE OF A FLAGRANT NATURE.

 PLAY 1 Third-and-10 on the Falcons' 30. The Falcons' Jamal Anderson runs to his 33, where he is tackled by the Bills' Gabe Northern, who incidentally grasps Andersons' face mask on the tackle, but it is not a twist, turn, or pull.

Ruling 1: Falcons' ball, third-and-two, on their 38. It is not an automatic first down. Five-yard penalty.

RUNNING
INTO KICKER

Article 6 No defensive player may run into or rough a kicker who kicks from behind his line unless such contact:

(a) is incidental to and after he has touched the kick in flight;

(b) is caused by the kicker's own motions;

(c) occurs during a quick kick;

(d) occurs during a kick or after a run behind the line;

(e) occurs after the kicker recovers a loose ball on the ground; or

(f) is caused because a defender is blocked into the kicker.

PENALTY: FOR RUNNING INTO THE KICKER: LOSS OF FIVE YARDS FROM THE PREVIOUS SPOT, NO AUTOMATIC FIRST DOWN. (THIS IS NOT A PERSONAL FOUL. FOR ROUGHING THE KICKER OR HOLDER, LOSS OF 15 YARDS FROM THE PREVIOUS SPOT. (THIS IS A PERSONAL FOUL, AND ALSO DISQUALIFICATION IF FLAGRANT.)

SUPPLEMENTAL NOTES

(1) Avoiding the kicker is a primary responsibility of defensive players if they do not touch the kick.

(2) Any contact with the kicker by a single defensive player who has not touched the kick is running into the kicker.

(3) Any unnecessary roughness committed by defensive players is roughing the kicker. Severity of contact and potential for injury are to be considered.

(4) When two defensive players are making a bona fide attempt to block a kick from scrimmage (punt, drop kick, and/or placekick) and one of them runs into the kicker after the kick has left the kicker's foot at the same instant the second player blocks the kick, the foul for running into the kicker shall *not* be enforced, unless in the judgment of the referee, the player running into the kicker was clearly the direct cause of the kick being blocked.

(5) If in the judgment of the referee any of the above action is unnecessary roughness, the penalty for roughing the kicker *shall* be enforced from the previous spot as a foul during a kick.

PLAY ① Bears' kicker Todd Sauerbraun in punt formation muffs a snap. He recovers on the ground and then kicks. Sauerbraun is run into, blocked or tackled by the Patriots' Ty Law who had started his action when Sauerbraun first recovered.

PLAY ② The Bears' Todd Sauerbraun receives a snap. He starts to run but after a few strides, he kicks from behind his line. As Sauerbraun kicks, he is tackled or run into.

PLAY ③ Fourth-and-12 on the Patriots' 30. On a field goal attempt which is not good, Patriots' defender Ty Law runs into the kicker without touching the ball.

Ruling 1: Legal action by Law.

Ruling 2: The kicker is to be protected, but the referee should use his judgment when ordinary line play carries an opponent into such a kicker or at any time when it is not obvious that a kick is to be made (quick kick).

Ruling 3: Bears' ball fourth-and-7 on the Patriots' 25. Running into the kicker. If the field goal had been good, no penalty would be enforced on the succeeding kickoff, since it was not a personal foul.

NO PILING ON   **Article 7**   There shall be no piling on (3-22).

PENALTY: FOR PILING ON: LOSS OF 15 YARDS.

NOTE: AN OFFICIAL SHOULD PREVENT PILING ON A PROSTRATE OR HELPLESS RUNNER BEFORE THE BALL IS DEAD. WHEN OPPONENTS IN CLOSE PROXIMITY TO SUCH A RUNNER ARE ABOUT TO PILE ON, AND FURTHER ADVANCE IS IMPROBABLE, THE OFFICIAL COVERING SHOULD SOUND HIS WHISTLE FOR A DEAD BALL IN ORDER TO PREVENT FURTHER PLAY AND ROUGHNESS. SEE 7-4-1-D.

PLAY ① The holder of a Try-kick is run into or piled on and the act is not incidental to blocking the kick.

Ruling 1: Unnecessary roughness. Such a player is obviously out of play unless the kick is blocked, and even then until he arises and participates in play. See 14-1-14 and 14-6, Exception 6.

UNNECESSARY
ROUGHNESS

Article 8 There shall be no unnecessary roughness. This shall include, but will not be limited to:

STRIKING

(a) striking an opponent anywhere above the knee with the foot or any part of the leg below the knee with a whipping motion;

(b) tackling the runner when he is clearly out of bounds;

(c) throwing the runner to the ground after the ball is dead. A member of the receiving team cannot go out of bounds and contact a kicking team player out of bounds. If this occurs on a kick from scrimmage, post-possession rules would apply if appropriate (9-1-7);

(d) running or diving into, or throwing the body against or on a ball carrier who falls or slips to the ground untouched and makes no attempt to advance, before or after the ball is dead;

(e) running or diving into, or throwing the body against or on a player obviously out of the play, before or after the ball is dead; also a member of the receiving team cannot go out of bounds and contact a kicking-team player out of bounds;

CONTACTING
RUNNER OUT
OF BOUNDS

(f) contacting a runner out of bounds. Defensive players must make an effort to avoid contact. Players on defense are responsible for knowing when a runner has crossed the boundary line, except in doubtful cases where he might step on a boundary line and continue parallel with it;

IMPERMISSIBLE
USE OF HELMET
AND
FACEMASK

(g) using any part of a player's helmet (including the top/crown and forehead/"hairline" parts) or facemask to violently and unnecessarily butt, spear or ram an opponent; although such violent and unnecessary use of the facemask is impermissible against any opponent, game officials will give special attention in administering this rule to protecting those players who are in virtually defenseless postures (e.g., a player in the act of or just after throwing a pass, a receiver catching or attempting to catch a pass, a runner already in the grasp of a tackler, a kickoff or punt returner attempting to field a kick in the air, or a player on the ground at the end of a play). All players in virtually defenseless postures are protected by the same prohibitions against use of the helmet and facemask that are described in the roughing-the-passer rules (see Article 11, subsection 3 below of this Rule 12, Section 2);

(h) any player who hooks his fingers under the helmet of an opponent and forcibly twists his head.

PENALTY: FOR UNNECESSARY ROUGHNESS: LOSS OF 15 YARDS. *THE PLAYER MAY BE DISQUALIFIED IF THE ACTION IS JUDGED BY THE OFFICIAL(S) TO BE FLAGRANT.*

NOTE: IF IN DOUBT ABOUT A ROUGHNESS CALL OR POTENTIALLY DANGEROUS TACTICS, THE COVERING OFFICIAL(S) SHOULD ALWAYS CALL UNNECESSARY ROUGHNESS.

 PLAY **1** Third-and-20 on the Cowboys' 30. The Cowboys' Emmitt Smith runs to his 33, where he is tackled by a Giants' defensive end, who hooks his fingers under the front of Smith's helmet, but not his facemask, and forcibly twists his head.

Ruling 1: 15 yards for unnecessary roughness. It is an automatic first down. Cowboys' ball, first-and-10, on their 48.

CLIPPING

Article 9 There shall be no clipping from behind below the waist against a non-runner. This does not apply to offensive blocking in close-line play where it is legal to clip above the knee(s), but it is illegal to clip at or below the knee(s).

PENALTY: FOR CLIPPING: LOSS OF 15 YARDS.

CLOSE LINE PLAY

SUPPLEMENTAL NOTES

(1) Close line play is that which occurs in an area extending laterally to the position originally occupied by the offensive tackles and longitudinally three yards on either side of each line of scrimmage.

Exception: An offensive lineman may not clip a defender who, at the snap, is aligned on the line of scrimmage opposite another offensive lineman who is more than one position away when the defender is responding to the flow of the ball away from the blocker.

Example: Tackle cannot clip nose tackle on sweep away.

(2) Doubtful cases involving a side block or the opponent turning his back as the block is being made are to be judged according to whether the opponent was able to see or ward off the blocker.

(3) The use of hands from behind above the waist on a non-runner is illegal use of hands (see 12-1-3).

(4) The use of hands on the back is not clipping when it is by:

   a) one of the kickers in warding off a receiver, while going downfield under a kick, or

   b) any player in an actual personal legal attempt to recover a loose ball.

(5) It is not considered clipping if:

   a) a blocker is moving in the same direction as the opponent, and while his head is in advance of the opponent he then contacts the opponent from behind with any part of his body, or

   b) in any case if an official has not observed the blocker's initial contact.

PLAY **1** Second-and-10 on the Seahawks' 30. The Seahawks' Cortez Kennedy is hit from behind, below the waist at the Seahawks' 25 by the Saints' Willie Roaf throwing his body across the back of Kennedy's legs. Saints' running back Ricky Williams is downed on the Seahawks' 15.

PLAY **2** Second-and-10 on the Seahawks' 30. The Saints' Willie Roaf pushes the Seahawks' Cortez Kennedy from behind above the waist at the Seahawks' 25. Saints' running back Ricky Williams is down on the Seahawks' 15.

Ruling 1: Clipping. Saints' ball second-and-20 on Seahawks' 40.

Ruling 2: Illegal use of hands. Saints' ball second-and-15 on the Seahawks' 35.

CRACKBACK
(ILLEGAL)

Article 10 At the snap, an offensive player who is aligned in a position more than two yards laterally outside an offensive tackle, or a player who is in a backfield position at the snap and then moves to a position two or more yards outside a tackle, may not clip an opponent anywhere, nor may he contact an opponent below the waist if the blocker is moving toward the position where the ball was snapped from, and the contact occurs within an area five yards on either side of the line of scrimmage.

> NOTE 1: A PLAYER ALIGNED TWO OR MORE YARDS OUTSIDE A TACKLE AT THE SNAP IS DESIGNATED AS BEING FLEXED.

> NOTE 2: IF A RUNNER (PASSER) SCRAMBLES ON THE PLAY, SIGNIFICANTLY CHANGING THE ORIGINAL DIRECTION (BROKEN PLAY), THE CRACKBACK BLOCK IS LEGAL.

PENALTY: ILLEGAL CRACKBACK BLOCK: LOSS OF 15 YARDS.

MAKE THE RIGHT CALL

PLAY ❶ Second-and-10 on the Saints' 40. Saints' flanker Keith Poole sets up five yards outside of offensive tackle Willie Roaf. At snap Poole comes back and crackback blocks the Seahawks' Cortez Kennedy. Contact is made at the Saints' 38 behind the offensive tackle's original position. Runner goes to 50.

Ruling 1: Saints' ball second-and-25 on their 25. Illegal crackback block. Penalize from previous spot.

ROUGHING
THE PASSER

Article 11 Because the act of passing often puts the quarterback (or any other player attempting a pass) in a position where he is particularly vulnerable to injury, special rules against roughing the passer apply. The referee has principal responsibility for enforcing these rules. Any physical acts against passers during or just after a pass which, in the referee's judgement, are unwarranted by the circumstances of the play will be called as fouls. The referee will be guided by the following principles:

PASS LEAVING
PASSER'S
HAND; 1-STEP
RULE

(1) Roughing will be called if, in the referee's judgement, a pass rusher clearly should have known that the ball had already left the passer's hand before contact was made; pass rushers are responsible for being aware of the position of the ball in passing situations; the referee will use the release of the ball from the passer's hand as his guideline that the passer is now fully protected; once a pass has been released by a passer, a rushing defender may make direct contact with the passer only up through the rusher's first step after such release (prior to second step hitting the ground); thereafter the rusher must be making an attempt to avoid contact and must not continue to "drive through" or otherwise forcibly contact the passer; incidental or inadvertent contact by a player who is easing up or being blocked into the passer will not be considered significant;

UNNECESSARY
ACTS AGAINST
PASSER

(2) A rushing defender is prohibited from committing such intimidating and punishing acts as "stuffing" a passer into the ground or unnecessarily wrestling or driving him down after the passer has thrown the ball, even if the rusher makes his initial contact with the passer within the one-step limitation provided for in (1) above. When tackling a passer who is in a virtually defenseless posture (e.g., during or just after throwing a pass), a defensive player must not unnecessarily and violently throw him down and land on top of him with all or most of the defender's weight. Instead, the defensive player must strive to wrap up or cradle the passer with the defensive player's arms;

HITS TO PASSER'S HEAD AND USE OF HELMET AND FACEMASK

(3) In covering the passer position, referees will be particularly alert to fouls in which defenders impermissibly use the helmet and/or facemask to hit the passer, or use hands, arms, or other parts of the body to hit the passer in the head, neck, or face (see also the other unnecessary-roughness rules covering these subjects). A defensive player must not use his facemask or other part of his helmet against a passer who is in a virtually defenseless posture—for example, (a) forcibly hitting the passer's head, neck, or face with the helmet or facemask, regardless of whether the defensive player also uses his arms to tackle the passer by encircling or grasping him, or (b) lowering the head and violently and unnecessarily making forcible contact with the "hairline" or forehead part of the helmet against any part of the passer's body. This rule does not prohibit incidental contact by the mask or non-crown parts of the helmet in the course of a conventional tackle on a passer. A defensive player must not "launch" himself (spring forward and upward) into a passer, or otherwise strike him, in a way that causes the defensive player's helmet or facemask to forcibly strike the passer's head, neck, or face—even if the initial contact of the defender's helmet or facemask is lower than the passer's neck. Examples: (a) a defender buries his facemask into a passer's high chest area, but the defender's trajectory as he leaps into the passer causes the defender's helmet to violently strike the passer in the head or face; (b) a defender, using a face-on posture or with head slightly lowered, hits a passer in an area below the passer's neck, then the defender's head moves upward, resulting in a strong contact by the defender's mask or helmet with the passer's head, neck, or face (one example of this is the so-called "dip-and-rip" technique).

CLUBBING PASSER'S ARM

(4) A defensive player is prohibited from clubbing the arm of a passer during a pass or just after a pass has been thrown; however, a defensive player may grasp, pull, or otherwise make normal contact with a passer's arm in attempting to tackle him;

HITTING PASSER'S KNEES

(5) A rushing defender who has an unrestricted path to the passer from any direction is prohibited from forcibly hitting the passer in the knee area or below;

GRASP AND CONTROL

(6) The referee must blow the play dead as soon as the passer is clearly in the grasp and control of any tackler behind the line and the passer's safety is in jeopardy;

PASSER OUT OF PLAY

(7) A passer who is standing still or fading backwards after the ball has left his hand is obviously out of the play and must not be unnecessarily contacted by the defense through the end of the play or until the passer becomes a blocker, or until he becomes a runner upon taking a lateral from a teammate or picking up a loose ball, or, in the event of a change of possession on the play, until the passer assumes a distinctly defensive position;

PASSER OUT OF POCKET

(8) When a passer goes outside the pocket area and either continues moving with the ball (without attempting to advance the ball as a runner) or throws on the run, he loses the protection of the one-step rule provided for in (1) above, but he remains covered by all the other special protections afforded to a passer in the pocket (Numbers 2,3,4,5,6, and 7), as well as the regular unnecessary-roughness rules applicable to all player positions. If the passer stops behind the line and clearly establishes a passing posture, he will then be covered by all of the special protections for passers.

PENALTY: FOR ROUGHING THE PASSER, LOSS OF 15 YARDS FROM THE PREVIOUS SPOT; DISQUALIFICATION IF FLAGRANT.

NOTE 1: IF IN DOUBT ABOUT A ROUGHNESS CALL OR POTENTIALLY DANGEROUS TACTIC ON THE QUARTERBACK, THE REFEREE SHOULD ALWAYS CALL ROUGHING THE PASSER.

NOTE 2: SEE 8-3-3,4 FOR PERSONAL FOULS PRIOR TO COMPLETION OR INTERCEPTION.

PLAY **1** Chiefs' passer Todd Collins is run into or tackled by the Packers' Vonnie Holiday after a pass. Holiday had started his action prior to the pass.

PLAY **2** The Packers' Vonnie Holiday bats or punches the ball out of the potential passer's hand.

Ruling 1: A legal action, unless the official rules that Holiday had a reasonable chance to avoid or minimize the contact and made no attempt to do so.

Ruling 2: Illegal bat or punch. Loss of 10 yards from the previous spot (12-1-6).

BLOCKING BELOW WAIST ON KICKS AND CHANGE OF POSSESSION

Article 12 Only players on the receiving team are prohibited from blocking below the waist during a down in which there is a kickoff, safety kick, punt, field goal attempt, or Try (kick).

Exception: Only immediately at the snap on a punt, field goal attempt, or Try (kick), those defensive players on the line of scrimmage lined up on or inside the normal tight end position can block low.

All players on the kicking team are prohibited from blocking below the waist after a kickoff, safety kick, punt, field goal attempt, or Try (kick). After a change of possession, neither team may block below the waist.

PENALTY: LOSS OF 15 YARDS.

PLAY **1** Third-and-6 on the Raiders' 26. The Raiders' Charles Woodson intercepts a forward pass in the end zone and runs it out to his 31. During Woodson's run, the Dolphins' Bernie Parmalee blocks the Raiders' Greg Biekert low from the side at the Raiders' 28, so that the Dolphins' Yatil Green could tackle Woodson at the Raiders' 31.

Ruling 1: Illegal block. Raiders' ball first-and-10 on their 46 (12-2-12).

USE OF HELMET AS A WEAPON

Article 13 A player may not use a helmet (that is no longer worn by anyone) as a weapon to strike, swing at, or throw at an opponent.

PENALTY: FOR ILLEGAL USE OF A HELMET AS A WEAPON: LOSS OF 15 YARDS AND AUTOMATIC DISQUALIFICATION.

Article 14 A chop block is a foul by the offense in which one offense player (designated as A1 for purposes of this rule) blocks a defensive player in the area of the thigh or lower while another offensive player (A2) occupies that same defensive player in one of the circumstances described in sub-sections (1) through (6) below.

CHOP BLOCK
ON PASS
(ENGAGEMENT)

(1) On a forward pass play, A1 chops a defensive player while the defensive player is physically engaged by the blocking attempt of A2.

CHOP BLOCK ON
PASS (AFTER
ENGAGEMENT)

(2) On a forward pass play in which A2 physically engages a defensive player with a blocking attempt, A1 chops the defensive player after the contact by A2 has been broken and while A2 is still confronting the defensive player.

CHOP BLOCK
ON PASS (WITH
"LURE")

(3) On a forward pass play, A1 chops a defensive player while A2 confronts the defensive player in a pass-blocking posture but is not physically engaged with the defensive player (a "lure").

REVERSE
CHOP BLOCK
ON PASS

(4) On a forward pass play, A1 fires out aggressively and blocks a defensive player in the area of the thigh or lower, and A2, simultaneously or immediately after the block by A1, engages the defensive player high.

NOTE: EACH OF THE ABOVE CIRCUMSTANCES IN SUB-SECTIONS (1) THROUGH (4), WHICH DESCRIBES A CHOP-BLOCK FOUL ON A FORWARD-PASS PLAY, ALSO APPLIES ON A PLAY IN WHICH AN OFFENSIVE PLAYER INDICATES AN APPARENT ATTEMPT TO PASS BLOCK BUT THE PLAY ULTIMATELY BECOMES A RUN.

CHOP BLOCK
ON RUN (BY A
BACK)

(5) On a running play, A1 is lined up in the backfield at the snap and subsequently chops a defensive player engaged above the waist by A2, and such a block occurs on or behind the line of scrimmage in an area extending laterally to the positions originally occupied by the tight end on either side.

CHOP BLOCK
ON RUN (BY A
LINEMAN)

(6) On a running play, A1, an offensive lineman, chops a defensive player after the defensive player has been engaged by A2 (high or low), and the initial alignment of A2 is more than one position away from A1. This rule applies only when the block occurs at a time when the flow of the play is clearly away from A1.

PENALTY: FOR CHOP BLOCK: LOSS OF 15 YARDS.

Section 3   Unsportsmanlike Conduct

Article 1   There shall be no unsportsmanlike conduct. This applies to any act which is contrary to the generally understood principles of sportsmanship. Such acts specifically include, among others:

(a) The use of abusive, threatening or insulting language or gestures to opponents, teammates, officials, or representatives of the League.

TAUNTING

(b) The use of baiting or taunting acts or words that engender ill will between teams.

CONTACT-GAME
OFFICIAL

(c) Unnecessary physical contact with a game official.

REMOVAL OF
HELMET

(d) Removal by a player of his helmet after a play. (Exceptions: The player is not in the game or he is in or has returned to his bench area; or, the player is in the game and a time out has been called for reasons of injury, television break, charged team time out, or it is between periods.

NOTE: UNDER NO CONDITION IS AN OFFICIAL TO ALLOW A PLAYER TO SHOVE, PUSH, STRIKE OR LAY A HAND ON HIM IN AN OFFENSIVE OR UNSPORTSMANLIKE MANNER. ANY SUCH ACTION MUST BE REPORTED TO THE COMMISSIONER.

PENALTY: (A), (B), (C) AND (D): LOSS OF 15 YARDS FROM SUCCEEDING SPOT OR WHAT-EVER SPOT THE REFEREE, AFTER CONSULTING WITH THE CREW, DEEMS EQUITABLE.

> NOTE: VIOLATIONS OF (A) OR (B) (ABOVE), WHICH OCCUR BEFORE OR DURING THE GAME MAY RESULT IN DISQUALIFICATION IN ADDITION TO THE YARDAGE PENALTY. ANY VIOLATIONS AT THE GAME SITE ON THE DAY OF THE GAME, INCLUDING POSTGAME, MAY RESULT IN DISCIPLINE BY THE COMMISSIONER. ANY VIOLATION OF (C) (ABOVE) RESULTS IN DISQUALIFICA-TION AND ALSO WILL INCLUDE DISCIPLINE BY THE COMMISSIONER.

(e) The defensive use of acts or words designed to disconcert an offensive team at the snap. An official must blow his whistle immediately to stop play.

(f) Concealing a ball underneath the clothing or using any article of equipment to simulate a ball.

LINGERING

(g) Using entering substitutes, legally returning players, substitutes on sidelines, or withdrawn players to confuse opponents. The clarification is also to be interpreted as covering any lingering by players leaving the field when being substituted for. See 5-2-1.

HIDE OUT

(h) An offensive player lines up or is in motion less than five yards from the sideline in front of his team's designated bench area. However, an offensive player can line up less than five yards from the sidelines on the same side as his team's player bench, as long as he is not in front of the designated bench area.

(i) Repeatedly abusing the substitution rule (time in) in attempts to conserve time. See 5-2-2.

(j) More than two successive 40/25 second penalties (after warning) during same down.

LEVERAGE

(k) Jumping or standing on a teammate or opponent to block or attempt to block an opponent's kick.

(l) Placing a hand or hands on a teammate to gain additional height in the block or attempt to block an opponent's kick.

(m) Being picked up by a teammate in a block or an attempt to block an opponent's kick.

(n) Throwing a punch, or a forearm, or kicking at an opponent even though no con-tact is made.

LEAPING

(o) Clearly running forward and leaping in an obvious attempt to block a field goal or Try-kick after touchdown and landing on players, unless the leaping player was originally lined up within one yard of the line of scrimmage when the ball was snapped.

GOAL TENDING

(p) Goal-tending by any player leaping up to deflect a kick as it passes above the crossbar of a goalpost is prohibited. The referee could award three points for a palpably unfair act (12-3-3).

(q) A punter, placekicker, or holder who simulates being roughed or run into by a defensive player.

(r) A member of the kicking team who goes out of bounds, whether forced out or voluntarily, must attempt to return inbounds in a reasonable amount of time.

PENALTY: FOR UNSPORTSMANLIKE PLAYER CONDUCT (E) THROUGH (R): LOSS OF 15 YARDS FROM:
A) THE SUCCEEDING SPOT IF THE BALL IS DEAD.
B) THE PREVIOUS SPOT IF THE BALL WAS IN PLAY.
IF THE INFRACTION IS FLAGRANT, THE PLAYER IS ALSO DISQUALIFIED.

FOULS TO
PREVENT
SCORE

Article 2   The defense, when near its goal line, shall not commit successive or continued fouls (half distance penalties) to prevent a score.

PENALTY: FOR CONTINUOUS FOULS TO PREVENT A SCORE: IF THE VIOLATION IS REPEATED AFTER A WARNING, THE SCORE INVOLVED IS AWARDED TO THE OFFENSIVE TEAM.

PALPABLY
UNFAIR ACT
(PLAYER)

Article 3   A player or substitute shall not interfere with play by any act which is palpably unfair.

PENALTY: FOR A PALPABLY UNFAIR ACT: OFFENDER MAY BE DISQUALIFIED. THE REFEREE, AFTER CONSULTING HIS CREW, ENFORCES ANY SUCH DISTANCE PENALTY AS THEY CONSIDER EQUITABLE AND IRRESPECTIVE OF ANY OTHER SPECIFIED CODE PENALTY. THE REFEREE COULD AWARD A SCORE. 15-1-6.

CHAPTER 13

NON-PLAYER CONDUCT

This rule applies the same standard of conduct to bench personnel, a coach, or a player out of uniform that applies in the previous chapter to players. No unsportsmanlike actions will be tolerated.

Jerry Seeman
NFL DIRECTOR OF OFFICIATING

Rule 13 Non-Player Conduct

Section 1   Non-Player Conduct

NON-PLAYER FOULS

Article 1   There shall be no unsportsmanlike conduct by a substitute, coach, attendant, or any other non-player (entitled to sit on a team's bench) during any period or time out (including between halves).

SUPPLEMENTAL NOTES

(1) "Loud speaker" coaching from the sidelines is not permissible.

(2) A player may communicate with a coach provided the coach is in his prescribed area during dead ball periods.

ATTENDANTS ON FIELD ONLY ON TEAM TIME OUTS

Article 2   Either or both team attendants and their helpers may enter the field to attend their team during a team time out by either team. No other non-player may come on the field without the referee's permission, unless he is an incoming substitute (5-2-1).

BENCH CREDENTIALS

Article 3   With the exception of uniformed players eligible to participate in the game, all persons in a team's bench area must wear a visible credential clearly marked "BENCH." For all NFL games—preseason, regular-season, and postseason—the home club will be issued a maximum of 27 credentials and the visiting club will be issued a maximum of 25 credentials for use in its bench area. Such credentials must be worn by coaches, players under contract to the applicable club but ineligible to participate in the game, and team support personnel (trainers, doctors, equipment men). From time to time, persons with game-services credentials (e.g., oxygen technicians, ball boys) and authorized club personnel not regularly assigned to the bench area may be in a team's bench area for a brief period without bench credentials. Clubs are prohibited from allowing into their bench areas any persons who are not officially affiliated with the club or otherwise serving a necessary game day function.

RESTRICTED AREAS

Article 4   All team personnel must observe the zone restrictions applicable to the bench area and the border rimming the playing field. The only persons permitted within the solid six-foot white border (1-1) while play is in progress on the field are game officials. For reasons involving the safety of participating players whose actions may carry them out of bounds, officials' unobstructed coverage of the game, and spectators' sightlines to the field, the border rules must be observed by all coaches and players in the bench area. Violators are subject to penalty by the officials.

MOVEMENT ON SIDELINES

Article 5   Coaches and other non-participating team personnel (including uniformed players not in the game at the time) are prohibited from moving laterally along the sidelines any further than the points that are 18 yards from the middle of the bench area (i.e., 32-yard lines to left and right of bench areas when benches are placed on opposite sides of the field). Lateral movement within the bench area must be behind the solid six-foot white border (see Article 4 above).

NON-BENCH
AREAS

Article 6 Clubs are prohibited from allowing into the non-bench areas of field level any persons who have not been accredited to those locations by the home club's public-relations office for purposes related to news-media coverage, stadium operations, or pregame and halftime entertainment. The home club is responsible for keeping the field level cleared of all unauthorized persons. Photographers and other personnel accredited for field-level work must not be permitted in the end zones or any other part of the official playing field while play is in progress.

PENALTY: FOR ILLEGAL ACTS UNDER ARTICLES 1 THROUGH 6 ABOVE: LOSS OF 15 YARDS FROM TEAM FOR WHOSE SUPPOSED BENEFIT FOUL WAS MADE. (UNSPORTSMANLIKE CONDUCT).

ENFORCEMENT IS FROM:

A) SUCCEEDING SPOT IF THE BALL IS DEAD;

B) PREVIOUS SPOT IF THE BALL WAS IN PLAY; OR

C) WHATEVER SPOT THE REFEREE, AFTER CONSULTING WITH CREW, DEEMS EQUITABLE.

FOR A FLAGRANT VIOLATION, THE REFEREE MAY EXCLUDE OFFENDER OR OFFENDERS FROM THE PLAYING FIELD ENCLOSURE FOR THE REMAINDER OF THE GAME.

NOTE: SEE 4-1-4, NOTE FOR A FOUL BY NON-PLAYERS BETWEEN HALVES.

PALPABLY
UNFAIR ACT
(NON-PLAYER)

Article 7 A non-player shall not commit any act which is palpably unfair.

PENALTY: FOR A PALPABLY UNFAIR ACT, SEE 12-3-3. THE REFEREE, AFTER CONSULTING THE CREW, SHALL MAKE SUCH RULING AS THEY CONSIDER EQUITABLE (15-1-6 AND NOTE) (UNSPORTSMANLIKE CONDUCT).

NOTE: VARIOUS ACTIONS INVOLVING A PALPABLY UNFAIR ACT MAY ARISE DURING A GAME. IN SUCH CASES, THE OFFICIALS MAY AWARD A DISTANCE PENALTY IN ACCORDANCE WITH 12-3-3, EVEN WHEN IT DOES NOT INVOLVE DISQUALIFICATION OF A PLAYER OR SUBSTITUTE. SEE 17-1.

Article 8 Non-player personnel of a club (e.g., management personnel, coaches, trainers, equipment men) are prohibited from making unnecessary physical contact with or directing abusive, threatening, or insulting language or gestures at opponents, game officials, or representatives of the League.

PENALTY: LOSS OF 15 YARDS. (UNSPORTSMANLIKE CONDUCT). ENFORCEMENT IS FROM:

A) SUCCEEDING SPOT IF THE BALL IS DEAD;

B) PREVIOUS SPOT IF THE BALL WAS IN PLAY; OR

C) WHATEVER SPOT THE SPOT REFEREE, AFTER CONSULTING WITH THE CREW, DEEMS EQUITABLE (PALPABLY UNFAIR ACT).

NOTE: VIOLATIONS WHICH OCCUR BEFORE OR DURING THE GAME MAY RESULT IN DISQUALIFICATION IN ADDITION TO THE YARDAGE PENALTY. ANY VIOLATION AT THE GAME SITE ON THE DAY OF THE GAME, INCLUDING POSTGAME, MAY RESULT IN DISCIPLINE BY THE COMMISSIONER.

CHAPTER 14
PENALTY ENFORCEMENT

This rule covers the different types of penalty enforcement situations not covered by other chapters here.

We've simplified the rules a great deal in recent years in order to make them easier for fans, coaches, players, and officials to understand and apply.

Jerry Seeman
NFL DIRECTOR OF OFFICIATING

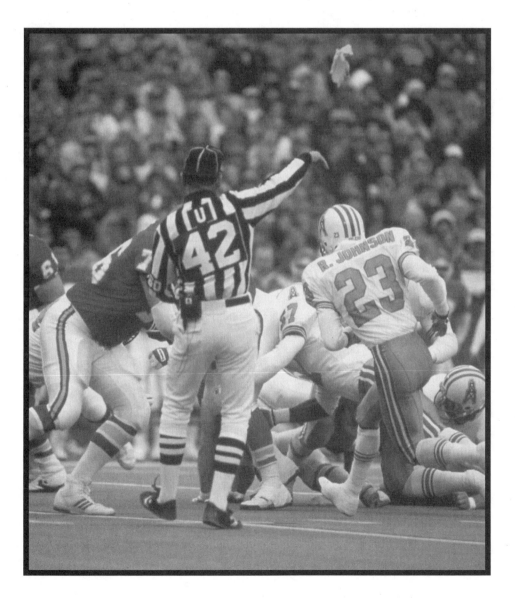

(Governing all cases not otherwise specifically provided for)

Section 1   Spot From Which Penalty in Foul is Enforced

SPOTS OF ENFORCEMENT

Article 1   The general provisions of Rule 14 govern all spots of enforcement.

> NOTE: THE SPOT OF ENFORCEMENT FOR FOULS BY PLAYERS OR THE ACTUAL DISTANCE PENALTY OR BOTH, WHEN NOT SPECIFIC, ARE SUBORDINATE TO THE SPECIFIC RULES GOVERNING A FOUL DURING A FUMBLE, PASS OR KICK. THESE IN TURN ARE BOTH SUBORDINATE TO RULE 14.

PLAY **1**   Second-and-15 on the Buccaneers' 4. Buccaneers' quarterback Trent Dilfer throws a legal pass which is incomplete. The Buccaneers' Karl Williams held in end zone.

Ruling 1: Safety or Buccaneers' ball third-and-15 on their 4.

FOULS BETWEEN DOWNS

Article 2   When a foul by a player occurs between downs, enforcement is from the succeeding spot (14-5-S.N. 3).

FOULS BY NON-PLAYERS

Article 3   Penalties for fouls committed by non-players shall be enforced as specifically provided under Rule 13.

ENFORCEMENT SPOT NOT GOVERNED

Article 4   When the spot of enforcement is not governed by a general or specific rule, it is the spot of the foul.

BASIC SPOTS OF ENFORCEMENT

Article 5   The basic spots of enforcement (3-11-1) are:

(a) The previous spot for a forward pass (8-3-2); a scrimmage kick (9-1-17); or a free kick (6-2-5).

(b) The succeeding spot on a running play (14-1-12).

(c) The spot of snap, backward pass, or fumble (8-4-4).

(d) The spot of the foul (14-1-4, 14-1-13).

> NOTE: IF A FOUL IS COMMITTED DURING A RUN, A FUMBLE, OR A BACKWARD PASS, THE PENALTY IS ASSESSED FROM THE BASIC SPOT IF:
>
> I) DEFENSE FOULS IN ADVANCE OF THE BASIC SPOT
>
> II) DEFENSE FOULS BEHIND THE BASIC SPOT
>
> III) OFFENSE FOULS IN ADVANCE OF THE BASIC SPOT

If the offense fouls behind the basic spot, enforcement is from the spot of the foul (3 and 1).

Exceptions:

1) All fouls committed by the offensive team behind the line of scrimmage (except in the end zone) shall be penalized from the previous spot. If the foul is in the end zone, it is a safety (14-1-11-b).

2) If a runner (3-27-1) is downed behind the line of scrimmage (except in the end zone) and the foul by an offensive player is beyond the line of scrimmage, enforcement shall be from the previous spot. If the runner is down in the end zone, it is a safety (11-4-1-a).

PLAY 1 Second-and-10 on the Rams' 30. The Rams' June Henley is downed on his 35. The Vikings' Corey Miller illegally uses his hands on the Rams' 45 during run.

PLAY 2 Second-and-10 on the Rams' 30. The Rams' June Henley is downed on his 35. Teammate Isaac Bruce uses his hands illegally on his 45.

PLAY 3 Second-and-10 on the Rams' 30. The Rams' June Henley is downed on his 40. An offensive player illegally uses his hands on the Rams' 35.

PLAY 4 Second-and-10 on the Rams' 30. Rams' quarterback Trent Green is downed on his 40. Teammate Kevin Knox held on his 25.

PLAY 5 Second-and-10 on the Rams' 30. The Rams' June Henley is downed on his 25. An offensive player held on the Rams' 32.

Ruling 1: The defensive foul is in advance of the basic spot (Rams' 35 where downed). Penalize from the basic spot (Rams' 35). Rams' ball first-and-10 on their 40.

Ruling 2: The offensive foul is in advance of the basic spot (Rams' 35 where downed). Penalize from the basic spot (Rams' 35). Rams' ball second-and-15 on their 25.

Ruling 3: The offensive foul is behind the basic spot (spot where downed). Penalize from the spot of the foul (Rams' 35). Rams' ball second-and-15 on their 25.

Ruling 4: Penalize 10 yards from the previous spot as the offensive foul was behind the line of scrimmage. Rams' ball second-and-20 on their 20.

Ruling 5: Rams' ball second-and-20 on their 20. Henley was downed behind the line of scrimmage. Enforcement is from the previous spot. Defense has option of refusing the penalty and taking the play which would then be Rams' ball third-and-15 on their 25 (14-6).

FOULS OUT OF BOUNDS

Article 6 When the spot of a player foul is out of bounds between the end lines, it is assumed to be at an inbounds line on a yard line (extended) through the spot where the foul was committed. If this spot is behind an end line, it is assumed to be in the end zone. See 7-3-7 and 14-1-11.

CONTINUING ACTION FOULS WHEN GAME CLOCK IS STOPPED

Article 7 The penalty is enforced from the succeeding spot as a foul between downs (14-5) if there is a continuing action foul (subsequent foul) (3-11-2-a) after:

(a) a ball is dead in touch;

(b) an out of bounds;

(c) a kick is (legally or illegally) recovered by the kickers;

(d) an incompletion; or

(e) a ball is dead when caught after a fair catch signal or interference with one.

See 9-1-4, Note for Exception to (c).

PLAY ❶ Second-and-10 on the Bills' 30. The Bills' Antowain Smith goes out of bounds on his 35. Teammate Sam Gash then clips the Vikings' John Randle either on the Bills' 40 or Bills' 30.

PLAY ❷ Fourth-and-10 on the Rams' 30. A punt goes to the Vikings' 30 where Rams' kicking team player Todd Lyght illegally touches the ball and then falls on it there, after which:
a) Rams' kicking team player Ricky Proehl clips any place on the field.
b) Vikings' receiver Randy Moss commits a personal foul any place on the field.

PLAY ❸ Fourth-and-8 on the Vikings' 12. A legal forward pass by the Rams is incomplete behind the goal line. During continuing action:
a) a Vikings' player roughs passer.
b) the Rams' Isaac Bruce clips.

Ruling 1: Enforce from the succeeding spot (out of bounds) as a foul between downs. Continuing action foul. The down is counted as the foul occurred after the ball was dead from Smith going out of bounds. Bills' ball third-and-20 on their 20.

Ruling 2a: Vikings' ball first-and-10 on their 45.

Ruling 2b: Vikings' ball first-and-10 on their 15.

Ruling 3a: Enforce from the succeeding spot (Vikings' 12) as the pass was incomplete in the end zone on fourth down (8-1-5-a) (14-1-7). Vikings' ball first and-10 on their 6.

Ruling 3b: Enforce from the succeeding spot (Vikings' 12). Vikings' ball first-and-10 on their 27.

CONTINUING ACTION BY BOTH TEAMS

Article 8 Continuing action fouls by both teams, after the ball is dead anywhere, are offset except when one or both are disqualifying or as provided in 4-1-9. See 14-3-2.

PLAY ❶ Fourth-and-5 on the Vikings' 14. A legal forward pass is incomplete behind the goal line, after which:
a) a Rams' player clips the Vikings' Todd Steussie and a Vikings' player roughs the Rams' Trent Green.
b) a Rams' player punches the Vikings' Todd Steussie and Steussie punches him in return.

PLAY ❷ Second-and-10 on the Rams' 30. A legal forward pass is incomplete, after which (during continuing action):
a) the Vikings' David Palmer clips the Rams' Isaac Bruce and Bruce punches Palmer.
b) a Rams' receiver clips a Vikings' defensive back and the Vikings' defensive back punches the Rams' receiver.

PLAY ❸ Vikings' receiver Randy Moss is offside on the kickoff. The kickoff is legally out of bounds on the Vikings' 30 (last touching a receiving team player) after which:
a) a Rams' player is penalized for roughness.
b) Moss is penalized for roughness.

Ruling 1a: Fouls are offset. They occurred during continuing action and the succeeding spot is Vikings' 14. Vikings' ball first-and-10 on their 14.

Ruling 1b: Continuing action fouls. Offsetting fouls; in addition, both players are disqualified. Vikings' ball first-and-10 on their 14.

Ruling 2a: Disqualify Bruce. Penalties offset. The down counts as the foul occurred after the down had ended. Rams' ball third-and-10 on their 30. See 14-1-8.

Ruling 2b: Disqualify the Vikings' defensive back. Penalties offset. Rams' ball third-and-10 on their 30.

Ruling 3a: Rekick. Double foul (14-3-1, 14-1-9).

Ruling 3b: Choice for the Rams. Rekick from the Rams' 40 (offside penalty) or Vikings' ball first- and-10 on their 15. A continuing action foul is penalized from the succeeding spot (Vikings 30). If the kick is illegally out of bounds, it is a rekick in either case (14-3-2).

FOUL AND
CONTINUING
ACTION FOUL

Article 9   If there has been a foul by either team during a down not including:

(a) an incompletion, or

(b) an illegal recovery of a kick (other than a free kick). Then there is a continuing action foul by the opponents after the down ends, Articles 7 and 8 are not enforced and if it is a double foul (14-3-1), except when the scoring team commits the continuous action foul after a score.

MAKE THE RIGHT CALL   PLAY **1**   Second-and-10 on the Panthers' 30. The Panthers' Fred Lane is out of bounds on his 40, after which teammate Rae Carruth clips any place. The Vikings were offside.

Ruling 1: Panthers' ball second-and-25 on their 15. See 14-3-1, Exception 1.

LEGAL ACTS
AFTER
CONTINUING
ACTION

Article 10 There is no penalty unless the contact was avoidable and it is deemed unnecessary roughness, if a player:

(a) uses his hands, arms, or body in a manner ordinarily illegal (other than striking) during continuing action after a down ends, or

(b) completes a legal action (blocking or tackling) started during the down.

MAKE THE RIGHT CALL   PLAY **1**   Second-and-10 on the Broncos' 30. The Broncos' Terrell Davis goes out of bounds on his 35 after which:
a)   the Broncos' Mark Schlereth holds on his 30.
b)   Schlereth clips on his 30.
c)   a Broncos' lineman strikes the 49ers' Junior Bryant on the Broncos' 30.

Ruling 1a: Ignore the foul as it was illegal use of hands and not a personal foul. Broncos' ball third-and-five their 35.

Ruling 1b: A personal foul on continuing action penalized as stated in 14-1-7. Broncos' ball third-and-20 on their 20.

Ruling 1c: Disqualify the Broncos' lineman. Penalize from the succeeding spot as in 14-1-7. Broncos' ball third-and-20 on their 20.

Article 11 When a spot of enforcement is behind the offensive goal line, and the foul is:

(a) by the defense, a distance penalty is measured from the goal line (unless a touch-back, one during a backward pass, or fumble, or 12-1-4 Penalty Exception), or

(b) by the offense, it is a safety. See 8-4-4 for Exception.

NOTE: DURING A LOOSE BALL THERE IS ALWAYS AN OFFENSIVE AND DEFENSIVE TEAM, AND ENFORCEMENT IS PROVIDED FOR IN THE SPECIFIC SECTION GOVERNING PASSES, FUMBLES, AND KICKS. SEE 3-2-3, 3-16, 3-35-1, AND 14-1-5.

PLAY **1** The 49ers' Tommy Vardell fumbles a punt on his one-yard line. The ball enters the end zone where Vardell recovers. During a run in the end zone, he fumbles. The Broncos' Tyrone Braxton clips anywhere during the last fumble. Vardell is downed in the end zone.

PLAY **2** Second-and-15 on the Broncos' 4. The Broncos' Derick Loville is downed in the end zone. During the run teammate Shannon Sharpe held on the Broncos' 10.

PLAY **3** Second-and-goal on the 49ers' 2. The Broncos' Derick Loville fumbles into the 49ers' end zone. The 49ers' Ray Brown recovers in his end zone (downed) or goes out of bounds from there. While Brown is a runner, teammate Tim McDonald fouls in the end zone.

Ruling 1: Enforce from the goal line. 49ers' ball first-and-10 on their 15.

Ruling 2: Safety. Decline penalty.

Ruling 3: Safety.

Article 12 When a foul occurs during a running play (3-27-2) and the run in which the foul occurs is not followed by a change of team possession during the down, the spot of enforcement is the spot where the ball is dead.

Exceptions:

1) When the spot of a foul by the offense is behind the spot where dead, enforcement is from the spot of the foul.

2) When the spot of a foul by the offense is behind the line of scrimmage, enforcement is from the previous spot unless in offensive's end zone. Then it is a safety (14-1-11-b).

3) When the spot of a foul by the offense is beyond the line of scrimmage and a runner (3-27-1) is downed behind the line, enforcement is from the previous spot unless he is downed in the end zone. Then it is a safety, the result of the play (11-4-1).

4) When the spot of foul is that of an illegal forward pass, enforcement is from the spot of the foul. This does not apply to a second forward pass from behind the line, or a pass after the ball had gone beyond the line, which is enforced from the previous spot.

5) If the spot of a defensive foul occurs on or beyond the line of scrimmage and the ball becomes dead behind the line, penalty is enforced from the previous spot.

6) When the spot of enforcement for the defense is behind the offensive goal line, enforcement is from the goal line. See 14-1-11-a.

DEFENSIVE
FOUL BEHIND
LINE

7) When the spot of a foul by the defense is behind the line of scrimmage and the ball becomes dead behind the line, enforcement is from the spot of the foul or the spot where the ball is dead, whichever is more advantageous to the offense. If such foul incurs a penalty that results in the offended team being short of the line, the ball will be advanced to the previous spot and no additional yardage assessed.

 PLAY **1**   While the 49ers' Tommy Vardell is returning a kickoff, teammate Greg Clark holds on the 49ers' 30. Vardell is downed on his 20.

Ruling 1: The offensive foul is in advance of the dead ball; enforce from the dead ball spot (49ers' 20). First-and-10 on 49ers' 10.

FOUL
ENFORCEMENT
ON RUNNING
PLAY WITH
POSSESSION
CHANGE

Article 13 When a defensive foul occurs during a running play (3-27-2) and the run in which the foul occurs is followed by a change of possession, the spot of enforcement is the spot of the foul and ball reverts to offensive team. See 14-1-12- Exception, 5.

Exceptions:

1) When the spot of a foul is in advance of the spot where the offensive player lost possession, the spot of enforcement is the spot where player possession was lost and the ball reverts to offensive team.

2) When the spot of a foul by the defense is behind the line of scrimmage, and such foul incurs a penalty that results in the offensive team being short of the line, the ball will be advanced to the previous spot.

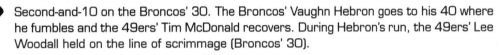

PLAY **1**   Second-and-10 on the Broncos' 30. The Broncos' Vaughn Hebron goes to his 40 where he fumbles and the 49ers' Tim McDonald recovers. During Hebron's run, the 49ers' Lee Woodall held on the line of scrimmage (Broncos' 30).

PLAY **2**   Second-and-10 on the Broncos' 30. The Broncos' Vaughn Hebron goes to his 40 where he fumbles and the 49ers' Tim McDonald recovers. During Hebron's run, the 49ers' Lee Woodall held on the Broncos' 45.

PLAY **3**   Second-and-10 on the Broncos' 30. Broncos' quarterback Bubby Brister scrambles to his 20, fumbles and the 49ers' Travis Jervey recovers. During Brister's scramble, the 49ers' Lee Woodall holds at the Broncos' 22.

Ruling 1: Penalize from the spot of the foul on change of possession. Broncos' ball first- and-10 on their 35.

Ruling 2: Enforce from the spot where Hebron lost possession as the foul was in advance of where Milburn lost possession. If the Broncos had been the only one to foul, the 49ers would refuse the penalty and keep the ball. Broncos' ball first-and-10 on their 45.

Ruling 3: Broncos' ball first-and-10 on their 30. See 14-1-13. Exc. 2

SUPPLEMENTAL NOTES

PASS AND KICK
ENFORCEMENTS

(1) A foul during a run prior to a kick or forward pass from behind the line, is enforced as if it had occurred during a pass or kick which follows. See 8-4-4, 8-3-2,3,4; 9-1-17, and 14-1-5.

(2) If an offensive player fouls behind the defensive goal line during a running play in which the runner crosses that line, the penalty is enforced from the spot where the runner crossed the goal line. See 7-3-7.

(3) After a penalty for a foul during a running play, the general provisions of 14-8-1, relative to the number of the ensuing down, always apply.

(4) Any foul prior to possession by a runner is enforced as otherwise specified.

PLAY **1** Second-and-10 on the Broncos' 30. The Broncos' Howard Griffith crosses the goal line. During Griffith's run:
a) the Broncos' Shannon Sharpe clips on the 49ers' 20.
b) Sharpe clips in the 49ers' end zone before Griffith crosses the goal line.
c) Sharpe clips on the 49ers' 10 after Griffith crosses the goal line.

Ruling a: Enforce from the spot of the foul. Broncos' ball first-and-10 on the 49ers' 35.

Ruling b: Enforcement is from the goal line. Broncos' ball first-and-10 on the 49ers' 15.

Ruling c: Touchdown. Kick off on the Broncos' 15.

SCORE AND
PERSONAL
FOUL OR
UNSPORTSMAN-
LIKE CONDUCT
FOUL BY
OPPONENT

Article 14 If a team scores and the opponent commits a personal or unsportsmanlike conduct foul or a palpably unfair act during the down, the penalty is enforced on the succeeding free kick unless the enforcement resulted in the score.

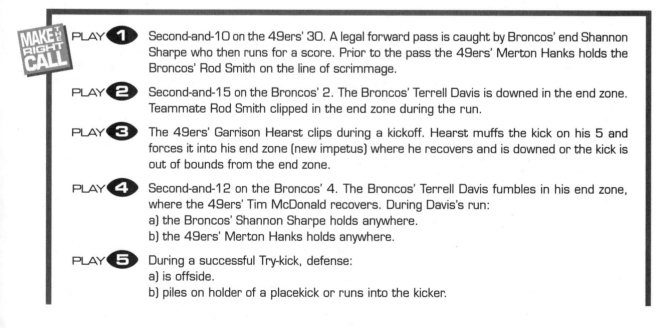

PLAY **1** Second-and-10 on the 49ers' 30. A legal forward pass is caught by Broncos' end Shannon Sharpe who then runs for a score. Prior to the pass the 49ers' Merton Hanks holds the Broncos' Rod Smith on the line of scrimmage.

PLAY **2** Second-and-15 on the Broncos' 2. The Broncos' Terrell Davis is downed in the end zone. Teammate Rod Smith clipped in the end zone during the run.

PLAY **3** The 49ers' Garrison Hearst clips during a kickoff. Hearst muffs the kick on his 5 and forces it into his end zone (new impetus) where he recovers and is downed or the kick is out of bounds from the end zone.

PLAY **4** Second-and-12 on the Broncos' 4. The Broncos' Terrell Davis fumbles in his end zone, where the 49ers' Tim McDonald recovers. During Davis's run:
a) the Broncos' Shannon Sharpe holds anywhere.
b) the 49ers' Merton Hanks holds anywhere.

PLAY **5** During a successful Try-kick, defense:
a) is offside.
b) piles on holder of a placekick or runs into the kicker.

Ruling 1: Touchdown. Kick off on the Broncos' 30. No enforcement of penalty as it was not a personal foul but defensive holding.

Ruling 2: Safety. Free kick from the Broncos' 10. The personal foul is penalized from the succeeding spot (Broncos' 20) as the foul did not result in a score.

Ruling 3: Safety. The 49ers free kick from their 10 as the penalty is also enforced for the clip from the succeeding spot (49ers' 20). The Broncos have the choice to rekick from their 45 if they refuse the other option.

Ruling 4a: Touchdown 49ers. Kickoff at the 49ers' 30.

Ruling 4b: Enforce from the goal line. Broncos' ball first-and-10 on their 5. (14-1-13).

Ruling 5a: Point awarded. Enforce five-yard penalty against defense on kickoff. See 11-3-3 or retry at defense's 1.

Ruling 5b: Point awarded. Enforce the penalty on the succeeding kickoff (11-3-e) or retry at defense's 1.

Section 2   Location of Foul

HALF
DISTANCE
PENALTY

Article 1   If a distance penalty, enforced from a specific spot between the goal lines would place the ball more than half the distance to the offender's goal line, the penalty shall be half the distance from that spot to their goal line.

NOTE: THIS GENERAL RULE SUPERSEDES ANY OTHER GENERAL OR SPECIFIC RULE OTHER THAN FOR A PALPABLY UNFAIR ACT OR THE ENFORCEMENT FOR INTENTIONAL GROUNDING, IF APPROPRIATE.

PLAY **1**   Second-and-20 on the Steelers' 24. A legal forward pass is caught by Lions' end Herman Moore on the Steelers' 12 and he runs to the Steelers' 10. A Steelers' player roughed the passer.

Ruling 1: Half the distance from the end of the run. Lions' ball first-and-goal on the Steelers' 5.

LOCATION OF
FOUL

Article 2

(a) If a foul occurs behind a goal line during a down, the penalty shall be enforced as provided for under the specific running play, pass or fumble rule involved.

(b) If a foul occurs between downs, enforcement is from the succeeding spot (14-5).

(c) If any enforcement leaves or places the ball behind a line, Rule 11, Section 3, 4, and 6 govern. See 14-1-11 and Note.

Section 3   Fouls by Both Teams

DOUBLE FOUL
WITHOUT
CHANGE OF
POSSESSION

Article 1   If there is a double foul (3-11-2-c) without a change of possession, the penalties are offset and the down is replayed at the previous spot. If it was a scrimmage down, the number of the next down and the necessary line is the same as for the down for which the new one is substituted.

PENALTY ENFORCEMENT

Exceptions:

15 YARDS VERSUS 5 YARDS

1) If one of the fouls is of a nature that incurs a 15-yard penalty and the other foul of a double foul normally would result in a loss of 5 yards *only* (15 yards versus 5 yards), the major penalty yardage is to be assessed from the previous spot.

NOTE: IF A SCORE OCCURS ON A PLAY THAT WOULD NORMALLY INVOLVE A 5 VS. 15 YARD ENFORCEMENT, ENFORCE THE MAJOR PENALTY FROM THE PREVIOUS SPOT.

2) Any disqualified player is removed immediately, even when one or both fouls are disqualifying or are disregarded otherwise. See 14-1-8.

DOUBLE FOUL DISQUALIFICATION

3) If both fouls involve disqualification, the down is replayed at the previous spot. If both fouls occur during the continuing action or are treated as such (14-1-8), the fouls are disregarded and the ball is next put in play at the succeeding spot. See Exception 1 in either case.

ILLEGAL TOUCHING AND FOUL

4) If the one foul by the kickers during a down is illegal touching of a scrimmage kick, the down is not replayed at the previous spot. The foul (illegal touching) by the kickers is disregarded provided the distance penalty for a foul by the receivers is enforced. If not enforced, the receivers next put the ball in play at any spot of illegal touching or at any other spot where they are entitled to possession at the end of the down.

NOTE: ANY FOUL BY EITHER TEAM AFTER A KICK ENDS IS ENFORCED AS ORDINARY. SEE 9-1-17.

MAKE THE RIGHT CALL

PLAY 1 Second-and-20 on the Lions' 30. The Lions' Ron Rivers goes to his 35. During the run the Lions' Herman Moore holds a Steelers' linebacker who punches Moore.

PLAY 2 Third-and-eight on the Steelers' 10. The Lions' Herman Moore is offside and a Steelers' linebacker slugs on the Steelers' 6 during the play. The Lions' Charlie Batch scored on the play.

PLAY 3 Second-and-10 on the Lions' 30. The Steelers' Jason Gildon is offside. The Lions' Ron Rivers goes to the Steelers' 30. During Rivers' run teammate Herman Moore clips at the 50.

PLAY 4 Second-and-10 on the Lions' 30. After the ball is dead anywhere a Lions' player and a Steelers' player strike each other with their fists during continuing action. Moore was downed on his 35.

PLAY 5 Fourth-and-10 on the Steelers' 18. A forward pass alights in the end zone, after which the Lions' Herman Moore clips. A Steelers' defensive lineman then strikes Moore.

PLAY 6 A kickoff is illegally out of bounds on the Steelers' 30. During continuing action:
a) The Lions' Mark Carrier clips and the Steelers' Hines Ward blocks below the waist.
b) The Lions' Mark Carrier clips and a Steelers' player punches Carrier.

Ruling 1: *Disqualify the Steelers' linebacker. Penalties offset. Lions' ball second-and-20 on their 30.*

Ruling 2: *Disqualify the Steelers' linebacker. Lions' ball first-and-goal on the Steelers' 5.*

Ruling 3: *Lions' ball second-and-25 on their 15. See 14-3-1, Exc. 1.*

Ruling 4: *Fouls are disregarded except for disqualifying both players. Lions' ball third- and-five on their 35.*

Ruling 5: Disqualify Steelers' defensive lineman. Steelers' ball first-and-10 on their 18.

Ruling 6a: Replay. A kickoff out of bounds is an offensive foul.

Ruling 6b: Lions rekick from the 30. Steelers' player disqualified.

DOUBLE FOUL WITH CHANGE OF POSSESSION (CLEAN HANDS)

Article 2   If there is a double foul (3-11-2-c) during a down (including kickoffs, punts, field goals, and safety kicks) in which there is a change of possession, the team gaining possession must keep the ball after enforcement for its foul, provided its foul occurred after the change of possession (clean hands).

If a score would result from a foul by a team gaining possession, the down is replayed at the previous spot.

If the team gaining possession fouls and loses possession, the penalties offset and the down is replayed at the previous spot.

DOUBLE FOUL PRIOR TO CHANGE OF POSSESSION (NOT CLEAN HANDS)

If the team gaining possession fouls prior to the change of possession (not clean hands), the penalties offset and the down is replayed at the previous spot.

DOUBLE FOUL AFTER CHANGE OF POSSESSION

Article 3   If a double foul occurs after a change in possession, the team in possession retains the ball at the spot where the team in possession's foul occurred so long as that spot is not in advance of the dead ball spot. In that event, ball is spotted at dead ball spot.

(a) If this spot is normally a touchback, the ball is placed on the 20-yard line.

(b) If normally a safety, place the ball on 1-yard line.

(c) This enforcement also applies if one of the fouls is a post-possession foul.

SUPPLEMENTAL NOTES

DOUBLE FOUL DISREGARDED

(1) When enforcement for a double foul is disregarded, the number of the next down, if a scrimmage down, is the same as if no foul had occurred. See 14-3-2.

(2) If there is a foul by the defensive team from the start of a snap until a legal forward pass ends, it is not treated as a double foul except as provided in 8-3-3,4.

(3) Change of possession refers to the physical change of possession from one team to the other except for kicks from scrimmage (9-1-17), and free kick (4-3-1- Note 4).

(4) If a team fouls before it gains possession on a double foul, it cannot score.

(5) Illegal touching, while technically a foul, does not offset a foul committed by its opponent. It is *not* considered part of a double foul. See 14-3-1-Exc. 4.

(6) If there is a continuing action foul by the defensive team after a legal forward pass becomes incomplete, both penalties are enforced. See 14-1-7.

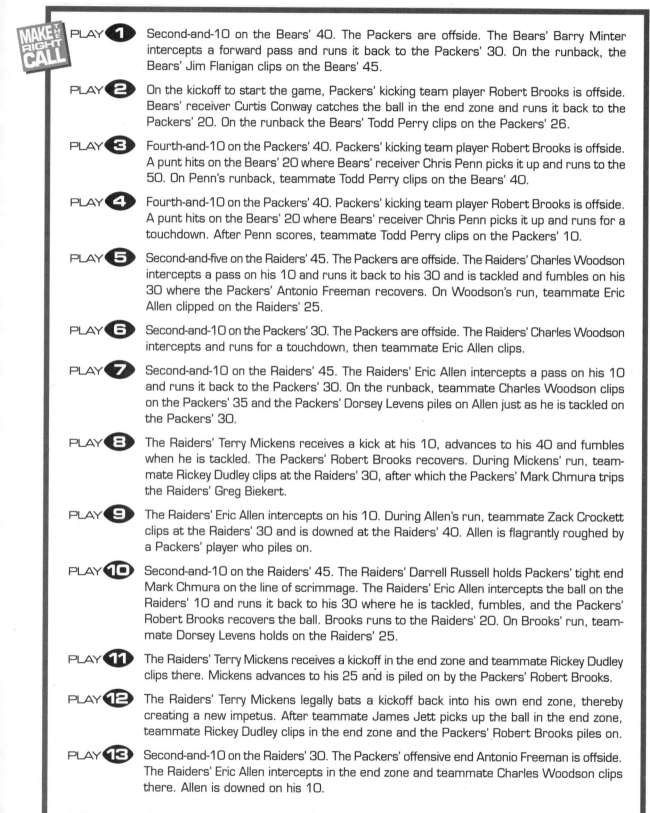

PLAY 1 Second-and-10 on the Bears' 40. The Packers are offside. The Bears' Barry Minter intercepts a forward pass and runs it back to the Packers' 30. On the runback, the Bears' Jim Flanigan clips on the Bears' 45.

PLAY 2 On the kickoff to start the game, Packers' kicking team player Robert Brooks is offside. Bears' receiver Curtis Conway catches the ball in the end zone and runs it back to the Packers' 20. On the runback the Bears' Todd Perry clips on the Packers' 26.

PLAY 3 Fourth-and-10 on the Packers' 40. Packers' kicking team player Robert Brooks is offside. A punt hits on the Bears' 20 where Bears' receiver Chris Penn picks it up and runs to the 50. On Penn's runback, teammate Todd Perry clips on the Bears' 40.

PLAY 4 Fourth-and-10 on the Packers' 40. Packers' kicking team player Robert Brooks is offside. A punt hits on the Bears' 20 where Bears' receiver Chris Penn picks it up and runs for a touchdown. After Penn scores, teammate Todd Perry clips on the Packers' 10.

PLAY 5 Second-and-five on the Raiders' 45. The Packers are offside. The Raiders' Charles Woodson intercepts a pass on his 10 and runs it back to his 30 and is tackled and fumbles on his 30 where the Packers' Antonio Freeman recovers. On Woodson's run, teammate Eric Allen clipped on the Raiders' 25.

PLAY 6 Second-and-10 on the Packers' 30. The Packers are offside. The Raiders' Charles Woodson intercepts and runs for a touchdown, then teammate Eric Allen clips.

PLAY 7 Second-and-10 on the Raiders' 45. The Raiders' Eric Allen intercepts a pass on his 10 and runs it back to the Packers' 30. On the runback, teammate Charles Woodson clips on the Packers' 35 and the Packers' Dorsey Levens piles on Allen just as he is tackled on the Packers' 30.

PLAY 8 The Raiders' Terry Mickens receives a kick at his 10, advances to his 40 and fumbles when he is tackled. The Packers' Robert Brooks recovers. During Mickens' run, teammate Rickey Dudley clips at the Raiders' 30, after which the Packers' Mark Chmura trips the Raiders' Greg Biekert.

PLAY 9 The Raiders' Eric Allen intercepts on his 10. During Allen's run, teammate Zack Crockett clips at the Raiders' 30 and is downed at the Raiders' 40. Allen is flagrantly roughed by a Packers' player who piles on.

PLAY 10 Second-and-10 on the Raiders' 45. The Raiders' Darrell Russell holds Packers' tight end Mark Chmura on the line of scrimmage. The Raiders' Eric Allen intercepts the ball on the Raiders' 10 and runs it back to his 30 where he is tackled, fumbles, and the Packers' Robert Brooks recovers the ball. Brooks runs to the Raiders' 20. On Brooks' run, teammate Dorsey Levens holds on the Raiders' 25.

PLAY 11 The Raiders' Terry Mickens receives a kickoff in the end zone and teammate Rickey Dudley clips there. Mickens advances to his 25 and is piled on by the Packers' Robert Brooks.

PLAY 12 The Raiders' Terry Mickens legally bats a kickoff back into his own end zone, thereby creating a new impetus. After teammate James Jett picks up the ball in the end zone, teammate Rickey Dudley clips in the end zone and the Packers' Robert Brooks piles on.

PLAY 13 Second-and-10 on the Raiders' 30. The Packers' offensive end Antonio Freeman is offside. The Raiders' Eric Allen intercepts in the end zone and teammate Charles Woodson clips there. Allen is downed on his 10.

Ruling 1: The Bears keep the ball as its foul was not prior to change of possession and foul enforced. Bears' ball first-and-10 on their 30.

Ruling 2: Bears' ball first-and-10 on the Packers' 41 (14-3-2).

Ruling 3: Bears' ball first-and-10 on their 25 (14-3-2).

Ruling 4: Touchdown Bears. Kickoff Bears' 15 (14-3-2).

Ruling 5: Packers' ball second-and-5 on the Raiders' 45 (14-3-2).

Ruling 6: Touchdown. Penalize the Raiders' on the kickoff. Kickoff from their 15-yard line as the foul did not result in a score.

Ruling 7: The Raiders retain ball at spot of its foul. Raiders' ball first-and-10 on the Packers' 35.

Ruling 8: Double foul following change of possession. Raiders' ball at spot of its foul, first-and-10 on the Raiders' 30.

Ruling 9: Packers' player disqualified. Raiders' ball first-and-10 on their 30.

Ruling 10: Packers keep the ball as they gained possession prior to their foul. Packers' ball first-and-10 on the Raiders' 35.

Ruling 11: Raiders' ball first-and-10 on their 1. See 14-3-3-b.

Ruling 12: Both fouls occurred after the Raiders gained possession. Normally, if this spot was in the end zone, the succeeding spot would be the Raiders' 20. In this case, Mickens created the impetus which would have resulted in a safety if the fouls had not been committed. The ball is transferred to the one-yard line. Raiders' ball first-and-10 on their 1. See 14-3-3-b.

Ruling 13: Replay. A score cannot result from one of the fouls of a double foul. Packers' ball second-and-10 on the Raiders' 30. See 14-3-2.

Section 4   Choice of Penalties

ONLY ONE
PENALTY
ENFORCED

If there is a multiple foul (3-11-2-b) or a foul and a forward pass violation by the same team during the same down, only one penalty may be enforced after the referee has explained the alternatives. The captain of the offended team shall make the choice.

Exceptions: A continuing action foul by:

1) passers after an incompletion or the team whose foul results in a touchback or safety, enforcement is from the succeeding spot.

2) kickers after a fair catch or interference with one, enforcement is from the succeeding spot.

3) kickers after a free kick is illegally out of bounds between the goal lines or is illegally recovered, enforcement is from the succeeding spot (6-3-1, Pen.).

DISQUALIFIED
PLAYER
REMOVED

NOTE: A DISQUALIFIED PLAYER IS ALWAYS REMOVED, REGARDLESS OF ANY CAPTAIN'S CHOICE. SEE 5-1-3 AND 5-1-5-A.

PLAY **1**   Second-and-10 on the Bills' 30. The Bills' Thurman Thomas goes to his 35. During the run, teammate Andre Reed clipped on the Bills' 30. The Bills were offside.

PLAY **2**   After a fair catch signal, receiver Steelers' Courtney Hawkins who did or did not signal, catches. After the catch he (a) comes to a reasonable stop or (b) unduly advances. In either case there is a foul after the catch.

PLAY **3** The Seahawks' Shawn Springs intercepts a pass in the end zone. He runs and is downed in the end zone. Teammate Chad Brown holds in the end zone during Springs' run. Teammate Cortez Kennedy clips after the ball is dead.

PLAY **4** The Seahawks' Ahman Green fumbles a punt on his 2-yard line. In attempting to recover in the end zone, he deliberately kicks the ball out of bounds behind the goal line.
   a) Seahawks' Shawn Springs clips on his 4 during the fumble.
   b) Springs clips on his 4 after the ball is out of bounds.

Ruling 1: *A multiple foul and only one penalty can be enforced. Option for defense. Bills' ball second-and-15 on their 25 or Bills' ball second-and-25 on their 15. If both declined, it is third-and-five on their 35.*

Ruling 2: *Enforcement is from the succeeding spot in either case. In (b) it is either a double or multiple foul.*

Ruling 3: *If the penalty for holding is declined, it is Seahawks' ball on its 10 (touchback minus 10). If the penalty for holding is enforced (which it would be), it is a safety and Seahawks free kick from their 10 (14-1-14).*

Ruling 4a: *If Chiefs accept the penalty for clipping, it is Seahawks' ball on their one-yard line. Otherwise, it is a safety. Safety kick from Seahawks' 10.*

Ruling 4b: *Safety. Seahawks' free kick from its 10 (14-1-14) (continuous action foul).*

Section 5   Time of Foul

TIME OF FOUL   If a foul occurs between downs (3-11-2-d), a distance penalty is enforced from the succeeding spot. If it is a continuing action foul (3-11-2-a) at the end of a play from scrimmage, a down is charged provided the ball is not dead in touch. See 14-1-7 to 10.

PLAY **1** Second-and-10 on the Bills' 30. The Bills' Thurman Thomas goes out of bounds on his 35, after which teammate Antowain Smith clips on the Bills' 30.

PLAY **2** Third-and-five on the Bills' 30. The Bills are offside and the Bills' Thurman Thomas fails to gain. Teammate Jay Riemersma clips just as the ball is declared dead.

PLAY **3** Fourth-and-10 on the Bills' 40. Bills' kicking team player Eric Moulds first touches and recovers a scrimmage kick on the Seahawks' 10:
   a) after an illegal recovery by Moulds, teammate Sam Gash roughs an opponent.
   b) after an illegal recovery by Moulds, the Seahawks' Shawn Springs roughs an opponent.

Ruling 1: *The down counts and enforce from the succeeding spot (14-1-7-b). Bills' ball third-and-20 on their 20.*

Ruling 2: *If defense declines both penalties, it is fourth-and-five on the Bills' 30. If the penalty for clipping is enforced, it is third-and-20 on the Bills' 15.*

Ruling 3a: *Seahawks' ball first-and-10 on their 25.*

Ruling 3b: *Seahawks' ball first-and-10 on their 5.*

SUPPLEMENTAL NOTES

CONTINUING
ACTION FOUL

(1) When a foul occurs simultaneously with an out of bounds or after a loose ball crosses the plane of the boundary line in the air and then first touches anything out of bounds, it is considered to be a continuing action foul.

FOUL AFTER
TOUCHDOWN

(2) The succeeding spot for a foul after a touchdown and before a whistle for a Try for point(s) is the next kickoff (3-11-2-d).

FOUL
BETWEEN
DOWNS

(3) The time between downs is the interval during all time outs (including intermissions) and from the time the ball is dead until it is next put in play (time in). See 3-36-1, 2.

DEFENSIVE
FOUL
CONTINUING
ACTION

(4) For a continuing action foul by the defensive team or by either team at the end of a play not from scrimmage, see 14-8-5 and 6.

SPECIAL
ENFORCEMENT
BETWEEN
DOWNS

(5) See 5-1-5-S.N. 2 for a special enforcement between downs.

MAKE THE RIGHT CALL

PLAY **1** Third-and-20 on Seahawks' 40. The Bills' Thurman Thomas is out of bounds on the Seahawks' 15, after which teammate Andre Reed clips on the Seahawks' 20.

PLAY **2** Third-and-10 on the Seahawks' 30. A forward pass is out of bounds on the Seahawks' 10, after which the Bills' Andre Reed clips on the Seahawks' 15.

PLAY **3** The Bills have made a first down and its captain calls time out for the fourth time in the half without making a substitution for an injured player.

PLAY **4** Seahawks' Joey Galloway catches a punt on his 30 and goes out of bounds on the Seahawks' 40, after which teammate Cortez Kennedy clips on the Seahawks' 35.

PLAY **5** Second-and-15 on the Bills' 30. The Bills' Thurman Thomas steps out of bounds on his 40, after which teammate Andre Reed clips on 50.

PLAY **6** Second-and-15 on the Bills' 30. The Bills' Thurman Thomas steps out of bounds on the 50, after which teammate Andre Reed clips on his 40.

Ruling 1: The Bills had made its first down, and as it was a continuing action foul, enforce from the succeeding spot (14-1-7-b). Bills' ball first-and-25 on the Seahawks' 30.

Ruling 2: Bills' ball fourth-and-25 on the Seahawks' 45.

Ruling 3: Bills' ball first-and-15.

Ruling 4: Continuing action foul (14-1-7-b). Seahawks' ball first-and-10 on their 25. Also see 14-8-6.

Ruling 5: Enforce from the dead ball spot (Bills' 40)(14-1-7). Bills' ball third-and-20 on their 25.

Ruling 6: Enforce from dead ball spot (50)(14-1-7). First-and-25 on the Bills' 35.

Section 6   Refusal of Penalties

REFUSAL OF
PENALTIES

Penalties for all fouls, unless otherwise expressly provided for, may be declined by the Captain of the offended team, in which case play proceeds as though no foul had been committed.

NOTE: THE YARDAGE DISTANCE FOR ANY PENALTY MAY BE DECLINED, EVEN THOUGH THE PENALTY IS ACCEPTED.

PLAY ❶ Second-and-10 on the Bills' 30. A legal forward pass is completed to Bills' end Andre Reed on his 45 where he is downed. The Seahawks' Shawn Springs held Bills' flanker Eric Moulds on the Bills' 35 prior to the pass.

Ruling 1: Declines holding penalty which would have been five yards from the previous spot and a first down. Bills' ball first-and-10 on their 45.

Exceptions:

DISQUALIFICA-
TION FOUL
REMOVES
PLAYER

1) A disqualified or suspended player is always removed, even when an accompanying distance penalty is declined, or when a penalty for another foul is chosen (multiple foul).

2) During a down a foul occurs (includes an incomplete forward pass) for which the ball is dead immediately.

3) The penalty for certain illegal actions prior to or pertaining to a snap or to a free kick may not be declined, i.e., the ball remains dead.

    a) 40/25-second violations (4-3-9).

    b) Snap made before the referee can assume his normal stance (7-3-3-c-2).

DISTANCE
PENALTY
DECLINED

4) When a 40/25-second penalty occurs prior to the snap, the defensive team may decline a distance penalty, in which case the down is replayed from the previous spot.

5) If fouls are committed by both teams during the same down (double foul), no penalty may be declined, except as provided for kickers when their only foul is illegal touching of a scrimmage kick. See 14-3-1-Exception 4.

6) If the defensive team commits a foul during an unsuccessful try, the offensive team may decline the distance penalty and the down is replayed from the previous spot.

PLAY ❶ Second-and-10 on the Bills' 30. On a legal forward pass the Seahawks' Shawn Springs interferes with Bills' eligible end Andre Reed on the Seahawks' 40 where the ball falls incomplete. A Seahawks' player strikes the Bills' Jay Riemersma on the line of scrimmage.

PLAY ❷ During time in, the Bills' Eric Moulds illegally recovers a kick, unduly advances, and fumbles. The Seahawks' Joey Galloway recovers and advances beyond the spot where the penalty for delay by Moulds would place the ball.

Ruling 1: Disqualify the Seahawks' player although the penalty for interference is taken. Bills' ball first-and-10 on the Seahawks' 40.

Ruling 2: Seahawks may not decline the penalty as ball is dead when Moulds recovers.

Section 7   On Incomplete Forward Pass

ILLEGAL
FORWARD
PASS AND
INCOMPLETE
FORWARD
PASS

An illegal forward pass is a foul, but an incomplete forward pass is not classed as a foul and the penalties provided therefore may not be declined.

Exception: If a team commits a foul during the same play in which it makes an incomplete forward pass, the captain of the offended team may elect which of the penalties is to be enforced (14-4).

NOTE: IF THERE IS A CONTINUING ACTION FOUL BY EITHER TEAM AFTER AN INCOMPLETION, ENFORCEMENT IS FROM THE SUCCEEDING SPOT. SEE 14-5.

Section 8   Number of Down After Penalty

NUMBER OF
DOWN AFTER
PENALTY

Article 1   After a distance penalty (not combined with a loss-of-down penalty) for a foul by the offensive team prior to (between downs) or during a play from scrimmage which results in the ball being in its possession behind the necessary line, the number of the ensuing down is the same as that of the down before which or during which the foul occurred.

COMBINATION
PENALTY

Article 2   A combination penalty involving both distance and loss of down is enforced for certain forward pass fouls by the offensive team.

LOSS OF
DISTANCE AND
DOWN

Examples: Loss of Distance and Down

(a) from beyond the line (8-1-1, Penalty, c); or

(b) intentionally grounded (8-3-1).

NOTE: AFTER A LOSS-OF-DOWN PENALTY (PRIOR TO FOURTH DOWN), THE NUMBER OF THE ENSUING DOWN IS ONE GREATER THAN THAT OF THE PREVIOUS DOWN. IF IT OCCURS ON FOURTH DOWN, IT IS LOSS OF THE BALL TO THE DEFENSIVE TEAM UNLESS IT IS A COMBINATION PENALTY, IN WHICH CASE THE DISTANCE PENALTY IS ENFORCED IN ADDITION TO THE LOSS OF THE BALL. SEE 8-1-1 AND S.N. 4.

FOUL AND
CHANGE OF
POSSESSION

Article 3   When a foul occurs during a play from scrimmage, the necessary line remains the same regardless of any change of team possession thereafter.

PLAY **1**   Second-and-10 on the Bills' 30. Bills are offside. A legal forward pass is intercepted by the Falcons' Eugene Robinson on the 50. Robinson runs to the Bills' 40, fumbles, and the Bills' Antowain Smith recovers there.

Ruling 1: Bills' ball second-and-15 on their 25. (If Falcons refused the penalty, it would have been Bills' ball first-and-10 on their 40).

ADVANCE OF
NECESSARY
LINE FIRST-
AND -10

Article 4   After a distance penalty for a foul by the offensive team during a play from scrimmage which results in the ball being in advance of the necessary line, it is a first-and-10 for the offensive team.

Articles 4 and 6 also apply to a continuing action foul of the offensive team at the end of a play from scrimmage during which it has been constantly in possession. For exceptions, see 14-1-7.

PLAY 1 Second-and-4 on the Bills' 30. The Bills' Thurman Thomas goes to the Seahawks' 45. During the run, teammate Andre Reed clipped on the 50.

Ruling 1: After the penalty, the ball is still in advance of the necessary line for the first down. Bills' ball first-and-10 on their 35.

DEFENSIVE FOUL FIRST-AND-10 FOR OFFENSE

DEFENSIVE FOUL AND NO FIRST DOWN

Article 5   After a penalty for a foul by the defense prior to (between downs) or during a play from scrimmage, the ensuing down is first-and-10 for the offense.

Exceptions are:

1) offside;
2) encroachment;
3) neutral zone infraction;
4) delay of game;
5) illegal substitution;
6) excess time out;
7) running into kicker; and
8) incidental facemask.

In the above eight exceptions the number of the down and the necessary line remain the same unless a distance penalty places the ball on or in advance of that line, in which case it is first-and-10 for A.

PLAY 1 Second-and-15 on the Bills' 30. The Bills' Thurman Thomas is downed on his 35. During the run the Seahawks' Cortez Kennedy held on the line of scrimmage.

PLAY 2 Third-and-goal on the Seahawks' 4. The forward rod of the chains is one yard past the goal line. The Seahawks are offside and the Bills' Thurman Thomas gains one yard.

Ruling 1: Bills' ball first-and-10 on their 40.

Ruling 2: Bills' ball third-and-goal on the Seahawks' 2 (14-2-1).

FOUL AFTER
CHANGE OF
POSSESSION

Article 6 After a distance penalty for a foul which occurs during a play after team possession has changed following a snap or free kick, it is first-and-10 for the team that was in possession at the time of the foul or at the time of the continuing action foul.

MAKE THE RIGHT CALL

PLAY **1** On a kickoff the Seahawks' Joey Galloway runs to his 45 where he steps out of bounds, after which teammate Cortez Kennedy clips on the 50.

Ruling 1: Seahawks' ball first-and-10 on their 30.

ENFORCEMENT
AND FIRST-
AND-10

Article 7 After a loss of ball penalty, it is first-and-10 for the offended team after enforcement, unless the offended team free kicks following the fair catch interference.

NOTE: LOSS OF BALL RESULTS ONLY FROM ILLEGAL TOUCHING OF KICK (OTHER THAN A FREE KICK) OR A FAIR CATCH INTERFERENCE. SEE 6-2-4 AND 10-1-4.

MAKE THE RIGHT CALL

PLAY **1** Second-and-10 on the Bills' 30. The Falcons' Eugene Robinson intercepts a legal forward pass on the Bills' 40. He fumbles and the Bills' Andre Reed recovers on his 25. Reed runs to his 45. During Reed's run teammate Eric Moulds clipped on the 50.

Ruling 1: Bills' ball first-and-10 on their 30 (change of possession).

MAKE THE RIGHT CALL

CHAPTER 15
OFFICIALS

To make correct calls you've got to be in the correct position.

An official in one position may be able to help another make a call — let's say the play moves downfield and the covering official gets tied up pursuing the play. If the runner pitches the ball forward — an illegal pass — maybe an official from across the field might have a better line of vision to make that call.

Jerry Seeman
NFL DIRECTOR OF OFFICIATING

Section 1   Officials

OFFICIALS'
MANUALS

Article 1   By League action, the officials' manual is an integral part of the Official rules, especially in regard to the specific duties, mechanics and procedures for each official during any play situations. For that reason, many such specific items are omitted in Sections 1 to 7 to avoid needless repetition, and only the primary duties of each official are stated. Some of the technical terms used hereafter are defined only in the manual.

NOTE: THE TERMS "ON BALL" OR "COVER" IMPLY THAT AN OFFICIAL IS NEAREST OR IN CLOSE PROXIMITY TO A LOOSE BALL OR RUNNER AND IS IN POSITION TO DECLARE THE BALL DEAD WHEN THE DOWN ENDS BY RULE. SEE 15-1-11-S.N.

GAME
OFFICIALS

Article 2   The game Officials are: referee, umpire, head linesman, line judge, back judge, side judge, and field judge.

NOTE: IN THE ABSENCE OF SEVEN OFFICIALS, THE CREW IS TO BE REARRANGED, ON THE MOST FEASIBLE BASIS, ACCORDING TO THE OTHER MEMBERS OF CREW.

Article 3   All officials are to wear uniforms prescribed by the League (including a black cap with visor and piping for all except the Referee, who will wear a white cap). All officials will carry a whistle and a weighted bright gold flag.

SOUND
WHISTLE

Article 4   An official is to sound his whistle:

(a) for any foul for which ball remains dead or is dead immediately;

(b) to signal time out at end of a down, during which he has indicated a foul, by means of dropping his flag and provided no other official signalled time out at end of down;

(c) to indicate dead ball when he is covering a runner. See 7-4-1, 2, 3, 4, 5;

(d) at any other time, when he is nearest to ball, when a down ends. See 15-8-3.

NOTE: THE FLAG IS TO BE USED TO INDICATE A FOUL. SEE 7-4-5-NOTE.

CREW
MEETING

Article 5   Members of the crew are required to meet in their dressing quarters at least 2 hours and 15 minutes before game time.

OFFICIALS'
DRESSING
ROOM

NOTE: BY ORDER OF THE COMMISSIONER, FROM ANY TIME ANY OFFICIAL FIRST ENTERS THE DRESSING ROOM, AND UNTIL ALL OFFICIALS HAVE LEFT IT AT THE END OF THE GAME, NO PERSON OTHER THAN CLUBHOUSE ATTENDANTS OR THOSE INDIVIDUALS INVITED BY THE REFEREE SHALL BE ALLOWED TO ENTER IT. THIS PROHIBITION INCLUDES COACHES, PLAYERS, OWNERS, AND OTHER MANAGEMENT PERSONNEL.

OFFICIALS'
RESPONSIBILITY
AND CREW
CONFERENCE

Article 6   All officials are responsible for any decision involving the application of a rule, its interpretation or an enforcement. If an official errs in his interpretation of a rule, the other officials must check him before play is resumed, otherwise they are equally responsible. In the event of a disagreement, the crew should draw aside for a conference.

NOTE: IF BECAUSE OF INJURY, THE OFFICIALS' VOTE IS TIED, REFEREE'S DECISION WILL BE THE DECIDING FACTOR. ANY DISSENTING OPINION IS TO BE REPORTED TO THE SUPERVISOR.

Article 7   All officials have concurrent jurisdiction over any foul, and there is no fixed territorial division in this respect. When an official signals a foul, he must report it to referee, informing him of its nature, position of ball at time of foul, the offender (when known), the penalty and spot of enforcement.

RECORDING
FOULS

Article 8   Each official is to record every foul he signals and the total number of officials signalling the same foul. During the game, these are to be recorded on white game cards provided by league. They are to be preserved after each game in case they should be needed to revise an officials final game card.

LEAGUE
GAME
REPORTS

Article 9   At the end of the game the officials are to record their own fouls on the yellow game cards provided by the league, and are to check them with other officials, for duplications, before leaving the dressing room.

NOTE: BOTH WHITE AND YELLOW GAME CARDS ARE TO BE MADE OUT IN ACCORDANCE WITH THE YEARLY BULLETIN ISSUED FOR THAT PURPOSE.

CREW ERRORS

Article 10 All members of a crew are equally responsible for any errors in Officiating Mechanics as prescribed by the Manual and are required to call the attention of this fact to an official who had been remiss.

NOTE: THIS APPLIES TO SUCH ERRORS, IN MECHANICS OR APPLICATIONS OF RULES, AS TEND TO INCREASE THE LENGTH OF THE GAME (ELAPSED TIME) AND PARTICULARLY SO TO THOSE WHICH RESULT IN UNDUE LOSS OF PLAYING TIME (CREW TIME). IN THE LATTER CASE, IF THE REFEREE HAS CLEARLY FAILED TO SIGNAL A REFEREE'S TIME OUT AS SPECIFIED BY RULE, ANY OFFICIAL SHOULD DO SO. SEE 4-3-7 AND 4-3-9.

COIN TOSS

Article 11 Ten minutes before the opening kickoff, the entire crew is to appear on the field. Three minutes prior to the kickoff, the referee is to make the toss of the coin. He is to indicate which team is to receive and is to do the same when teams first appear on the field prior to the start of the second half. See 4-2-1 and S.N.

NOTE: ALL OFFICIALS RECORD RESULTS OF COIN TOSS AND OPTIONS CHOSEN.

SUPPLEMENTAL NOTES

(1) During any running play (includes runbacks), or a loose ball, the nearest official is to cover and remain with the ball or runner, unless outdistanced until end of down. In such case any nearer official is to cover. See 15-2-9-Note, for referee entering a side zone and 15-3-4 for umpire.

(2) When a ball is dead inbounds near a sideline, during time in, the official covering is to use the clock signal to indicate this fact.

(3) Any officials not involved in an enforcement are to see that all players other than captains remain aside during any conference between referee and captains. See 15-2-5.

RECORDING TIME OUTS

Article 12 All officials must record charged team time outs.

Section 2   Referee

REFEREE AUTHORITY

Article 1   The referee is to have general oversight and control of game. He is the final authority for the score, and the number of a down in case of a disagreement. His decisions upon all matters not specifically placed under the jurisdiction of other officials, either by rule or the officials' manual, are to be final. See 15-1-6, Note, and 15-1-10.

Article 2   Prior to the kickoff to start each half and after every time out, the referee shall sound his whistle for play to start without asking captains if they are ready. In such cases where time is in with his whistle, he is to indicate it by use of clock signal.

BALL PUT IN PLAY

Article 3   He is to see that the ball is properly put in play and shall decide on all matters pertaining to its position and disposition at end of down. If any official sounds his whistle, the ball is dead (7-4-1). In case the referee is informed or believes that ball was dead before such signal or down ends, he has the authority to make a retroactive ruling after consulting the crew or the official involved.

Article 4   The referee must notify the coach and field captain when their team has used its three charged time outs, signal both coaches when two minutes remain in a half, and positively inform the coach of any disqualified player. He may not delegate any such notifications to any other person. He will announce on the microphone when each period is ended. See 4-3-8-Exception.

FOUL OPTIONS

Article 5   After a foul, the referee (in the presence of both captains) must announce the penalty and explain to the offended captain the decision and choice (if any) as well as number of next down and distance (usually approximate) to necessary line for any possible positions of ball. See 7-1-2. The referee is to designate the offending player, when known. After an enforcement (7-3-2) he shall signal to spectators the nature of penalty by means of the visual signals specifically provided for herein.

NOTE: IT IS NOT NECESSARY FOR THE REFEREE TO EXPLAIN TO BOTH CAPTAINS THE DECISION AND DISTANCE TO THE NECESSARY LINE IN SUCH CASES WHEN: THE ENFORCEMENT IS ENTIRELY AUTOMATIC AND/OR WHEN THERE IS OBVIOUSLY NO CHOICE.

FIELD CAPTAINS ONLY MAY APPEAL TO REFEREE, AND THEN SOLELY ON QUESTIONS OF INTERPRETATION OF THE RULES. THEY SHALL NOT BE ALLOWED TO QUESTION THE JUDGMENT OF JURISDICTION OF ANY PARTICULAR OFFICIAL IN REGARD TO A FOUL OR IN SIGNALLING DEAD BALL.

REFEREE'S POSITION

Article 6 Prior to the snap, the referee shall assume such a stance that he is in the clear of and behind any backfield player. This is also to be construed as including the normal path of any player in motion behind the line as well as the line of vision between such a player and the maker of a pass (forward or backward). He shall also favor the right side (if the passer is right-handed). He will count offensive players.

MEASUREMENT

Article 7 At the end of any down, the referee may (when in doubt or at the request of a captain unless obviously unnecessary) request the linesman and his assistants to bring the yardage chains on field to determine whether the ball has reached the necessary line. See 4-3-10-S.N. 3.

Article 8 Prior to each snap, the referee is to positively check the number of the ensuing down and distance to be gained with the linesman, signal the field judge when to start his watch for the timing of 25 seconds (when appropriate), and know the eligible pass receivers.

SPOTTING BALL

Article 9 He is primarily responsible for spotting the ball at the inbounds spot on plays from scrimmage, and should not enter a side zone to cover a runner (other than the quarterback) when the linesman, back judge or line judge is in position to do so. See 15-1-11-S.N. 1.

NOTE: WHEN THE BALL IS DEAD NEAR THE SIDELINE DURING TIME IN, HE IS NOT TO ASSIST IN A RELAY TO THE INBOUNDS SPOT, UNLESS THE UMPIRE HAS BEEN REMISS OR DELAYED IN DOING SO (15-1-10- NOTE, AND 15-3-4). IN SUCH A CASE, THE UMPIRE IS TO SPOT. SEE RULE 2, NOTE IN REGARD TO USING A NEW BALL AT START OF SECOND AND FOURTH PERIODS IN CASE OF A WET BALL.

Section 3   Umpire

Article 1 The umpire has primary jurisdiction over the equipment and the conduct and actions of players on the scrimmage line.

EQUIPMENT INSPECTION

Article 2 Before the game, the umpire with assistance of other officials shall inspect the equipment of players. He may order any changes he deems necessary to any proposed equipment which is considered dangerous or confusing (5-3). This authority extends throughout the game.

Article 3 He shall assist in relaying the ball:

(a) to the inbounds spot when it is dead near a sideline during time in when feasible (15-2-9-Note);

(b) to the previous spot after an incompletion; and

(c) to the spot of a free kick when indicated. See 15-1-11-S.N.

DUTIES OF UMPIRE

Article 4 The umpire shall record:

(a) all charged team time outs during the game;

(b) the winner of the toss; and

(c) the score.

He is to assist the referee on decisions involving possession of the ball in close proximity to the line, after a loose ball or runner has crossed it. He and the linesman are to determine whether ineligible linesmen illegally cross the line prior to a pass, and he must wipe a wet ball in accordance with the proper timing. He should count the offensive players on the field at the snap.

Section 4   Linesman

LINESMAN POSITION

Article 1   The linesman operates on the side of field designated by the referee during the first half and on opposite side during the second half unless ordered otherwise. See 1-4, Note for exception.

Article 2   He is responsible for illegal motion, offside, encroaching, and any actions pertaining to scrimmage line prior to or at snap; and for covering in his side zone. See 15-1-11-S.N. 1, 15-2-9 and 15-3-4. He will count offensive players.

Article 3   Prior to the game, he shall see that his chain crew is properly instructed as to their specific duties and mechanics.

> NOTE: EACH HOME TEAM APPOINTS THE OFFICIAL CHAIN CREW (BOXMAN, TWO RODMEN AND ALTERNATE, DRIVE START AND FORWARD STAKE INDICATOR) SUBJECT TO APPROVAL BY THE LEAGUE OFFICE. EACH MEMBER CARRIES A WORKING PASS TO THAT EFFECT AND IT IS PROHIBITED FOR ANYONE ELSE TO WORK AS SUCH. THE STANDARDIZED YARDAGE CHAINS AND DOWNS BOX MUST BE USED AND IF ANY OTHERS ARE FURNISHED THIS FACT IS TO BE REPORTED TO THE COMMISSIONER.

Article 4   The linesman shall use a clamp on the chain when measuring for first down.

MARKING AND CHAINS

Article 5   The linesman is to mark with his foot (when up with ball) the yard line touched by forward point of ball at end of each scrimmage down. At the start of each new series of downs, he and the rodmen set the yardage chains when the referee so signals. He positively must check with the referee as to the number of each down that is about to start.

> NOTE: IT IS MANDATORY FOR LINESMAN TO PERSONALLY SEE THAT REAR ROD IS ACCURATELY SET AND ALSO TO SEE THAT THE FORWARD RODMAN AND BOXMAN HAVE SET THE SAFETY MARKERS FOR THE FORWARD ROD AND THE PREVIOUS SPOT, DURING ANY SERIES OF DOWNS, AS PRESCRIBED BY THE OFFICIALS' MANUAL.

LINESMAN DUTIES

Article 6   On his own side, he is to assist the line judge as to illegal motion or a shift and umpire in regard to holding or illegal use of hands on end of line (especially during kicks or passes), and know eligible pass receivers.

Article 7   He and the umpire are to determine whether ineligible linemen illegally cross the line prior to a pass. He is to mark out of bounds spot on his side of field when within his range and is to supervise substitutions made by team seated on his side of field during either half.

> NOTE: SEE 15-1-11-S.N. 1, 15-2-9 AND 15-3-4.

Section 5   Line Judge

LINE JUDGE DUTIES

Article 1   The line judge is to operate on side of field opposite the linesman.

Article 2   He is responsible for the timing of game. He also is responsible for illegal motion, illegal shift, and for covering in his side zone. See 15-1-11-S.N. 1 and 15-2-9. He will count offensive players.

Article 3   He is responsible for supervision of the timing and in case the game clock becomes inoperative, or for any other reason is not being operated correctly, he shall take over the official timing on the field.

Article 4   He is to time each period and intermission between halves (4-1-3, 4), signal the referee when two minutes remain in a half and leave in ample time with the back judge to notify their respective teams of five minutes before the start of the second half.

Article 5   He shall advise the referee when time has expired at end of a period.

Article 6   He must notify both captains, through the referee, of the time remaining for play not more than 10 or less than five minutes before the end of each half and must signal referee when two minutes remain in each half.

> NOTE: UPON INQUIRY OF A FIELD CAPTAIN, HE MAY STATE THE APPROXIMATE TIME REMAINING FOR PLAY AT ANY TIME DURING THE GAME, PROVIDED HE DOES NOT COMPLY WITH SUCH REQUEST MORE THAN THREE TIMES DURING THE LAST FIVE MINUTES OF EITHER HALF, AND PROVIDED IT WILL NOT AFFECT PLAYING TIME NEAR THE END OF A HALF (4-3-10).

Article 7   On his own side, he is to:

(a) assist the linesman as to offside or encroaching;

(b) assist the umpire as to holding or illegal use of hands on the end of the line (especially during kicks or passes);

(c) assist the referee as to forward laterals behind the line and false starts; and

(d) be responsible for knowing the eligible pass receivers.

Article 8   He is to:

(a) mark the out of bounds spot of all plays on his side, when within his range (see 15-1-11-S.N. and 15-2-9);

(b) supervise substitutions made by the team seated on his side of the field during either half (see 5-2-1);

NOTIFY HOME
TEAM COACH

(c) notify the home team head coach with the back judge five minutes before the start of the second half.

Section 6   Back Judge

BACK JUDGE'S
POSITION AND
DUTIES

Article 1   The back judge will operate on the same side of the field as line judge, 20 yards deep.

Article 2   The back judge shall count the number of defensive players on the field at the snap.

Article 3   He shall be responsible for all eligible receivers on his side of the field.

Article 4   After receivers have cleared line of scrimmage, the back judge will concentrate on action in the area between the umpire and field judge. Be aware of "trapped balls" in this vital area.

Article 5   In addition to the specified use of the whistle by all officials (15-1-4), the back judge is also to use his whistle when upon his positive knowledge he knows:

(a) that ball is dead;

(b) that time is out;

(c) that time is out at the end of a down, during which a foul was signaled by a marker, no whistle has sounded in such cases; and

(d) that even in the presence of a whistle up or down field, he is to sound his whistle when players are some distance from such signal. This will help prevent continuing action fouls.

Article 6   The back judge will assist referee in decisions involving any catching, recovery, out of bounds spot, or illegal touching, of a loose ball, after it has crossed scrimmage line and particularly so for such actions that are out of the range of the line judge and umpire. See 15-1-11, S.N. 1.

POSITION ON
FIELD GOAL
ATTEMPT
AND TRY

Article 7   On field goal attempts or try-kick attempts, the back judge will station himself on the end line and cover the upright opposite the field judge. He, along with the field judge, is responsible for indication to the referee whether the kick is high enough and through the uprights.

Section 7   Side Judge

SIDE JUDGE'S
POSTION AND
DUTIES

Article 1   The side judge will operate on the same side of the field as the head linesman, 20 yards deep.

Article 2   The side judge shall count the number of defensive players on the field at the snap.

Article 3   He shall be responsible for all eligible receivers on his side of the field.

Article 4   After receivers have cleared line of scrimmage, the side judge will concentrate on action in the area between the umpire and field judge. Be aware of "trapped balls" in this vital area.

Article 5   In addition to the specified use of the whistle by all officials (15-1-4), the side judge is also to use his whistle when upon his positive knowledge he knows:
- (a) that ball is dead;
- (b) that time is out;
- (c) that time is out at the end of a down, during which a foul was signaled by a marker, no whistle has sounded in such cases; and
- (d) that even in the presence of a whistle up or down field, he is to sound his whistle when players are some distance from such signal. This will help prevent continuing action fouls.

Article 6   The side judge will assist referee in decisions involving any catching, recovery, out of bounds spot, or illegal touching, of a loose ball, after it has crossed scrimmage line and particularly so for such actions that are out of the range of the head linesman and umpire.

Article 7   The side judge will line up in a position laterally from the umpire on punts, field goals, and try-kick attempts.

Section 8   Field Judge

DUTIES OF
FIELD JUDGE

Article 1   The field judge is primarily responsible in regard to: covering kicks from scrimmage (unless a try-kick) or forward passes crossing the defensive goal line and all such loose balls, out of the range of umpire, back judge and linesman, noting an illegal substitution or withdrawal during dead ball with time in (see 5-2-1-Notes), and a foul signalled by a flag or cap during down. He will count defensive team.

Article 2   He is to time the intermission between the two periods of each half (4-1-2), the length of all team time outs (4-3-4-S.N. 1 and 2), and the 40/25 seconds permitted Team A to put ball in play (4-3-10-S.N. 1). He is to utilize the 40/25 second clock provided for by the home team. If this clock is inoperative he should take over the official timing of the 40/25 seconds on the field.

Article 3   In addition to the specified use of the whistle by all officials (15-1-4), the Field Judge is also to use his whistle, when upon his own positive knowledge he knows:

(a) that ball is dead;

(b) time is out; or

(c) is out at end of down, during which a foul was signalled by a flag or cap, and no whistle has sounded in such cases.

Even in the presence of a whistle upfield, he is to sound his when downfield players are some distance away from such signal, and in order to prevent continuing action fouls. He should be particularly alert for item (c).

Article 4   He shall assist the referee in decisions involving any catching, recovery, out of bounds spot, or illegal touching, of a loose ball, after it has crossed scrimmage line and particularly so for such actions as are out of the range of the back judge, linesman and umpire. See 15-1-11-S.N. 1. He should count the defensive players on the field at the snap.

Article 5   The field judge has the absolute responsibility:

(a) to instruct kicker and/or placekicker that "kickoff" *must* be made by placekick or dropkick.

(b) that the height of the tee (artificial or natural) used for the kickoff conforms to the governing rules.

NOTE: HE IS TO NOTIFY THE VISITING TEAM AT LEAST FIVE MINUTES BEFORE THE START OF THE SECOND HALF.

NOTIFY
VISITING
TEAM COACH

INSTANT
REPLAY

Section 9   Instant Replay

For 1999 only, the League will employ a system of Referee Replay Review to aid officiating for reviewable plays as defined below. Prior to the two-minute warning of each half, a Coaches' Challenge System will be in effect. After the two-minute warning of each half, and throughout any overtime period, a Referee Review will be initiated by a Replay Assistant from a Replay Booth comparable to the location of the coaches' booth or Press Box. The following procedures will be used:

Coaches' Challenge. In each game, a team will be permitted a maximum of two challenges that will initiate Referee Replay reviews. Each challenge will require the use of a team timeout. If a challenge is upheld, the timeout will be restored to the challenging team, but a challenge will never be restored. No challenges will be recognized from a team that has exhausted its timeouts.

Replay Assistant's Request for Review. After the two-minute warning of each half, and throughout any overtime period, any Referee Review will be initiated by a Replay Assistant. There is no limit to the number of Referee Reviews that may be initiated by the Replay Assistant. His ability to initiate a review will be unrelated to the number of timeouts that either team has remaining, and no timeout will be charged for any review initiated by the Replay Assistant.

CHAPTER 16
SUDDEN DEATH

In the regular season, the sudden death period is one 15-minute period in which the first team to score wins. If there's no score at the end of that period, the game ends in a tie.

In the playoffs, the first team to score also wins, however many periods are necessary.

Jerry Seeman
NFL DIRECTOR OF OFFICIATING

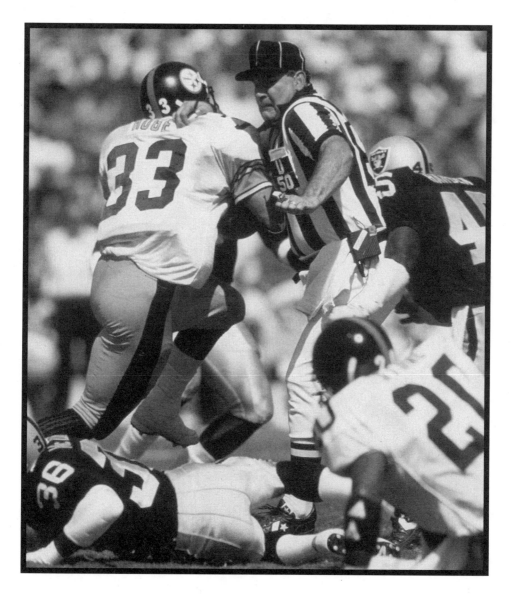

Section 1   Sudden-Death Procedures

SUDDEN-
DEATH
PROCEDURE

Article 1   The sudden-death system of determining the winner shall prevail when the score is tied at the end of the regulation playing time of *all NFL games.* Under this system, the team scoring first during overtime play herein provided for, shall be the winner of the game and the game is automatically ended upon any score (including a safety) or when a score is awarded by the referee for a palpably unfair act.

Article 2   At the end of regulation playing time, the referee shall immediately toss a coin at the center of the field, in accordance with rules pertaining to a usual pregame toss (4-2-1). The visiting team captain is to again call the toss.

Article 3   Following a three-minute intermission after the end of regular game, play shall continue by 15-minute periods with a two-minute intermission between each such overtime period with no halftime intermission.

Exception: Preseason and regular season league games shall have a maximum of one fifteen (15) minute period with the rule for 2 time outs instead of 3 as in a regular game and include the general provisions for the fourth quarter of a regular game.

At the end of each extra 15-minute period, starting with the end of the first one, teams must change goals in accordance with rule 4-2-2. Disqualified player(s) may not re-enter during overtime period(s).

Article 4   During any intermission or team time out a player may leave the field.

Article 5   If there is an excess time out during the first and second, third and fourth, etc., extra periods, the usual rules shall apply (4-3-3 to 7).

Article 6   Near the end of any period or during the last two (2) minutes of the second, fourth, etc., extra periods, the usual rules in regard to attempts to conserve time shall apply (4-3-10 and 5-2-1).

The rules for time outs shall be the same as in a regular game, including the last two (2) minutes of the second and fourth quarters.

Article 7   The clock operator shall time all extra fifteen (15) minute periods (4-3-1).

The field judge shall time the three (3) and two (2) minute intermissions, and is to sound his whistle 30 seconds before the expiration of each intermission. The referee shall sound his whistle for play to start, immediately upon the field judge's signal. See 4-3-9 and 4-3-10-S.N.

Article 8   Except as specifically provided for above, all other general and specific rules shall apply during any extra period.

CHAPTER 17
EMERGENCIES, UNFAIR ACTS

Basically this chapter covers things such as unusual weather conditions, spectators entering the field, power failures, and similar events.

Jerry Seeman
NFL DIRECTOR OF OFFICIATING

Section 1   Emergencies

NON-PLAYER
ON FIELD

Article 1   If any non-player, including photographers, reporters, employees, police or spectators, enters the field of play or end zones, and in the judgment of an official said party or parties interfere with the play, the referee, after consulting his crew (12-3-3 and 15-1-6), shall enforce any such penalty or score as the interference warrants.

FIELD CONTROL

Article 2   If spectators enter the field and/or interfere with the progress of the game in such a manner that in the opinion of the referee the game cannot continue, he shall declare time out. In such a case he shall record the number of the down, distance to be gained, and position of ball on field. He shall also secure from the line judge the playing time remaining and record it. He shall then order the home club through its management to have the field cleared, and when it is cleared and order restored and the safety of the spectators, players and officials is assured to the satisfaction of the referee, the game must continue even if it is necessary to use lights.

GAME CALLED

Article 3   If the game must be called due to a state or municipal law, or by darkness if no lights are available, an immediate report shall be made to the Commissioner by the home club, visiting club and officials. On receipt of all reports the Commissioner shall make a decision which will be final.

EMERGENCY
SITUATIONS

Article 4   The NFL affirms the position that in most circumstances all regular-season and postseason games should be played to their conclusion. If, in the opinion of appropriate League authorities, it is impossible to begin or continue a game due to an emergency, or a game is deemed to be imminently threatened by any such emergency (e.g., severely inclement weather, lightning, flooding, power failure), the following procedures (Articles 5 through 11) will serve as guidelines for the Commissioner and/or his duly appointed representatives. The Commissioner has the authority to review the circumstances of each emergency and to adjust the following procedures in whatever manner he deems appropriate. If, in the Commissioner's opinion, it is reasonable to project that the resumption of an interrupted game would not change its ultimate result or adversely affect any other inter-team competitive issue, he is empowered to terminate the game.

LEAGUE
AUTHORITY

Article 5   The League employees vested with the authority to define emergencies under these procedures are the Commissioner, designated representatives from his League office staff, and the game referee. In those instances where neither the Commissioner nor his designated representative is in attendance at a game, the referee will have sole authority; provided, however, that if a referee delays the beginning of or interrupts a game for a significant period of time due to an emergency, he must make every effort to contact the Commissioner or the Commissioner's designated representative for consultation. In all cases of significant delay, the League authorities will consult with the management of the participating clubs and will attempt to obtain appropriate information from outside sources if applicable (e.g., weather bureau, police).

LATER DATE

Article 6   If, because of an emergency, a regular-season or postseason game is not started at its scheduled time and cannot be played at any later time that same day, the game nevertheless must be played on a subsequent date to be determined by the Commissioner.

PREGAME THREAT

Article 7 If there is deemed to be a threat of an emergency that may occur during the playing of a game (e.g., an incoming tropical storm), the starting time of such game will not be moved to an earlier time unless there is clearly sufficient time to make an orderly change.

INTERRUPTED GAME

Article 8 If, under emergency circumstances, an interrupted regular-season or post-season game cannot be completed on the same day, such game will be rescheduled by the Commissioner and resumed at that point.

ALTERNATE DATES, SITES

Article 9 In instances under these emergency procedures which require the Commissioner to reschedule a regular-season game, he will make every effort to set the game for no later than two days after its originally scheduled date, and he will attempt to schedule the game at its original site. If unable to do so, he will schedule it at the nearest available facility. If it is impossible to schedule the game within two days after its original date, the Commissioner will attempt to schedule it on the Tuesday of the next calendar week in which the two involved clubs play other clubs (or each other). Further, the Commissioner will keep in mind the potential for competitive inequities if one or both of the involved clubs has already been scheduled for a game following the Tuesday of that week (e.g., Thanksgiving).

POSTSEASON INTERRUPTION

Article 10 If an emergency interrupts a postseason game and such game cannot be resumed on that same date, the Commissioner will make every effort to arrange for its completion as soon as possible. If unable to schedule the game at the same site, he will select an appropriate alternate site. He will terminate the game short of completion only if in his judgment the continuation of the game would not be normally expected to alter the ultimate result.

GAME RESUMPTION

Article 11 In all instances where a game is resumed after interruption, either on the same date or a subsequent date, the resumption will begin at the point at which the game was interrupted. At the time of interruption, the referee will call time out and he will make a record of the following: the team possessing the ball, the direction in which its offense was headed, position of the ball on the field, down, distance, period, time remaining in the period, and any other pertinent information required for an efficient and equitable resumption of play.

Section 2   Extraordinarily Unfair Acts

COMMISSIONER AUTHORITY

Article 1 The Commissioner has the sole authority to investigate and take appropriate disciplinary and/or corrective measures if any club action, non-participant interference, or calamity occurs in an NFL game which he deems so extraordinarily unfair or outside the accepted tactics encountered in professional football that such action has a major effect on the result of the game.

NO CLUB PROTESTS

Article 2 The authority and measures provided for in this entire Section 2 do not constitute a protest machinery for NFL clubs to avail themselves of in the event a dispute arises over the result of a game. The investigation called for in this Section 2 will be conducted solely on the Commissioner's initiative to review an act or occurrence that he deems so extraordinary or unfair that the result of the game in question would be inequitable to one of the participating teams. The Commissioner will not apply his authority in cases of complaints by clubs concerning judgmental errors or routine errors of omission by game officials. Games involving such complaints will continue to stand as completed.

PENALTIES
FOR UNFAIR
ACTS

Article 3   The Commissioner's powers under this Section 2 include the imposition of monetary fines and draft-choice forfeitures, suspension of persons involved in unfair acts, and, if appropriate, the reversal of a game's result or the rescheduling of a game, either from the beginning or from the point at which the extraordinary act occurred. In the event of rescheduling a game, the Commissioner will be guided by the procedures specified in Rule 17, Section 1, Articles 5 through 11, above. In all cases, the Commissioner will conduct a full investigation, including the opportunity for hearings, use of game videotape, and any other procedure he deems appropriate.

CHAPTER 18
GUIDELINES FOR CAPTAINS

At least one and as many as six captains can come out for the coin toss. Captains have to decide things like accepting or declining penalties, so we're very careful to communicate closely with these people.

Jerry Seeman
NFL DIRECTOR OF OFFICIATING

Section 1   Guidelines for Captains

Article 1   One hour prior to kickoff:

Respective coaches designate the captain(s)—a maximum of six per team.

COIN TOSS
OPTIONS

Article 2   Coin toss:

(a) Up to six captains per team can participate in the coin toss ceremony; only one captain from the visiting team (or captain designated by Referee if there is no home team) can declare the choice of coin toss.

(b) The team that won the toss may then have only one captain declare its option.

(c) The team that lost the coin toss may then have only one captain declare its option.

PENALTY
OPTIONS

Article 3   Choice on Penalty Option:

Only one captain is permitted to indicate the team's penalty option.

CHANGE OF
CAPTAINS

Article 4   Change of Captains:

(a) The coach has prerogative of informing Referee when he wishes to make a change in team captains; or

(b) A captain who is leaving can inform the Referee which player will act as captain in his place when he is substituted for; or

(c) When a captain leaves the game, the incoming substitute is permitted to inform the Referee which player the respective coach has designated as captain.

NOTE: A CAPTAIN ON THE FIELD HAS NO AUTHORITY TO REQUEST A CHANGE OF FELLOW TEAM CAPTAIN WHEN THAT CAPTAIN REMAINS ON THE FIELD.

1. TOUCHDOWN, FIELD GOAL, OR SUCCESSFUL TRY
BOTH ARMS EXTENDED ABOVE HEAD.

2. SAFETY
PALMS TOGETHER ABOVE HEAD.

3. FIRST DOWN
ARM POINTED TOWARD DEFENSIVE TEAM'S GOAL.

4. CROWD NOISE, DEAD BALL, NEUTRAL ZONE ESTABLISHED
ONE ARM ABOVE HEAD WITH AN OPEN HAND. WITH FIST CLOSED: **FOURTH DOWN**.

5. BALL ILLEGALLY TOUCHED, KICKED, OR BATTED
FINGERTIPS TAP BOTH SHOULDERS.

6. TIME OUT
HANDS CRISSCROSSED ABOVE HEAD. SAME SIGNAL FOLLOWED BY PLACING ONE HAND ON TOP OF CAP: **REFEREE'S TIME OUT**. SAME SIGNAL FOLLOWED BY ARM SWUNG AT SIDE: **TOUCHBACK**.

7. NO TIME OUT OR TIME IN WITH WHISTLE
FULL ARM CIRCLED TO SIMULATE MOVING CLOCK.

8. DELAY OF GAME, ILLEGAL SUBSTITUTION, OR EXCESS TIME OUT
FOLDED ARMS.

9. FALSE START, ILLEGAL SHIFT, ILLEGAL FORMATION, OR KICKOFF OR SAFETY KICK OUT OF BOUNDS
FOREARMS ROTATED OVER AND OVER IN FRONT OF BODY.

10. PERSONAL FOUL
ONE WRIST STRIKING THE OTHER ABOVE HEAD.
SAME SIGNAL FOLLOWED BY SWINGING LEG: **ROUGHING KICKER**.
SAME SIGNAL FOLOWED BY RAISED ARM SWINGING FORWARD: **ROUGHING PASSER**.
SAME SIGNAL FOLOWED BY HAND STRIKING BACK OF CALF: **CLIPPING**.

11. HOLDING
GRASPING ONE WRIST, THE FIST CLENCHED, IN FRONT OF CHEST.

12. ILLEGAL USE OF HANDS, ARMS, OR BODY
GRASPING ONE WRIST, THE HAND OPEN AND FACING FORWARD, IN FRONT OF CHEST.

13. PENALTY REFUSED, INCOMPLETE PASS, PLAY OVER, OR MISSED GOAL

HANDS SHIFTED IN HORIZONTAL PLANE.

14. PASS JUGGLED INBOUNDS AND CAUGHT OUT OF BOUNDS

HANDS UP AND DOWN IN FRONT OF CHEST (FOLLOWING INCOMPLETE PASS SIGNAL).

15. ILLEGAL FORWARD PASS

ONE HAND WAVED BEHIND BACK FOLLOWED BY LOSS OF DOWN SIGNAL (23).

16. INTENTIONAL GROUNDING OF PASS

PARALLEL ARMS WAVED IN A DIAGONAL PLAN ACROSS BODY. FOLLOWED BY LOSS OF DOWN SIGNAL (23).

17. INTERFERENCE WITH FORWARD PASS OR FAIR CATCH

HANDS OPEN AND EXTENDED FORWARD FROM SHOULDERS WITH HANDS VERTICAL.

18. INVALID FAIR CATCH SIGNAL

ONE HAND WAVED ABOVE HEAD.

19. INELIGIBLE RECEIVER OR INELIGIBLE MEMBER OF KICKING TEAM DOWNFIELD
RIGHT HAND TOUCHING TOP OF CAP.

20. ILLEGAL CONTACT
ONE OPEN HAND EXTENDED FORWARD.

21. OFFSIDE, ENCROACHING, OR NEUTRAL ZONE INFRACTION
HANDS ON HIPS.

22. ILLEGAL MOTION AT SNAP
HORIZONTAL ARC WITH ONE HAND.

23. LOSS OF DOWN
BOTH HANDS HELD BEHIND HEAD.

24. CRAWLING, INTERLOCKING INTERFERENCE, PUSHING, OR HELPING RUNNER
PUSHING MOVEMENT OF HANDS TO FRONT WITH ARMS DOWNWARD.

25. TOUCHING A FORWARD PASS OR SCRIMMAGE KICK
DIAGONAL MOTION OF ONE HAND ACROSS ANOTHER.

26. UNSPORTSMANLIKE CONDUCT
ARMS OUTSTRETCHED, PALMS DOWN. (SAME SIGNAL MEANS CONTINUOUS ACTION FOULS ARE DISREGARDED.) CHOP BLOCK.

27. ILLEGAL CUT
HANDS STRIKING FRONT OF THIGH.

ILLEGAL BLOCK BELOW THE WAIST
HANDS STRIKING FRONT OF THIGH PRECEDED BY PERSONAL FOUL SIGNAL (10).

28. ILLEGAL CRACKBACK
STRIKE OF AN OPEN RIGHT HAND AGAINST THE RIGHT MID-THIGH PRECEDED BY PERSONAL FOUL SIGNAL (10).

29. PLAYER DISQUALIFIED
EJECTION SIGNAL.

30. TRIPPING
REPEATED ACTION OF RIGHT FOOT IN BACK OF LEFT HEEL.

31. UNCATCHABLE FORWARD PASS
PALM OF RIGHT HAND HELD PARALLEL TO GROUND ABOVE HEAD AND MOVED BACK AND FORTH.

32. ILLEGAL SUBSTITUTION, 12 MEN IN OFFENSIVE HUDDLE, OR TOO MANT MEN ON THE FIELD
BOTH HANDS ON TOP OF HEAD.

33. FACE MASK
GRASPING MASK WITH ONE HAND.

34. ILLEGAL SHIFT
HORIZONTAL ARCS WITH TWO HANDS.

35. RESET PLAY CLOCK— 25 SECONDS
PUMP ONE ARM VERTICALLY.

36. RESET PLAY CLOCK— 40 SECONDS
PUMP TWO ARMS VERTICALLY.

Jerry Seeman, Senior Director of Officiating
Al Hynes, Supervisor of Officials
Mike Pereira, Supervisor of Officials
Ron DeSouza, Supervisor of Officials
Larry Upson, Supervisor of Officials

No.	Name	Position	College
81	Anderson, Dave	Line Judge	Salem College
66	Anderson, Walt	Line Judge	Sam Houston State
108	Arthur, Gary	Line Judge	Wright State
34	Austin, Gerald	Referee	Western Carolina
22	Baetz, Paul	Field Judge	Heidelberg
91	Baker, Ken	Side Judge	Eastern Illinois
48	Balliet, Brian	Umpire	Lehigh
26	Baltz, Mark	Head Linesman	Ohio University
55	Barnes, Tom	Line Judge	Minnesota
56	Baynes, Ron	Line Judge	Auburn
32	Bergman, Jeff	Line Judge	Robert Morris
7	Blum, Ron	Referee	Marin College
18	Boston, Byron	Line Judge	Austin
110	Botchan, Ron	Umpire	Occidental
31	Brown, Chad	Umpire	East Texas State
126	Carey, Don	Back Judge	U.C.-Riverside
94	Carey, Mike	Referee	Santa Clara
39	Carlsen, Don	Side Judge	Cal State-Chico
63	Carollo, Bill	Referee	Wisconsin-Milwaukee
11	Carroll, Duke	Field Judge	Ithaca
41	Cheek, Boris	Field Judge	Morgan State
65	Coleman, Walt	Referee	Arkansas
99	Corrente, Tony	Referee	Cal State-Fullerton
71	Coukart, Ed	Umpire	Northwestern
75	Daopoulos, Jim	Umpire	Kentucky
70	Dawson, Scott	Umpire	Virginia Tech
53	DeFelice, Garth	Umpire	San Diego State
113	Dorkowski, Don	Back Judge	Cal State-Los Angeles
6	Dornan, Kirk	Back Judge	Central Washington
74	Duke, James	Umpire	Howard
89	Dunn, Neely	Side Judge	South Carolina State
3	Edwards, Scott	Field Judge	Alabama
47	Fincken, Tom	Side Judge	Kansas State
111	Frantz, Earnie	Head Linesman	No College
50	Gereb, Neil	Umpire	California
72	Gierke, Terry	Head Linesman	Portland State
19	Green, Scott	Back Judge	Delaware
23	Grier, Johnny	Referee	University of D.C.
104	Hamer, Dale	Head Linesman	California, Pa.
40	Hannah, Charles	Umpire	Middle Tennessee State
105	Hantak, Dick	Referee	Southeast Missouri
125	Hayes, Laird	Side Judge	Princeton
54	Hayward, George	Head Linesman	Missouri Western
97	Hill, Tom	Side Judge	Carson-Newman
28	Hittner, Mark	Head Linesman	Pittsburg State
85	Hochuli, Ed	Referee	Texas-El Paso
82	Horton, Albert	Back Judge	Oregon State
37	Howey, Jim	Back Judge	Erskine College
114	Johnson, Tom	Head Linesman	Miami, Ohio
106	Jury, Al	Field Judge	San Bernardino Valley
86	Kukar, Bernie	Referee	St. John's
120	Lane, Gary	Side Judge	Missouri
17	Lawing, Bob	Back Judge	North Carolina State
127	Leavy, Bill	Back Judge	San Jose State
130	Lewis, Darryll	Line Judge	Dartmouth
76	Liebsack, Ron	Side Judge	Regis
49	Look, Dean	Side Judge	Michigan State
98	Lovett, Bill	Field Judge	Maryland
59	Luckett, Phil	Referee	Texas-El Paso
102	Mack, Keven	Field Judge	Fort Valley State
92	Madsen, Carl	Umpire	Washington
107	Marinucci, Ron	Line Judge	Glassboro State
38	Maurer, Bruce	Line Judge	Ohio State
77	McAulay, Terry	Side Judge	Louisiana State
95	McElwee, Bob	Referee	Navy
35	McGrath, Bob	Field Judge	Western Kentucky
64	McPeters, Lloyd	Field Judge	Oklahoma State
80	Millis, Timmie	Field Judge	Millsaps
117	Montgomery, Ben	Line Judge	Morehouse
60	Moore, Tommy	Side Judge	Stephen F. Austin
135	Morelli, Peter	Field Judge	St. Mary's College

No.	Name	Position	College
20	Nemmers, Larry	Referee	Upper Iowa
124	Paganelli, Carl	Umpire	Michigan State
46	Paganelli, Perry	Back Judge	Hope College
15	Patterson, Rick	Side Judge	Wofford
10	Phares, Ron	Line Judge	Virginia Tech
79	Pointer, Aaron	Line Judge	Pacific Lutheran
5	Quirk, Jim	Umpire	Delaware
83	Reels, Richard	Back Judge	No College
44	Rice, Jeff	Umpire	Northwestern
121	Rivers, Sanford	Head Linesman	Youngstown State
128	Rose, Larry	Side Judge	Florida
58	Saracino, Jim	Field Judge	Northern Colorado
21	Schleyer, John	Head Linesman	Millersville
122	Schmitz, Bill	Back Judge	Colorado State
109	Semon, Sid	Head Linesman	Southern California
118	Sifferman, Tom	Field Judge	Seattle
73	Skelton, Bobby	Back Judge	Alabama
30	Slaughter, Gary	Head Linesman	East Texas State
2	Smith, Billy	Back Judge	East Carolina
90	Spanier, Michael	Line Judge	St. Cloud State
119	Spitler, Ron	Back Judge	Panhandle State
12	Spyksma, Bill	Side Judge	South Dakota
24	Stabile, Tom	Head Linesman	Slippery Rock
88	Steenson, Scott	Field Judge	North Texas
84	Steinkerchner, Mark	Line Judge	Akron
62	Stewart, Charles	Line Judge	Long Beach State
4	Toole, Doug	Side Judge	Utah State
42	Triplette, Jeff	Referee	Wake Forest
93	Vaughan, Jack	Back Judge	Mississippi State
36	Veteri, Tony	Head Linesman	Manhattan College
25	Waggoner, Bob	Back Judge	Juniata College
100	Wagner, Bob	Umpire	Penn State
43	Warden, David	Field Judge	Oklahoma State
87	Weidner, Paul	Head Linesman	Cincinnati
123	White, Tom	Referee	Temple
8	Williams, Dale	Head Linesman	Cal State-Northridge
43	Wilson, James	Head Linesman	Eastern Kentucky
29	Wilson, Steve	Umpire	Whitworth College
14	Winter, Ron	Referee	Michigan State
16	Wyant, David	Side Judge	Virginia

Numerical Roster

No.	Name	Position		No.	Name	Position		No.	Name	Position
2	Billy Smith	BJ		41	Boris Cheek	FJ		88	Scott Steenson	FJ
3	Scott Edwards	FJ		42	Jeff Triplette	R		89	Neely Dunn	SJ
4	Doug Toole	SJ		43	James Wilson	HL		90	Michael Spanier	LJ
5	Jim Quirk	U		44	Jeff Rice	U		91	Ken Baker	sj
6	Kirk Dornan	BJ		46	Perry Paganelli	BJ		92	Carl Madsen	u
7	Ron Blum	R		47	Tom Fincken	SJ		93	Jack Vaughan	BJ
8	Dale Williams	HL		48	Brian Balliet	u		94	Mike Carey	R
10	Ron Phares	lj		49	Dean Look	SJ		95	Bob McElwee	R
11	Duke Carroll	FJ		50	Neil Gereb	U		97	Tom Hill	SJ
12	Bill Spyksma	SJ		53	Garth DeFelice	U		98	Bill Lovett	FJ
14	Ron Winter	R		54	George Hayward	HL		99	Tony Corrente	R
15	Rick Patterson	SJ		55	Tom Barnes	LJ		100	Bob Wagner	U
16	David Wyant	SJ		56	Ron Baynes	LJ		102	Keven Mack	Fj
17	Bob Lawing	Bj		58	Jim Saracino	FJ		104	Dale Hamer	HL
18	Byron Boston	LJ		59	Phil Luckett	r		105	Dick Hantak	R
19	Scott Green	BJ		60	Tommy Moore	SJ		106	Al Jury	FJ
20	Larry Nemmers	R		62	Charles Stewart	LJ		107	Ron Marinucci	lj
21	John Schleyer	HL		63	Bill Carollo	r		108	Gary Arthur	lj
22	Paul Baetz	FJ		64	Lloyd McPeters	Fj		109	Sid Semon	HL
23	Johnny Grier	R		65	Walt Coleman	R		110	Ron Botchan	U
24	Tom Stabile	HL		66	Walt Anderson	LJ		111	Earnie Frantz	HL
25	Bob Waggoner	Bj		70	Scott Dawson	U		113	Don Dorkowski	BJ
26	Mark Baltz	HL		71	Ed Coukart	U		114	Tom Johnson	HL
27	David Warden	FJ		72	Terry Gierke	HL		117	Ben Montgomery	LJ
28	Mark Hittner	hl		73	Bobby Skelton	BJ		118	Tom Sifferman	FJ
29	Steve Wilson	U		74	James Duke	U		119	Ron Spitler	BJ
30	Gary Slaughter	HL		75	Jim Daopoulos	u		120	Gary Lane	SJ
31	Chad Brown	U		76	Ron Liebsack	SJ		121	Sanford Rivers	HL
32	Jeff Bergman	LJ		77	Terry McAulay	SJ		122	Bill Schmitz	BJ
33	Steve Zimmer	Fj		79	Aaron Pointer	LJ		123	Tom White	R
34	Gerry Austin	R		80	Timmie Millis	FJ		124	Carl Paganelli	U
35	Bob McGrath	FJ		81	Dave Anderson	LJ		125	Laird Hayes	SJ
36	Tony Veteri	HL		82	Albert Horton	BJ		126	Don Carey	BJ
37	Jim Howey	BJ		83	Richard Reels	BJ		127	Bill Leavy	BJ
38	Bruce Maurer	LJ		84	Mark Steinkerchner	LJ		128	Larry Rose	sj
39	Don Carlsen	SJ		85	Ed Hochuli	R		130	Darryll Lewis	LJ
40	Charles Hannah	U		86	Bernie Kukar	R		135	Peter Morelli	Fj
				87	Paul Weidner	HL				

DISTANCE PENALTIES

Loss of Five Yards

Each time out in each half being in excess of three unless not notified or unless a fourth time out for injured player as specified (see charged time out penalties) ...... 4-3-5 and 6

Delay of game, i.e.,

exceeding 40/25 seconds in putting ball in play 4-3-9

failing to play immediately when ordered 4-3-9

player exercising privileges of captain 4-3-9

repeatedly snapping ball before referee can assume normal position .... 4-3-9 and 7-3-3-(c)-(2)

runner repeatedly attempting to advance when securely held 4-3-9

runner remaining on ball or opponent remaining on runner to consume time 4-3-9

undue delay in assembling after a time out 4-3-9

repeatedly entering neutral zone when not otherwise encroaching 4-3-9

unduly delaying establishment of neutral zone especially during time in 4-3-9

illegal return 5-1-5

kickers advancing recovered kick (not behind line) causes delay .... 4-3-9 and 9-1-4

substituting while ball is in play unless interference .... 4-3-9 and 12-3-1

contacting snapper or ball 7-3-5

catcher unduly advancing after fair catch signal .... 4-3-9 and 10-1-2

attempting to conserve or consume time near end of period, especially during last two minutes of half (also stop or not to stop watch to nullify) 4-3-10

more than eleven players on field during play 5-1-1

Illegal substitution, i.e.

substitute entering during play, withdrawn player on field at snap or free kick (unless interference) or withdrawing on opponent's side or across end line 5-2-1

Illegal kick at free kick (ball remains dead and replay) 6-1-3

Violation of free kick formation (includes kickoff), i.e.

kickers failing to be behind ball or inbounds (except place kick holder) .... 6-1-3, and 6-1-5

receivers failing to be inbounds or behind their free kick line 6-1-5

Neutral zone infraction 7-2-2

Making short free kick 6-2-1

Illegally touching free kick (a) before it goes 10 yards or (b) after being out of bounds 6-2-4

kicking free kick out of bounds between goal lines unless B last touches 6-3-1

Illegal position of A players at snap, i.e., having fewer than seven players on line 7-2-1

Having player neither on nor one yard behind his line unless man under center 7-2-1

Player entering neutral zone contacts opponent, causes him to charge or be offside (encroaching) or repeatedly entering it after warning (when not otherwise encroaching) 7-2-2

Player not reporting change in eligibility 7-2-3

Being offside at snap 7-2-2

Illegal motion by A at snap, i.e., player not being stationary (except) one only in motion clearly backward 7-2-5

Single player not moving clearly backward at snap 7-2-5

Moving backward from on scrimmage line and not being one yard back at snap 7-2-4

Pausing less than one second after a shift 7-2-6

Being out of bounds at snap 7-2-7

Not snapping ball when prescribed 7-3-1

Illegally snapping ball, i.e., failing to make backward pass 7-3-3

Failing to place ball on ground as specified 7-3-3

Failing to give impulse by continuous motion or sliding hands along ball before snap 7-3-3

Snapper moving his feet before ball leaves his hands during the snap 7-3-3

False start 7-3-4

Player under center not receiving snap 7-3-4

Snap going to receiver on line 7-3-6

Making forward pass in field of play not from scrimmage 8-1-1

Making forward pass beyond line of scrimmage (also loss of down) 8-1-1

Ineligible player downfield on kick 9-1-3

Ineligible player downfield on pass 8-2-2

Making invalid fair catch signal 10-1-1

Catcher unduly advancing after fair catch signal, unless touched by kickers in flight or after ball strikes ground 10-1-2, 3

Illegal use of hands or arms by defense, i.e., to hold an opponent who is not the runner 12-1-4

other than to ward off an opponent, to push or pull him, to get a runner or ball or to block 12-1-4

Defensive player during pass behind line pushes potential receiver behind line 12-1-4-A.R.7

Running into kicker behind his line (not roughing) 12-2-6

Incidental grasp of face mask 12-2-5

Loss of 10 Yards

Pass touched or caught by an ineligible offensive player beyond line (or loss of down) 8-1-5

Pass interference by team A 8-2-5

Tripping, holding, illegal use of hands, arms or body on offense 12-1-3

Assisting runner 12-1-1

Batting or punching ball, when loose (unless a pass), towards opponent's goal line or in any direction if an end zone, or from possession of a runner 12-1-6

Illegally kicking ball 12-1-7

Loss of 15 Yards

Not being ready to start each half on scheduled time 4-1-5

Interfering with fair catch (and catch awarded) 10-1-4

Tackling or blocking maker of a fair catch or avoidable running into 10-1-5

Head slap 12-2-2

Striking, kneeling and kicking (also disqualification) .. 12-2-1

Striking an opponent on head, neck or face with palm of hands 12-2-2

Striking opponent below shoulders with forearm or elbow by turning or pivoting 12-2-4

Twisting, turning or pulling of opponent's face mask 12-2-5

Blocking below waist on kicks and change of possession 12-2-13

Roughing the kicker 12-2-6

Falling on or piling on a prostrate player 12-2-7

Unnecessary roughness (also disqualification when flagrant), i.e.,

    striking an opponent above knee with foot or shin 12-2-8

    tackling runner who is out of bounds 12-2-8

    running into, throwing body against a player obviously out of the play or after the ball is dead 12-2-8

    running into from behind or dropping body across back of legs of opponent who is not the runner (clipping) 12-2-9

    illegal crackback 12-2-10

    running into passer after ball leaves his hand 12-2-11

Chop block—passing play 12-2-14

Chop block—running play 12-2-15

Illegal block after fair catch signal 10-1-3

Unsportsmanlike conduct by players (also disqualification when flagrant), i.e.,

    using abusive or insulting language or gestures to players or officials or continuing acts engendering ill will 12-3-1

    attempting to disconcert A at snap by words or signals 12-3-1-d

    concealing the ball under clothing or substituting article for it 12-3-1-e

    leaping to attempt to block a field goal or point after touchdown unless the player was lined up on the line of scrimmage when the ball was snapped 12-3-1n

    a punter, placekicker, or holder who simulates being roughed or run into by a defensive player 12-3-1-o

    taunting 12-3-1-b

    lingering 12-3-1-f

    player pushing, shoving, or laying hand on official (Note) .... 12-3-1-Pen. (Note)

    using substitutes or withdrawn players to confuse opponents (5-2-1-1) 12-3-1

    repeatedly violating substitution rule in attempts to conserve time .... 5-2-2 and 12-3-1-h

    violating 25-second rule more than twice (same down) after a warning 12-3-1-i

Illegal conduct by non-players (also exclusion for flagrant violations), i.e.

    player on field communicating other than to coach in prescribed area 13-1-1

    team representatives using unsportsmanlike conduct during game or between halves or sitting on bench when not qualified 13-1-1

    non-players going on field without permission (other than team attendants during a team time out) 13-1-2

    non-players moving along boundary lines (unless substitute warming up or coach in prescribed area) 13-1-5

Loss of Half Distance to Goal Line

Pass interfering by B in its end zone and previous spot is inside their 2-yard line 8-2-5

Distance penalty enforced from a spot between goal lines carrying ball more than half the distance to either goal line 14-2-1

Ball Placed on 1-Yard Line

Pass interfering by B in its end zone and previous spot is outside its 2 yard line 8-2-5

Loss of Down Penalty

(Unless Touchback)

Making second forward pass from behind line (same scrimmage) 8-1-1

Pass after ball crossed line and returned 8-1-1

Pass touching ineligible A behind line .... 8-1-4 and 8-1-5

WITHDRAWAL PENALTIES

Requesting fourth or more time out for injury during last two minutes of either half .... 4-3-4 and 4-3-5

Player being disqualified, suspended (illegal equipment), or replaced 5-1-5

Injured player taking more than two minutes or repair of legal equipment taking more than three minutes .... 4-3-4 and 5-1-5

Player leaving field during time out .... 4-3-3 and 5-2-1

Illegal return (loss of five also) 5-1-5

DISQUALIFICATION PENALTIES

Disqualification always occurs in combination with a 15-yard penalty. Exceptions to distance penalties:

> Both teams committing disqualifying fouls
> (double foul) 14-3-1

Distance being declined 14-6

Loss of 15 Yards

Flagrant striking, kicking or kneeing an opponent or striking him on head or neck with heel, back or side of hand, wrist, elbow or forearm 12-2-1

Flagrant roughing of kicker 12-2-6

Flagrant roughing of passer 12-2-11

Flagrant unsportsmanlike conduct by players 12-3-1

Player using a helmet as a weapon 12-2-13

Disqualified player returning (exclusion from field enclosure) .... 5-1-5 and 13-1-4-Pen.

Suspended player illegally returning .... 5-1-5 and 13-1-4

LOSS OF BALL PENALTIES

Ball being behind necessary line at end of fourth down 7-1-1

Kickers first touching kick (not a free kick) in field of play 9-1-4

Interfering with fair catch (also fair catch allowed) .. 10-1-4

DISQUALIFICATION FOR ENTIRE GAME

Repeat violation by player wearing or displaying illegal equipment .... 5-3-8-Pen.

CHARGED TIME OUT PENALTIES

Player requesting time out (includes for injured player when one of first three time outs in each half) 4-3-3

Taking time out for injured player during last two minutes of either half (withdrawal only when fourth time out—also loss of five when fifth or more) 4-3-6

Taking time out for repair of legal equipment (also withdrawal if more than thee minutes) 4-3-4

TIME PENALTY

Illegal conserving or consuming time near end of period (stop or not stop watch) or start watch with whistle when intent is in doubt 4-3-10

Fouling by defense, illegal touching or fair catch interfering by offense or fouling by both teams at end of half during play in which time expires (extend quarter) 4-3-11

REPLAY PENALTIES

B fouling on try which fails 11-3-3

Committing double foul unless continuing action fouls by both teams after ball is dead, the one only disqualifying foul is by B .... 14-1-8 and 9; 14-3-1; and 14-3-2

SCORE PENALTIES

Try Awarded

Team B committing a foul during a try which would ordinarily result in a safety 11-3-3

Score Awarded

Repeated fouling by defense (near own goal line) to prevent score by halving distance 12-3-2

Touchdown Awarded

Committing palpably unfair act which deprives opponent of a touchdown .... 12-3-3 and 13-1-7

Safety

Offense fouling anywhere, and spot of enforcement is behind its own goal line .... 11-4-2 and 14-1-11

Intentional grounding in own end zone 8-3-1

Making a forward pass (not from scrimmage) from within passer's end zone .... 8-1-1 and 14-1-11

Score Not Allowed

Offending team scores after foul during down in which time expires for half (also no extension of time) 4-3-11

Unsuccessful Try

Attempted kick ceasing to be in play 11-3-1

Team A committing foul during a try which would ordinarily result:

> in loss of down or in a touchback 11-3-3
> in loss of ball in field of play (not during a kick) . 11-3-3
> B recovering ball 11-3-5

NEW SERIES PENALTIES

B committing a foul during play from scrimmage giving A first down irrespective of distance penalty 14-8-5

B committing a foul not giving A first down unless enforcement places ball in advance of necessary line, i.e.,

B interfering in field of play with a pass from behind line (distance penalty in addition when personal foul) .... 8-2-5 and 12-2-1

COMBINATION PENALTIES

Loss of Down and Five

Making a forward pass from scrimmage from beyond the line 8-1-1

Loss of Down and 10

Intentionally throwing pass (from behind line) out of bounds or to the ground or against any player behind line 8-3-1

Loss of Ball and 15

Interfering with a possible fair catch in field of play (also fair catch) 10-1-4

TOUCHBACK

Kickers illegally touching kick (not free kick) in receivers' end zone 9-1-4

Fair catch interfering or running into maker of in receivers' end zone 10-1-5

SCORE, DISTANCE OR DISQUALIFICATION

Referee makes equitable ruling: 15-2-1

MISCELLANEOUS SITUATIONS

Safety

Ball in possession of team behind or out of bounds behind own goal line and impetus which sent it in touch came from:

Player of that team (unless pass violation by A is enforced from previous spot)—Safety .... 11-4-1 and 2

Kickoff Out of Bounds Between Goal Lines

Receivers' ball at inbounds spot when last touched by them 6-3-1

Receivers' ball 30 yards from previous spot 6-3-1

Ball Remains Dead

Fouls relating to the start of a down (ball not being in play even if the action begins) 14-6

Actions which delay game .... 4-3-9 and 10

Snapping before Referee assumes normal position ... 7-3-3

Ball Dead Immediately

Committing acts designed to consume time (stop watch also) 4-3-10

Kickers recovering a short free kick 6-2-2

Down ending because of and at the time of a foul, i.e.,

any forward pass becoming incomplete anywhere 8-1-5

Kickers advancing after recovery of a scrimmage or return kick unless behind line other than a try-kick (9-1-4) .... 9-1-6 and 11-3-5

Any kick touching receivers' goal post or cross bar unless scoring field goal .... 6-3-2; 9-1-14; and 11-6-1

Official sounding whistle (even when accidental) 7-4-3

Any receiver catching after fair catch signal unless touched in flight by kickers 10-1-2

Penalty Enforced From goal Line

Defense fouling and spot of enforcement is behind goal line of offense 14-1-11

Runner crosses opponents' goal line and spot of enforcing foul by teammate during run is behind defense goal line 14-1-12

Penalty Enforced on Next Free Kick

A team scoring and opponents commit a personal or unsportsmanlike conduct foul or a palpably unfair act, during down 14-1-14

INDEX

MAKE THE RIGHT CALL